A CREATIVE APPROACH TO THE CLASSIC.

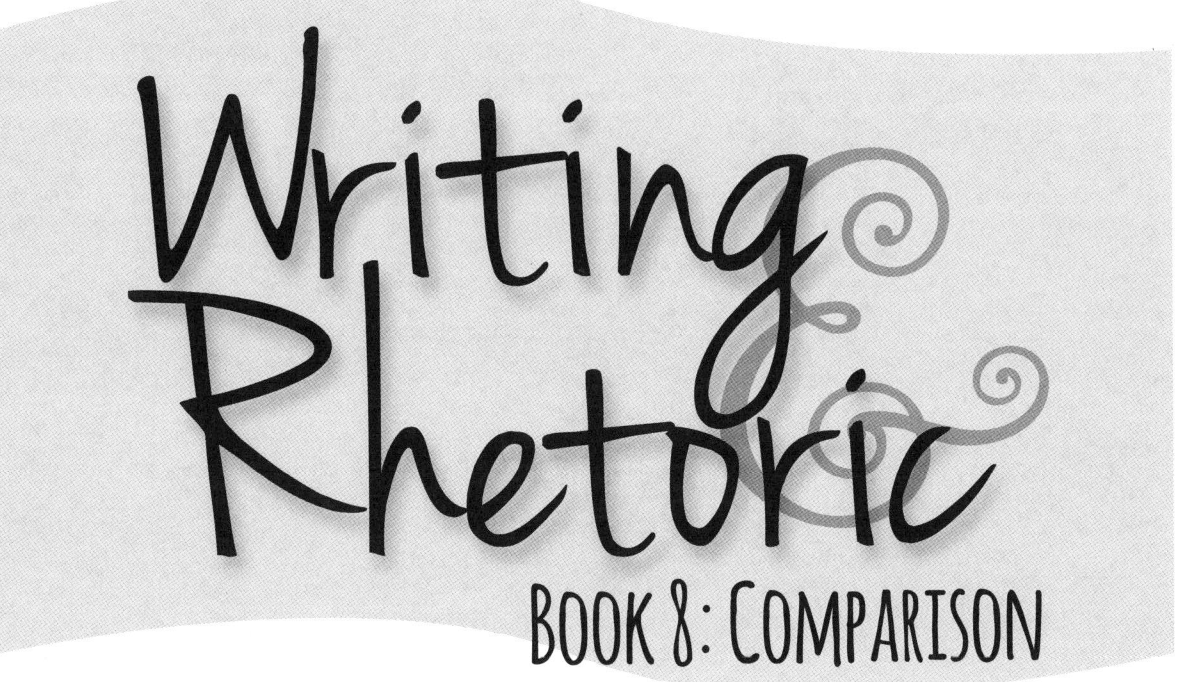

TOM PRIBLE
WITH PAUL KORTEPETER

Writing & Rhetoric Book 8: Comparison

Version 1.0

ISBN: 978-1-60051-308-4

Classical Academic Press
515 S. 32nd Street
Camp Hill, PA 17011

www.ClassicalAcademicPress.com

Series content editor: Christine Perrin
Series editor: Gretchen Nesbit
Illustrations: Jason Rayner
Book design: Lenora Riley

VP.03.24

Comparison

TABLE OF CONTENTS

A Typical Teaching Week v
Introduction to Students vii
Introduction viii
Best Foot Forward
The *Progym* and the Practice of Modern Writing x
Objectives for *Comparison* xiii

Lesson 1: What Is Comparison? 1

Lesson 2: Identifying Similarities & Differences 15

Lesson 3: The Tools of Metaphor & Simile 29

Lesson 4: Two Disasters: Fire & Ice 39

Lesson 5: Writing the Comparison Essay 53

Lesson 6: First Comparison: Roald Amundsen's Journey to the South Pole & Charles Lindbergh's Solo Transatlantic Flight 67

Lesson 7: Second Comparison: Helen Keller & Alice Paul 95

Lesson 8: Third Comparison: The Telephone & the Phonograph 123

Lesson 9: Fourth Comparison: Boxing & Baseball 149

Lesson 10: Fifth Comparison: The Love Letters of Napoleon & Keats 177

Comparison Essay Rubric 202
Get to the Point: Tips for Summarizing 203
Outlines: Your Very Own Story Maps 205
Memoria: Building Memory Muscle 207
Elocution Electrifies 209
Glossary 211
So Long 222

A Typical Teaching Week

These guidelines are intended to help bring some predictability to lesson planning.

Although the elements of grammar are important aspects of this course, its primary focus is writing and rhetoric. We recommend that you teach a simple, but rich, grammar curriculum in parallel with the lessons in *Writing & Rhetoric: Comparison*. By simple, we mean to suggest that you avoid a grammar program with a writing component. Two different writing methods would most likely work against each other and cause an imbalance in the school day. Instead, look for a grammar program that focuses on grammatical concepts, provides plenty of practice sentences, and encourages diagramming.

You may want to provide same-day grammar instruction several days a week, preferably separating Writing & Rhetoric from grammar study by an hour or two. Or, you may want to alternate weeks between a grammar program and Writing & Rhetoric. This requires some negotiation in your language arts program for the year. If you aim to do two Writing & Rhetoric books per school year, that would equal approximately twenty-four lessons. If you spend one week on each lesson, that leaves you with about eleven weeks to focus on grammar. However, as the reading selections grow longer and the writing tasks more extensive, you may need to spend more time on each Writing & Rhetoric lesson according to the needs of your students. You will have to choose a grammar program with these considerations in mind.

Please note that multiple opportunities for practice are built into the Writing & Rhetoric series. If you find that your students have mastered a particular form of writing, you should feel free to skip some lessons. In this case, some teachers choose to present the historical material from skipped lessons as part of their history lessons. Some teachers may also provide their students with practice in sentence manipulation by doing only the Sentence Play and Copiousness sections from skipped lessons.

Day One

1. The teacher models fluency by reading the text aloud while students follow along silently.
2. Tell It Back (Narration) and Talk About It should immediately follow the reading of the text, while the text is still fresh in the students' minds.

   Narration, the process of "telling back," can be done in a variety of ways. Pairs of students can retell the story to each other, or selected individuals can narrate orally to the entire class. Solo students can tell back the story into a recording device or to an instructor. At this age, written narrative summaries, outlines, and dramatic reenactments can be done with skill. The process of narration is intended to improve comprehension and long-term memory.

   Annotation is included under Tell It Back as a standard part of the reading process. Most lessons in this book contain two readings, and annotations can help a student easily locate vocabulary words, proper nouns, and important concepts for drafting essays.

   Talk About It is designed to help students analyze the meaning of their reading and to see analogous situations, both in the world and in their own lives. This book also includes several opportunities for picture analysis.
3. The "Memoria" feature can be discussed during class, and students can work on memorizing the quote and completing their commonplace notebooks as homework.

Days Two and Three

1. As time allows, the teacher can ask students to reread the text silently. If annotations were not completed on the first day, students can continue to mark the text for main ideas, vocabulary words, and important concepts.
2. Students work with the text through the Go Deeper and Writing Time exercises. Go Deeper is a feature in the first half of the book and is all about practicing important skills essential to each lesson. Writing Time, which appears in the second half of the book, includes sentence play, copiousness, and the comparison exercises themselves. You will probably want to take more than one day for this step.

Day Four

1. The lessons in the first half of the book are designed to move quickly. You may choose to wrap up these lessons after the third day, or you may complete any unfinished exercises during days four or five.
2. The second half of the book is more intensely focused on writing and takes more time. If students complete the first draft of their essays on day three, we recommend that they take a breather from writing while they work on their speaking skills. Keeping a day between essay completion and revision helps students to look at their work with fresh eyes. However, teachers may find it valuable to pair students together to read their essays out loud and give each other ideas for revision. A rubric is included in the Speak It section of lesson 6 and at the back of the book as an aid to partner feedback.
3. The Speak It section in the second half of the book creates opportunities for students to memorize, recite, discuss and debate, read dramatically, and playact. Please consider using a recording device whenever it suits the situation. When using electronics, the student should listen to his recording to get an idea of what sounds right and what needs to be improved. Have students read the elocution instructions at the back of the book to help them work on skill in delivery.

Day Five

At this level, students will continue to work toward a foundation in revision. In the second half of the book, the Revise It section provides basic exercises that introduce students to revision and proofreading. Revise It also provides a list that covers some of the most important steps toward improving an essay. Most students can do rudimentary self-editing at this age and provide some useful feedback to each other. However, teachers are still the best source for giving editorial feedback and requesting rewrites.

Introduction to Students

I don't know about you, but I love summer. School's out, and you can wear shorts and flip-flops all day long. You can fly down water slides and go water skiing across huge lakes. Nothing beats sitting by the pool with a cold glass of lemonade on a hot summer day. Of course, winter is pretty terrific as well. You can wear sweaters and woolly boots. You can fly down a hill on a sled, or you can ski down a huge mountain. You can also cozy up beside the fire with a book and a mug of hot cocoa. Now that I think about it, both summer and winter are great!

As you can see from my descriptions, summer and winter have similarities and differences. They both call for clothes that fit the season, for special outdoor sports and relaxation. On the other hand, summer is hot and winter is cold. Summer clothes are light and winter clothes are heavy. Summer sports involve water and winter sports involve snow.

Life is full of comparisons like this, isn't it? We can compare seasons, people, books, music, historical events, and ideas—just about anything, really. We do this all the time; we even do this without thinking about it. For example, have you ever stood in front of your closet, fretting over what to wear? You might lay out two outfits and try to judge between the two. You might even ask your sister, your dad, or your dog for advice! In this situation, you're actually making a comparison without realizing it. You're taking two (or more) objects, seeing their similarities and differences, and making a decision based on that comparison.

Making comparisons is a normal part of making a decision, but it is also an important skill that we have to learn and practice. As decisions become more complicated, the ability to compare is crucial. Leaders have to make big decisions all the time—such as whether or not to build a road or go to war. You also have to make big decisions, such as where to go to college or whom to marry or what to do for a living. Don't you think it's important that you're able to analyze things carefully and with sound judgment?

Additionally, comparison is a useful tool in helping us understand people and historical events in greater depth. By comparing two people or ideas or events, we can draw deeper conclusions about life in general. If you were to visit a museum and compare two great works of art—say, Monet's *Water Lilies* and Van Gogh's *Starry Night*—your ideas of beauty and creativity and art in general would be richer and stronger than if you just observed one of them.

In this book, you will do a lot of comparing. You will not be doing a persuasive comparison, in which you try to persuade people to see one thing as better than another (e.g., dogs are better than cats; cake is better than ice cream). Rather, you will be doing an expository comparison, in which you consider two things side-by-side and show their similarities and differences. The purpose of the comparison essay will be not to persuade, but simply to give your reader more information. In other words, you'll be comparing two things equally to reveal how they are alike and how they are different. You'll find that the process of comparison leads to strengthening your understanding of the topic, and in turn makes you a much better writer and speaker—which is, after all, what this Writing & Rhetoric series is all about.

So what are you waiting for? Turn the page and let's get to it!

Introduction

Two thousand-plus years ago, the Greeks developed a system of persuasive speaking known as rhetoric. The Romans fell in love with rhetoric because it was both practical for the real world and served the need of training orators in their growing republic. In order to prepare their students for oration, the Romans invented a complementary system of persuasive writing known as the *progymnasmata*: *pro-* meaning "preliminary" and *gymnas* meaning "exercises." The *progymnasmata* were the primary method in Graeco-Roman schools used to teach young people the elements of rhetoric. This happened in a grammar school (called a *grammaticus*) sometime after a student reached the age of ten.

There are several ancient "*progyms*" still in existence. The most influential *progyms* were by Hermogenes of Tarsus, who lived in the second century, and by Aphthonius of Antioch, who lived during the fourth century just as the western Roman Empire was collapsing. Even after the great cities of Rome lay in ruins, the *progym* continued as the primary method for teaching writing during the Middle Ages and even into early modern times.

The Writing & Rhetoric series is based on the *progymnasmata* of ancient Rome. This method assumes that students learn best by reading excellent examples of literature and by growing their writing skills through imitation. It is incremental, meaning that it goes from simpler exercises to more complex exercises, and it moves from the concrete to the abstract. One of the beauties of the *progym* is that it grows with the student through the stages of childhood development termed the "trivium"[1] by modern classical education, effectively taking a young writer from the grammar phase through the logic phase and finally to the rhetoric phase.

In a democracy such as Athens or a republic such as Rome, rhetoric was a powerful way to enter into public conversations. In the words of Yale rhetorician Charles Sears Baldwin, "Rhetoric is conceived by Aristotle as the art of giving effectiveness to the truth." He adds that "the true theory of rhetoric is the energizing of knowledge, the bringing of truth to bear upon men. . . ." Rhetoric thus had an intentional public purpose, that is, to persuade people to embrace truth and its corollaries: virtue and beauty. It is designed to enjoin right behavior by holding up to public scrutiny examples of goodness and wickedness.

There is an urgency and a real purpose to rhetoric. It was never meant to be empty forms of speaking and composition. It was never meant to be only eloquence and skill of delivery. It was certainly never meant to be manipulative soundbites and commercials made to benefit an unscrupulous political class. Rather, it was intended for every citizen as a means to engage articulately with the urgent ideas of the day. As the old saying goes, "Whoever does not learn rhetoric will be a victim of it."

1. In medieval times, the trivium was originally the lower division of the seven liberal arts. For the modern idea that these studies correspond to childhood development, please refer to Dorothy Sayers, *The Lost Tools of Learning*.

The best preparation for rhetoric is still the *progymnasmata*, the preliminary exercises. In this book you will find these exercises creatively updated to meet the needs of modern children. We have embraced the method both as it was used for Roman youth and as it develops the skills demanded by contemporary education.

- It teaches the four modes of discourse—narration, exposition, description, and argumentation—while at the same time blending them for maximum persuasive impact.
- It is incremental, moving from easier forms to harder forms. The level of challenge is appropriate for students as they mature with the program.
- It uses "living" stories, from ancient to modern, and is not stuck in any particular time period. Rather, it follows a timeline of history so that the stories can be integrated with history lessons.
- Its stories engage the imagination and also spark a desire in young people to imitate them. In this way, Writing & Rhetoric avoids the "blank-page syndrome" that can paralyze many nascent writers by giving students a model from which to write.
- It promotes virtue by lifting up clear-cut examples of good and bad character.
- It fosters the joy of learning by providing opportunities for creative play and self-expression as well as classroom fun.
- It uses speaking to enhance the development of persuasive composition.
- It teaches students to recognize and use the three persuasive appeals to an audience: pathos, ethos, and logos.
- It provides opportunities for students to learn from other students' work as well as to present their own work.

As educators, I think we need to admit that teaching writing is difficult. This is because writing makes big demands on cognitive function and, for many young writers, can easily become overwhelming. Our brains need to simultaneously

- utilize motor skills,
- process vocabulary,
- sequence and organize ideas,
- employ grammatical concepts,
- and draw upon a reservoir of good writing—hopefully the reservoir exists—as a template for new writing.

That's a tall order. Also, writing contains a subjective element. It's not as clear-cut as math. And when you add argumentation to the mix, you have a very complex process indeed. To be properly educated, every person needs to be able to make and understand arguments.

It is from this list of complexities that a desire for a relatively easy-to-implement curriculum was born. While the task of teaching writing is difficult, it is my sincere belief that reconnecting the tree of modern composition to its classical roots in rhetoric will refresh the entire process. Regardless of your personal writing history, I trust that these books will provide a happy and rewarding experience for your students.

The *Progym* and the Practice of Modern Writing

Although the *progym* are an ancient method of approaching writing, they are extraordinarily relevant today. This is because modern composition developed from the *progym*. Modern writing borrows heavily from many of the *progym's* various exercises. For example, modern stories are essentially unchanged from the ancient fable and narrative forms. Modern expository essays contain elements from the ancient commonplace, encomium/vituperation, and other *progym* exercises. Persuasive essays of today are basically the same as the ancient thesis exercises. In this series, you can expect your students to grow in all forms of modern composition—narrative, expository, descriptive, and persuasive—while at the same time developing unique rhetorical muscle.

The *progym* cover many elements of a standard English and Language Arts curriculum. In *Comparison* these include:[2]

- experiencing both the reading of a story (sight) and listening to it (hearing)
- identifying a variety of genres including history, biography, autobiography, and letter
- determining the meaning of words and phrases, including figures of speech, as they are used in a text
- gathering vocabulary knowledge when considering a word or phrase important to comprehension or expression
- analyzing text that is organized in sequential or chronological order
- demonstrating an understanding of texts by creating outlines, annotating, summarizing, and paraphrasing in ways that maintain meaning and logical order within a text
- gathering relevant information from multiple sources, and annotating sources
- drawing evidence from literary or informational texts to support analysis, reflection, and research
- articulating an understanding of several ideas or images communicated by the literary work
- identifying similarities and differences between two characters (historical figures), objects, and events, drawing on specific details in the text
- establishing a central idea or topic
- composing a topic sentence and creating an organizational structure in which ideas are logically grouped into coherent paragraphs to support the writer's purpose

2. This list was derived from the Texas Administrative Code (TAC), Title 19, Part II, Chapter 110: Texas Essential Knowledge and Skills for English Language Arts and Reading (http://ritter.tea.state.tx.us/rules/tac/chapter110/index.html), the Core Knowledge Foundation's Core Knowledge Sequence: Content and Skill Guidelines for Grades K-8 (http://www.coreknowledge.org/mimik/mimik_uploads/documents/480/CKFSequence_Rev.pdf), the English-Language Arts Content Standards for California Public Schools: Kindergarten Through Grade Twelve (http://www.cde.ca.gov/be/st/ss/documents/elacontentstnds.pdf), the English Language Arts Standards of the Common Core State Standards Initiative (http://www.corestandards.org/ELA-Literacy), the English/Language Arts Standards Grade 6, Indiana Department of Education (http://www.doe.in.gov/standards/englishlanguage-arts), and the English Standards of Learning for Virginia Public Schools, Grade 7 (http://www.doe.virginia.gov/testing/sol/standards_docs/english/2010/stds_all_english.pdf).

- supporting claim(s) with clear reasons and relevant evidence, using credible sources, facts, and details
- writing informative/explanatory texts to examine a topic and convey ideas and information clearly
- developing the topic with relevant facts, definitions, concrete details, quotations, or other information and examples
- providing a concluding statement or section that follows from the topic presented
- using precise language and domain-specific vocabulary
- establishing and maintaining a formal style
- using appropriate transitions to clarify the relationships among ideas and concepts
- producing clear and coherent writing in which the development, organization, and style are appropriate to task, purpose, and audience
- avoiding plagiarism and providing basic bibliographic information for sources
- with some guidance and support from peers and adults, developing and strengthening writing as needed by planning, revising, editing, rewriting, or trying a new approach
- using technology as an aid to revision and oration
- using pictures and photos to analyze and interpret the past
- participating civilly and productively in group discussions

While these standards are certainly worthwhile and are addressed in this curriculum, the *progym* derive their real strength from the incremental and thorough development of each form of writing. The Writing & Rhetoric series does not skip from form to form and leave the others behind. Rather, it builds a solid foundation of mastery by blending the forms. For example, no expository essay can truly be effective without description. No persuasive essay can be convincing without narrative. All good narrative writing requires description, and all good persuasive writing requires expository elements. Not only do the *progym* demand strong organization and implement many of the elements of modern language arts, but they also retain all of the power of classical rhetoric.

Here is how the *progym* develop each stage of modern composition:

1. Fable—Narrative
2. Narrative—Narrative with descriptive elements
3. Chreia & Proverb—Expository essay with narrative, descriptive, and persuasive elements
4. Refutation & Confirmation—Persuasive essay with narrative, descriptive, and expository elements
5. Commonplace—Persuasive essay with narrative, descriptive, and expository elements
6. Encomium & Vituperation—Persuasive essay with narrative, descriptive, and expository elements
7. Comparison—Comparative essay with narrative, descriptive, and expository elements
8. Description & Impersonation—Descriptive essays with narrative, expository, persuasive, and comparative elements
9. Thesis Part 1—Persuasive essay with narrative, descriptive, expository, and comparative elements
10. Thesis Part 2—Persuasive speech with narrative, descriptive, expository, and comparative elements, as well as the three rhetorical appeals
11. Declamation—Persuasive essay or speech that marshals all the elements of the *progym* and brings them to bear upon judicial matters

As you can see, the *progym* move quickly to establish the importance of one form to another.

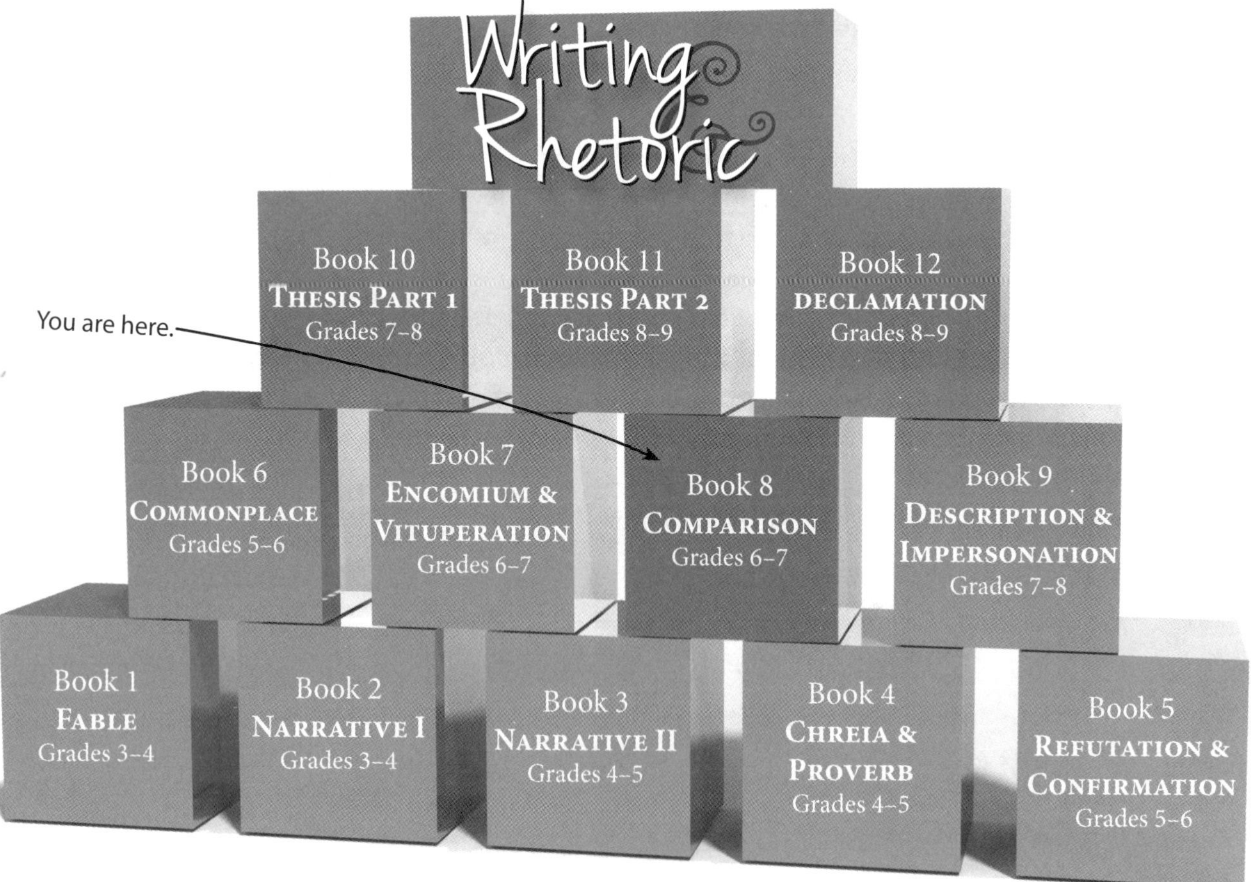

Objectives for *Comparison*

The following are some of the major objectives for the exercises found in each section of this book:

Reading

1. Expose students to various forms of biographical, autobiographical, epistolary, and nonfiction writing as well as culturally important narratives from American history during the Gilded Age until the Great Depression of the 1930s.
2. Model fluent reading for students and give them practice reading diverse texts.
3. Aid student reading and recall by teaching techniques for annotation.
4. Facilitate student interaction with well-written texts through discussions and exercises in evaluation and critical thinking.
5. Enhance research skills by giving students multiple texts to read and having them summarize, outline, lift quotes, and create a topic from the material.
6. Introduce students to the practice of identifying similarities and differences and making connections between people, ideas, objects, and historical events.

Writing

1. Support the development of invention (inventing topics and ideas to write about) and demonstrate how to use quotations in a crafted piece of writing.
2. Encourage students to map (pre-write) their information before they write a paragraph.
3. Support students in writing well-crafted, six-paragraph comparative essays—with introduction, body paragraphs, and conclusion—analyzing the similarities and differences between two subjects. These essays include the development of an awareness of transitions and tone.
4. Practice the concepts of topic sentence and narrative overview.
5. Strengthen the skill of deriving information from texts and organizing and summarizing it in expository paragraphs.
6. Strengthen the use of pathos to engage the emotions of readers, as introduced in the previous book in this series, *Encomium & Vituperation*. This includes the use of analogy, a rhetorical device.
7. Continue the development of revision, proofreading, and joint critiquing.
8. Reinforce grammatical concepts such as prepositional phrases and simple and compound sentences, as well as provide practice recognizing and repairing sentence fragments and run-on sentences.
9. Practice sentence manipulation and imitation, in particular simplifying sentences, creating appositive phrases, and changing passive voice to active.

Related Concepts

1. Aid in the development of vocabulary and analysis of language.
2. Reinforce the ability to summarize and paraphrase, as well as to amplify through description, for greater rhetorical flexibility.
3. Strengthen working memory through recitation (memoria), thus improving storage of information and rhetorical power.
4. Employ a number of rhetorical devices—analogy, simile, metaphor, chiasma, hypophora, parallelism, and anastrophe—for more thought-provoking writing and speaking.
5. Increase understanding of the flexibility and copiousness of language by practicing sentence variety.

Speaking

1. Strengthen students' oratory skills by providing opportunities for public speaking and for working on delivery—volume, pacing, and inflection.
2. Encourage students to see the relationship between writing and speaking as they consider their ideas orally and to use oration as an aid to the process of revision.
3. Practice tone and inflection by means of dramatic reading.

Lesson 1

What Is Comparison?

What are your favorite foods to eat? I have many. Sometimes I'm in the mood for a fresh, crisp salad, but more often I'd like a big, cheesy slice of deep-dish pizza. Sometimes I enjoy a gooey, warm brownie, and other times I feel like eating crunchy, salty pretzels. For breakfast I like fluffy scrambled eggs, and for dinner I like a grilled steak and fresh vegetables.

When you think about it, there is so much variety in food. Some foods, such as meat and poultry, are eaten cooked, while some foods—carrots and apples, for instance—can be eaten raw. Raisins are sweet, while popcorn is buttery and salty. Some foods come from plants, while others come from animals, and even factories. Some foods are very good for you, and others should only be eaten in small amounts. Different foods have different colors, shapes, sizes, and tastes. They may have some things in common—bananas and apples are both fruits, for instance—but they have a lot of differences too.

You probably don't realize it when you're standing there with the fridge wide open, but when you think about what food will taste the best, or what food will be the healthiest choice, you are making a comparison. **Comparison** is a way of looking at two or more people, objects, ideas, or events to identify how they are alike and different. Comparison helps us to look at—or observe—

To some people, the word "judgment" suggests meanness or offense, and to be honest, it can mean those things. No one wants to be called judgmental. We all know people who seem quick to criticize or who judge others before getting to know them. But don't confuse that kind of judgment with what I'm talking about here. Every day you and I make decisions, or judgments, about what seems best to us—what clothes to wear, who to talk to, what activities to give time to, and how to spend money. And, at a deeper level, all of us hold certain convictions or beliefs about right and wrong, how people should be treated, and so forth. These are judgments that you have made, hopefully after considerable thought, based on your background, the influence of your family, the experiences of others, your study, and your own experiences. Not all judgments are bad, and in fact many judgments are necessary and useful.

In Aphthonius's version of the *progym* (the version that this series is based on), comparison was seen as a third part to encomium and vituperation, which you learned about in the previous book in this series. (Remember, encomium praises a person for her admirable qualities, and vituperation disapproves of a person for her negative qualities.) With encomium and vituperation, Aphthonius's students learned to make judgments. Those students then went on to learn about comparison, or how to compare two people in order to make those judgments.

things more closely, and sometimes, such as when we decide what type of food is best for us, we use comparison to make judgments. You may think to yourself, *The leftover chocolate cake is more scrumptious, but the veggies and hummus is a healthier option,* or *The blueberries and the oranges both have good vitamins in them, so I will have some of each for a snack.* In these examples you are comparing your choices and deciding which one is the better choice, or deciding that both are good choices.

When we compare to make judgments, we use our observations to **evaluate** two persons, objects, or events. This means we weigh their good and bad. You'll notice that the word "evaluate" has the root word "value," which can help us understand its meaning. When we evaluate, we are assigning value to a particular subject, and we may even declare that one thing is more valuable than another. There are a variety of comparisons we might use to evaluate, or make judgments—Which is more helpful than the other? more healthy? more influential? more significant? You can imagine how difficult decision-making would be if you didn't feel comfortable making comparisons. You would never feel confident that you were making the right choice!

We don't always compare to make judgments, however. Sometimes we simply compare in order to make observations about two (or more) things. This kind of comparison helps us to understand things better. It helps us to pay attention to details and see things from different angles—which makes us appreciate those things in a deeper way.

Sometimes when we compare, we make connections between the things we are comparing. There is a delight that comes naturally to us when this happens. For instance, I stood in a museum a few days ago and studied a clay pull-toy from ancient Mesopotamia that dated back to 3,500 BC. It struck me with wonder that I myself had played with that same kind of toy when I was a kid—mine was a little plastic doggie with a string for its leash—and my own children have as well. I realized that we share something in common with people who lived over 5,000 years ago in a different part of the world. When I compare myself to a Mesopotamian child in this way, I am making a connection between the two of us that is in itself a source of joy.

When you compare two subjects in this way, you are simply noting how they are similar and how they are different. Your goal is to withhold judgment, which means you don't take sides. You aren't trying to determine which thing is better than the other. For example, if you were comparing maple syrup and a hard-boiled egg and trying to withhold judgment, you wouldn't say that maple syrup is tastier than the egg. You would simply say that maple syrup is sticky and sweet and often eaten on pancakes, and hard-boiled eggs are squishy, not sweet, and can be eaten on a salad. This is the type of comparison you will be doing for the essays in this book.

A Word about Words

Did you know that the Latin word *comparare* is the root word for "comparison" and means "to couple together, place side-by-side, or match"? Here are some common synonyms for "compare":

- When making an observation: observe, inspect, distinguish, examine
- When making a judgment: judge, evaluate, assess, appraise

For an example of comparison in literature, take a look at an excerpt from a book called *The Strange Case of Dr. Jekyll and Mr. Hyde* by Robert Louis Stevenson. It tells the story of a man who has two different personalities: He is both Dr. Jekyll, a professional, calm, and polite doctor, and Mr. Hyde, who is an evil murderer. He transforms from Jekyll into Hyde by drinking a potion, called a "draught." Today doctors might diagnose him with a mental disorder, but at the time that this text was written, people would have just referred to him as "mad." The following excerpt is a scene in which the narrator compares his two personalities. As you read, make note of any similarities or differences between the two.

Dr. Jekyll and Mr. Hyde

—adapted from *The Strange Case of Dr. Jekyll and Mr. Hyde* by Robert Louis Stevenson

Please note: This passage from *Dr. Jekyll and Mr. Hyde* can be found in updated language at the back of the book (see page 225). We recommend that you try to read and understand Stevenson's original writing first, but if you find yourself bogged down by the language, if the pictures aren't clear in your head, the updated version may help.

Note also that this is a difficult text, so if you find yourself struggling with challenging words, you can look them up in the glossary or, if you don't find them there, in a dictionary.

All things therefore seemed to point to this: that I was slowly losing hold of my original and better self (Jekyll), and becoming slowly **incorporated** with my second and worse (Hyde).

Between these two, I now felt I had to choose. My two natures had memory in common, but all other **faculties** were most unequally shared between them. Jekyll (who was **composite**) sometimes with the most sensitive **apprehensions**, other times with a greedy **gusto**, **projected** and shared in the pleasures and adventures of Hyde; but Hyde was indifferent to Jekyll, or but remembered him as the mountain bandit remembers the cavern in which he conceals himself from pursuit. Jekyll had more than a father's interest; Hyde had more than a son's **indifference**. To cast in my lot with Jekyll was to die to those appetites which I had long secretly indulged and had of late begun to pamper. To cast it in with Hyde was to die to a thousand interests and **aspirations** and to become, at a blow and forever, despised and friendless. I chose the better part and was found wanting in the strength to keep to it.

Yes, I preferred the elderly and **discontented** doctor, surrounded by friends and cherishing honest hopes; and bade a **resolute** farewell to the liberty, the comparative youth, the light step, leaping impulses and secret pleasures, that I had enjoyed in the disguise of Hyde. But soon enough I began to be tortured with **throes** and longings, as of Hyde struggling after freedom; and at last, in an hour of moral weakness, I once again mixed and swallowed the transforming draught.

I do not suppose that, when a drunkard reasons with himself upon his vice, he is once out of five hundred times affected by the dangers that he runs through his brutish, physical insensibility; neither had I, long as I had considered my position, made enough allowance for the complete moral insensibility and readiness to evil which were the leading characters of Edward Hyde. Yet it was by these that I was punished. My devil had been long caged, and he came out roaring.

Tell It Back—Narration

1. What is comparison? What are the two main purposes for making comparisons?
2. **ORAL NARRATION:** Without looking at the text, retell *Dr. Jekyll and Mr. Hyde* as best you remember it using your own words. Try not to leave out any important details.

   Here is the first sentence to help you get started:

   All things therefore seemed to point to this: that I was slowly losing hold of my original and better self (Jekyll), and becoming slowly incorporated with my second and worse (Hyde).

Talk About It—

1. We all have different parts to our personalities. Sometimes we are goofy, and other times we are serious. At school you might be well-behaved, but at home with your siblings you might sometimes be rude or self-centered. It is rare, however, that people have the extreme contrasts that we see between Jekyll and Hyde. Obviously, the main similarity between the two characters is that they are the same person. The text also notes that they share the same memories. How are the two personalities different?

2. We can all relate to the inner conflict between good and evil that happens between Jekyll and Hyde—although not in such an extreme way, I hope! We all have moments when part of us wants to give in to something that we know is wrong. Think of a time when you were tempted to do something wrong and describe that experience to a classmate.

3. It's easy to make a judgment about Dr. Jekyll and Mr. Hyde. Hyde is a villain, whereas Jekyll is an honest man. Hyde is bad, whereas Jekyll is good. In this book, however, you will focus on making comparisons without judgment. It's often difficult to realize when we are making a judgment and when we are just making observations—identifying how two things are similar and different. Some of the following statements are comparisons that make a judgment (that say one thing is better than another), and some are comparisons that make observations (that withhold judgment). With your class, or with a partner, identify whether each sentence makes a judgment or withholds judgment.
   a. The personalities of Jekyll and Hyde are very different.
   b. Hyde is a terrible man compared to Jekyll.
   c. Dr. Jekyll is an honest old man who has many friends. Hyde is young and friendless.
   d. A man who chooses to drink a potion that makes him evil is being foolish, but if he transforms accidentally, he is not to blame.

Memoria—

This icon points to more tips on memorization at the back of the book.

The Road Not Taken

—by Robert Frost

Two roads diverged in a yellow wood,
And sorry I could not travel both
And be one traveler, long I stood
And looked down one as far as I could
To where it bent in the undergrowth;

Then took the other, as just as fair,
And having perhaps the better claim,
Because it was grassy and wanted wear;
Though as for that the passing there
Had worn them really about the same,

And both that morning equally lay
In leaves no step had trodden black.
Oh, I kept the first for another day!
Yet knowing how way leads on to way,
I doubted if I should ever come back.

I shall be telling this with a sigh
Somewhere ages and ages hence:
Two roads diverged in a wood, and I—
I took the one less traveled by,
And that has made all the difference.

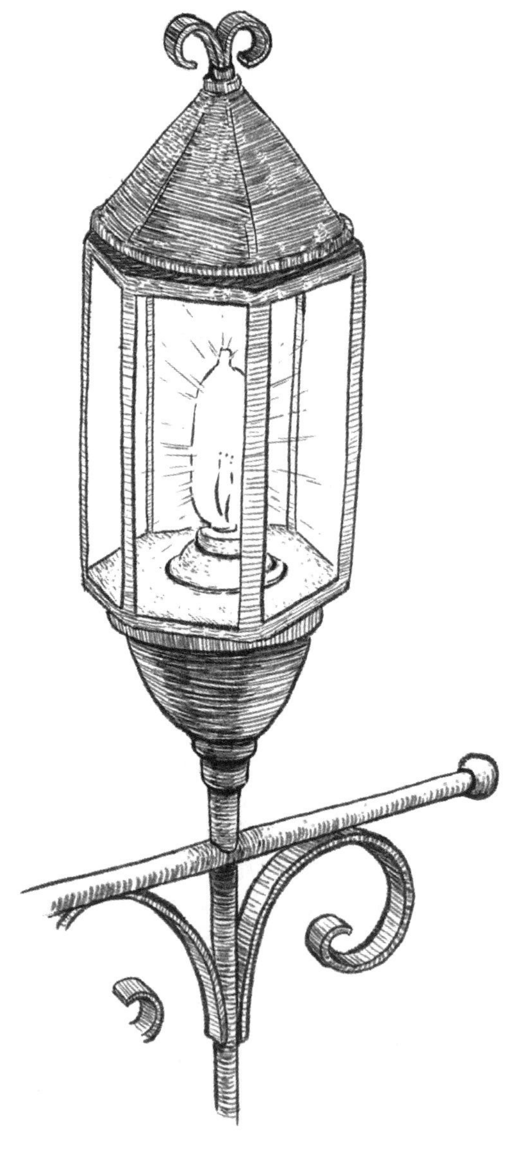

1. After reading this poem by Robert Frost, an American poet who lived during the nineteenth and twentieth centuries, define any words you may not know. Then discuss something particular that you like about this poem. You might choose a specific stanza, line, or phrase, a sound or rhythm, an image or a word. Make sure to explain why you like it.
2. Have you ever felt, like Frost, torn between two choices? Describe a time when comparing two things helped you make a decision.
3. Memorize a stanza of this poem and be prepared to recite it during your next class.
4. Write this poem in your commonplace book, along with any thoughts you have about it.

Go Deeper—

Now you will practice making comparisons between two subjects. First, you will compare characters from two different texts. Then you will compare two characters from the same text. Finally, you will compare what one character is like in the beginning of the text and what he is like at the end of the text. Read the passages and then use complete sentences to answer the questions that follow.

The Good Samaritan

—from Luke 10:30–37 in the Christian Scriptures (NIV)

"A man was going down from Jerusalem to Jericho, when he was attacked by robbers. They stripped him of his clothes, beat him and went away, leaving him half dead. A priest happened to be going down the same road, and when he saw the man, he passed by on the other side. So too, a **Levite**, when he came to the place and saw him, passed by on the other side. But a **Samaritan**, as he traveled, came where the man was; and when he saw him, he took pity on him. He went to him and bandaged his wounds, pouring on oil and wine. Then he put the man on his own donkey, brought him to an inn and took care of him. The next day he took out two denarii[1] and gave them to the innkeeper. 'Look after him,' he said, 'and when I return, I will **reimburse** you for any extra expense you may have.' "

1. denarii: a unit of money; in this story, equivalent to a full day's wage

Les Miserables

—adapted from *Les Miserables* by Victor Hugo

The main character of *Les Miserables* is Jean Valjean, an ex-prisoner who has spent twenty years in jail for stealing a loaf of bread. Upon his release, he is given a letter that must be shown at any place where he might seek employment. The letter basically calls him a thief. Shortly after, he is welcomed into a bishop's home to eat dinner with him and rest his weary bones. At dinner, he notices valuable pieces of silverware on the bishop's table. That night, he cannot sleep, because he keeps thinking about them. He knows that if he steals the silver, he will just be returning to a life of thievery, but he also realizes that this silver will give him money to eat and to sleep and perhaps to start a new life. After agonizing for quite some time, he gets up in the middle of the night, steals the items, and runs away from the bishop's home. The next morning he is caught by French police (gendarmes) and returned to the bishop, where he has a surprising conversation.

The door opened. A violent group made its appearance on the threshold. Three men were holding a fourth man by the collar. The three men were gendarmes; the other was Jean Valjean. The bishop advanced as quickly as his great age permitted.

"Ah! here you are!" he exclaimed, looking at Jean Valjean. "I am glad to see you. Well, but how is this? I gave you the candlesticks too, which are of silver like the rest, and for which you can certainly get two hundred **francs**. Why did you not carry them away with your forks and spoons?"

Jean Valjean opened his eyes wide and stared at the bishop with an expression which no human tongue can render any account of.

"Monseigneur,"[2] said the **brigadier** of gendarmes, "so what this man said is true, then? We came across him. He was walking like a man who is running away. We stopped him to look into the matter. He had this silver—"

"And he told you," interposed the bishop with a smile, "that it had been given to him by a kind old fellow of a priest with whom he had passed the night? I see how the matter stands. And you have brought him back here? It is a mistake."

"In that case," replied the brigadier, "we can let him go?"

"Certainly," replied the bishop.

The gendarmes released Jean Valjean, who shrank back.

"My friend," said the bishop to Jean Valjean, "before you go, here are your candlesticks. Take them."

2. Monseigneur: the proper title for addressing a French bishop

He stepped to the table, took the two silver candlesticks, and brought them to Jean Valjean.

Jean Valjean was trembling in every limb. He took the two candlesticks slowly, and with a bewildered air.

"Now," said the bishop, "go in peace. By the way, when you return, my friend, it is not necessary to pass through the garden. You can always enter and depart through the street door. It is never fastened with anything but a latch, either by day or by night."

Jean Valjean was like a man on the point of fainting.

The bishop drew near to him and said in a low voice: "Do not forget, never forget, that you have promised to use this money in becoming an honest man."

Jean Valjean, who had no recollection of ever having promised anything, remained speechless. The bishop had emphasized the words when he uttered them. He resumed with solemnity: "Jean Valjean, my brother, you no longer belong to evil, but to good. It is your soul that I buy from you; I withdraw it from black thoughts and I give it to God."

1. Compare the Good Samaritan and the bishop. What do their actions have in common?

____

____

____

____

____

2. Compare the Good Samaritan and the bishop. How are their actions different?

____

____

____

____

____

3. Think of a character from history or literature who is different from the Good Samaritan or the bishop, and write his or her name in the space provided. Then explain how this person is different from the Good Samaritan or the bishop.

   Example: Dr. Victor Frankenstein (fiction). Instead of using his medical skills to help suffering people, as the Samaritan and the bishop helped people, he created a dangerous monster.

   ____

   ____

   ____

   ____

   ____

   ____

   ____

   ____

   ____

   ____

The Town Mouse and the Country Mouse

—by Aesop

Now you must know that a Town Mouse once upon a time went on a visit to his cousin in the country. He was rough and ready, this cousin, but he loved his town friend and made him heartily welcome. Beans and bacon, cheese and bread, were all he had to offer, but he offered them freely. The Town Mouse rather turned up his long nose at this country fare, and said: "I cannot understand, Cousin, how you can put up with such poor food as this, but of course you cannot expect anything better in the country; come you with me and I will show you how to live. When you have been in town a week you will wonder how you could ever have stood a country life." No sooner said than done: the two mice set off for the town and arrived at the Town Mouse's residence late at night. "You will want some refreshment after our long journey," said the polite Town Mouse, and took his friend into the grand dining-room. There they found the remains of a fine feast, and soon the two mice were eating up jellies and cakes and all that was nice. Suddenly they heard growling and barking. "What is that?" said the Country Mouse. "It is only the dogs of the house," answered the other. "Only!" said the Country Mouse. "I do not like that music at my dinner." Just at that moment the door flew open, in came two huge **mastiffs**, and the two mice had to scamper down and run off. "Good-bye, Cousin," said the Country Mouse. "What! going so soon?" said the other. "Yes," he replied; "Better beans and bacon in peace than cakes and ale in fear."

1. What are the differences between the life of the Town Mouse and the life of the Country Mouse?

____

____

____

____

____

____

____

2. This fable from Aesop suggests that life in the country is better than life in the city if only because the country is safer than the city. However, many people have a natural preference for country or city living. Without making any judgments, explain how life in the city is different from life in the country. Make sure you consider both the positive and the negative qualities of each.

____

____

____

____

____

____

____

A Christmas Carol

—adapted from *A Christmas Carol* by Charles Dickens

Scrooge, as described at the beginning of the book:

Oh! But he was a tight-fisted hand, old Scrooge! a squeezing, wrenching, grasping, scraping, clutching, covetous, old sinner! Hard and sharp as flint, from which no steel had ever struck out generous fire; secret, and self-contained, and solitary as an oyster. The cold within him froze his old features, nipped his pointed nose, shriveled his cheek, stiffened his **gait**; made his eyes red, his thin lips blue; and spoke out shrewdly in his grating voice. Frost was on his head, and on his eyebrows, and his wiry chin. He carried his own low temperature always about with him; he iced his office in the dog-days[3] and didn't thaw it one degree at Christmas.

External heat and cold had little influence on Scrooge. No warmth could warm, no wintry weather chill him. No wind that blew was bitterer than he, no falling snow was more intent upon its purpose. Foul weather didn't know where to have him. The heaviest rain, and snow, and hail, and sleet, could boast of the advantage over him in only one respect. They often "came down" handsomely, and Scrooge never did.

Nobody ever stopped him in the street to say, with gladsome looks, "My dear Scrooge, how are you? When will you come to see me?" No beggars implored him for a little help, no children asked him what it was o'clock, no man or woman ever once in all his life inquired the way to such and such a place of Scrooge. Even the blind men's dogs appeared to know him; and when they saw him coming on, would tug their owners into doorways and up courts; and then would wag their tails as though they said, "No eye at all is better than an evil eye, dark master!"

But what did Scrooge care! It was the very thing he liked. To edge his way along the crowded paths of life, warning all human sympathy to keep its distance.

Scrooge, as described at the end of the book, after having been visited by three ghosts during the night and waking up to find that he has been given a second chance at life:

"I don't know what to do!" cried Scrooge, laughing and crying in the same breath. "I am as light as a feather, I am as happy as an angel, I am as merry as a schoolboy. I am as giddy as a drunken man. A merry Christmas to everybody! A happy New Year to all the world. Hallo here! Whoop! Hallo!"

3. "he iced his office in the dog-days": "Dog-days" refers to the very hottest of days. This phrase is used figuratively to mean that Scrooge was a "cold" person—he chilled even the hottest air with his presence.

"A merry Christmas, Bob!"[4] said Scrooge, with an earnestness that could not be mistaken, as he clapped him on the back. "A merrier Christmas, Bob, my good fellow, than I have given you, for many a year! I'll raise your salary and help your struggling family, and we will discuss your affairs this very afternoon, Bob! Make up the fires, and buy another bucket of coal before you dot another *i*, Bob Cratchit!"

Scrooge was better than his word. He did it all, and infinitely more; and to Tiny Tim,[5] who did NOT die, he was a second father. He became as good a friend, as good a master, and as good a man as the good old city knew, or any other good old city or town in the good old world. Some people laughed to see the change in him, but he let them laugh, and little heeded them; for he was wise enough to know that nothing ever happened on this globe, for good, at which some people did not have their fill of laughter. . . . His own heart laughed: and that was quite enough for him.

1. Compare Scrooge at the beginning of the story to Scrooge at the end of the story. In what ways is he different?

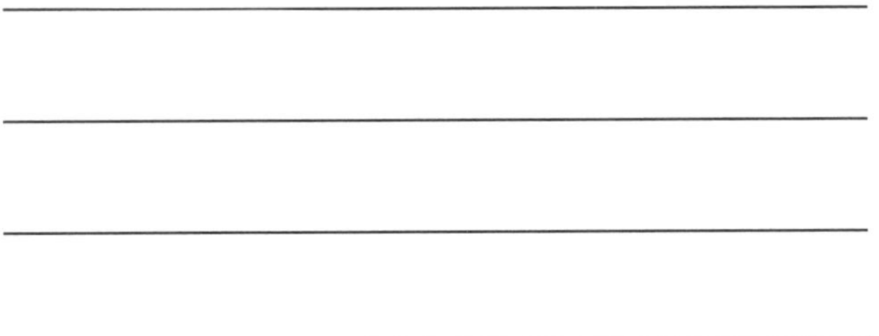

▲ Illustration of Bob Cratchit and Tiny Tim, reproduced from a c.1870s frontispiece to Charles Dickens's *A Christmas Carol*

4. Refers to Bob Cratchit, Scrooge's much-abused assistant.
5. Refers to Bob Cratchit's youngest son, who is crippled and unwell.

2. Based on the previous comparison, is Scrooge a better person at the beginning or the end of the story? Explain your answer.

3. Make a connection between Scrooge (either the old, stingy Scrooge or the new, generous one) and another person. In this case, think of someone who is similar to Scrooge in some way. This could be someone you know personally or a figure from history or literature. How is Scrooge similar to this person?

Lesson 2

Identifying Similarities & Differences

Ever since I was young, people have told me that I look just like my dad. It used to annoy me, especially when I was a teenager. The last thing I wanted was for my friends to hear someone say that I resembled my dad, who seemed like an uncool old guy. As I grew up, though, it bothered me less and less. My resemblance to my dad was just a fact I accepted because I knew it was true. I *did* look a lot like my dad. We had the same thick, wavy hair, the same pronounced chin and facial structure, the same blue eyes. We were—and still are—similar.

Just because we are similar, however, does not mean that we are exactly the same. We share *some* things in common, and we might resemble each other in *some* ways, but we are not identical. There are also many differences between my dad and me, even just in our physical appearance. I am taller than he is, for example. He has more facial hair than me. And, of course, he has a *lot* more gray hair!

Just as my dad and I look alike in some ways and different in other ways, two things you compare will usually have both similarities and differences. You may find that two objects of comparison are more similar than different, or more different than they are similar, but either way, you should be able to find both similarities and differences as you examine your subjects closely.

You may find that you are more interested in the ways your subjects are alike than how they are different, or vice versa. That's OK. While your goal is to write a balanced essay (you will be writing about an equal number of similarities and differences in your comparison essays), you will have a chance in the last paragraph of the essay to reflect on your observations.

Comparing two characters or objects can be easy when their similarities or differences are obvious. For example, a comparison between Winnie the Pooh and Dracula would show many glaring differences. Sometimes, however, it isn't as easy to find similarities or differences. For example, a comparison between two identical twins might show a lot of similarities, but it might be harder to find differences. When you can't find anything obvious to show as a similarity or difference, you may need to look at your subjects more closely. You may need to look for small similarities or differences, also called **nuances**, or you may need to look closer or gather more information in order to find a similarity or difference.

When you make a comparison your goal is to observe your subjects as skillfully and thoroughly as possible. Observation requires that you use your senses, pay attention, and record details, facts, and descriptions. Think of this kind of comparison as a bit like a science experiment. You don't just walk into science class, throw a few chemicals in a beaker, then sit back and eat popcorn while you watch what happens. You follow certain procedures, you record data and make observations, and then you reflect on what you observed. In a similar way, in order to write your essays you will need to make careful observations. When you are very careful in comparing two things, you will often see things you didn't notice right away.

The closer you look at something—and the better informed you are about its characteristics—the better you will be able to compare it with something else. Being a good and careful observer also shows your audience that you can be trusted to make accurate observations.

To understand how to compare two things carefully, consider the ideas of two prominent African American men who were social activists at the turn of the nineteenth century: Marcus Garvey and W.E.B. DuBois. At first glance these men may appear to have had very similar ideas. You may not see much difference between them. Both of them fought hard for African American rights and equality. While neither Garvey nor DuBois condoned violence, they both believed that achieving black equality would require a revolution of sorts. Yet if you look closer, you will see that these two activists did not agree on everything. Take a look at the following selections, one by Garvey and one by DuBois, and see if you can identify a major difference in their beliefs.

If You Believe the Negro[A] Has a Soul[1]

▲ Marcus Garvey, 1924.

[A]Please note that the use of the word "Negro" to identify people of the African American race is improper usage for today. For centuries it was considered the most common and least offensive word of choice, preferred even by black Americans, but during the civil rights movement of the 1950s and 1960s, some black leaders in the United States objected to the word. From that time onward, it began to be used less and less. Today some consider the word out of date or even offensive. In this instance, however, we have remained faithful to the reading selections' use of this term because it was the term that was chosen by Garvey and DuBois themselves to represent their race.

After World War I, thousands of African American soldiers returned home to face increased discrimination and **segregation**. The irony is that these men had just been fighting in Europe for the cause of **democracy**, yet in their homeland they themselves did not have freedom. Sensing this frustration, Marcus Garvey attracted many young black people to his Universal Negro Improvement Association (UNIA). Ultimately, Garvey and the UNIA wanted all the black people in the world to return to their homeland in Africa, free of white rule. Garvey even met with a leader of the Ku Klux Klan in Atlanta in 1922. He praised racial segregation laws and declared that the goal of the UNIA and the KKK was the same: completely separate black and white societies. The following reading selection is from a speech given by Garvey in 1921.

Fellow citizens of Africa, I greet you in the name of the Universal Negro Improvement Association (UNIA) and African Communities League of the World. You may ask, "What organization is that?" It is for me to inform you that the UNIA is an organization that seeks to unite, into one solid body, the 400 million Negroes in the world. To link up the 50 million Negroes in the United States of America, with the 20 million Negroes of the West Indies, the 40 million Negroes of South and Central America, with the 280 million Negroes of Africa, for the purpose of bettering our industrial, commercial, educational, social, and political conditions. As you are aware, the world in which we live today is divided into separate race groups and distinct nationalities. Each race and each

1. from the Marcus Garvey and UNIA Papers Project at the University of California, Los Angeles

nationality is endeavoring to work out its own destiny, to the exclusion of other races and other nationalities. We hear the cry of "England for the Englishman," of "France for the Frenchman," of "Germany for the German," of "Ireland for the Irish," of "Palestine[2] for the Jew," of "Japan for the Japanese," of "China for the Chinese." We of the UNIA are raising the cry of "Africa for the Africans," those at home and those abroad. There are 400 million Africans in the world who have Negro blood coursing through their veins, and we believe that the time has come to unite these 400 million people toward the one common purpose of bettering their condition. The great problem of the Negro for the last 500 years has been that of disunity. No one or no organization ever succeeded in uniting the Negro race. But within the last four years, the UNIA has worked wonders . . . . We want to unite the Negro race in this country. We want every Negro to work for one common object, that of building a nation of his own on the great continent of Africa. That all Negroes all over the world are working for the establishment of a government in Africa, means that it will be realized in another few years. We want the moral and financial support of every Negro to make this dream a possibility. Our race, this organization, has established itself in Nigeria, West Africa, and it endeavors to do all possible to develop that Negro country to become a great industrial and commercial commonwealth. Pioneers have been sent by this organization to Nigeria, and they are now laying the foundations upon which the 400 million Negroes of the world will build. If you believe that the Negro has a soul, if you believe that the Negro is a man, if you believe the Negro was endowed with the senses commonly given to other men by the Creator, then you must acknowledge that what other men have done, Negroes can do. We want to build up cities, nations, governments, industries of our own in Africa, so that we will be able to have a chance to rise from the lowest to the highest position in the African Commonwealth.

2. Palestine: an area of the Middle East, now known as Israel and the Palestinian Territories

The Way Forward

—adapted from *The Souls of Black Folk* by W.E.B. Dubois

W.E.B. DuBois was a black scholar who, like Garvey, was angered by the continued oppression of African Americans after World War I. He was very influential as the leader of the most prominent organization for African American equality, the NAACP (National Association for the Advancement of Colored People). Like Garvey, he fought for the independence of African colonies from the European powers. However, he disagreed sharply with Garvey's idea of **separatism**. He said that

▲ W.E.B. Dubois, 1918.

> Garvey is, without a doubt, the most dangerous enemy of the Negro race in America and in the world. He is either a lunatic or a traitor. He is sending all over this country tons of letters and pamphlets appealing to Congressmen, businessmen, philanthropists, and educators to join him on a platform whose half-concealed planks may be interpreted as follows:
>
> That no person of Negro descent can ever hope to become an American citizen.
>
> That forcible separation of the races and the banishment of Negroes to Africa is the only solution of the Negro problem.[3]

In fact, DuBois argued strenuously for the full integration of African Americans into American society and their full equality.

The following selection is from a book written by DuBois in 1903.

Chapter 1: Of Our Spiritual Strivings

A Negro ever feels his twoness, as an American and as a Negro—two souls, two thoughts, two unreconciled strivings. He has two warring ideals in one dark body. His dogged strength alone keeps it from being torn apart.

The history of the American Negro is the history of this strife,—this longing to attain self-conscious manhood, to merge his double self into a better and truer self. In this merging he wishes neither of the older selves to be lost. He would not Africanize America, for America has too much to teach the world and Africa. He would not bleach his Negro soul in a flood of white Americanism, for he knows that Negro blood has a message for the world. He simply wishes to make it possible for a man to be both a Negro and an American, without being cursed and spit upon by his fellows, without having the doors of Opportunity closed roughly in his face.

---

3. from "Marcus Garvey: A Lunatic or a Traitor?", originally published in the May 1924 edition of *The Crisis*, the official publication of the NAACP

This, then, is the end[4] of his striving: to be a co-worker in the kingdom of culture,[5] to escape both death and isolation, to husband[6] and use his best powers and his latent genius.

Chapter 6: Of The Training of Black Men

We may decry the color-prejudice of the South, yet it remains a heavy fact. Such curious kinks of the human mind exist and must be reckoned with soberly. They cannot be laughed away, nor always successfully stormed at, nor easily abolished by new laws. And yet they must not be left alone. They must be recognized as unpleasant facts; things that stand in the way of civilization and religion and common decency. They can be met in but one way,—by the breadth and broadening of human reason, by catholicity[7] of taste and culture. . . .

The one remedy of Education leaps to the lips of all:—such human training as will best use the labor of all men without enslaving or brutalizing; such training as will give us poise to encourage the prejudices that support society, and to stamp out those that in sheer barbarity deafen us to the wail of prisoned souls, and the mounting fury of shackled men.

But when we have vaguely said that Education will set this tangle straight, what have we uttered but a truth? Training for life teaches living; but what training for the profitable living together of black men and white? Today we have climbed to heights where we would open at least the outer courts of knowledge to all, display its treasures to many, and select the few to whom its mystery of Truth is revealed, not wholly by birth or the accidents of the stock market, but at least in part according to skill and aim, talent, and character.

4. By "end," DuBois means "goal"—the goal of his striving—rather than an end to his effort.
5. kingdom of culture: America. DuBois calls America "the kingdom of culture" to emphasize that his nation was a leading light and inspiration in the culture of the world.
6. husband: to manage carefully
7. catholicity: inclusiveness, broad-mindedness

Tell It Back—Narration

1. **MARK UP THE TEXT—Annotation:** Read through the two reading selections again. As you read, write in the margin of the text symbols that will help you understand the text better and find important details later. The following are some symbols you might use:
   - Underline the main idea of the reading or any important point.
   - Put a question mark in the margin to mark any part of the reading you don't understand.
   - Write any questions or thoughts you have in the margin.
   - Put an exclamation point in the margin to mark any part of the reading you find surprising or particularly interesting.
   - Circle any important or unfamiliar vocabulary words or proper nouns when they are first introduced. Remember, a proper noun is the name for any specific person, place, thing, or idea. How do you know which words to circle? Circle words that appear repeatedly, or words you can't understand from the context of the sentence alone. Look up any unfamiliar words in the glossary, or, if they aren't there, in a dictionary.

This icon points to more tips on summarizing, found on p. 203.

2. In the space provided, write a five- or six-sentence summary for each of the lesson readings. Use your annotations to help you identify the most important points in the readings, and be sure to include those points in your summaries.

Summary of *If You Believe the Negro Has a Soul*:

Summary of *The Way Forward*:

3. Tell back any similarities you see between the lives or ideas of Marcus Garvey and W.E.B. DuBois.

Talk About It—

1. What was the major difference between Garvey's ideas for helping African Americans and DuBois's? Provide evidence from the text to support this contrast.

2. The president of the United States during part of Garvey's and DuBois's careers (1913–1921) was Woodrow Wilson.[8] Wilson was a former university professor and leader. He was proud of the fact that while he was president of Princeton University, no black people had been admitted to the school. During his presidency of the United States, he segregated the federal government offices. He sympathized with the Ku Klux Klan and even organized a private screening at the White House of a racist film called *The Birth of a Nation*. He also promoted separation of the races, saying on one occasion: "Segregation is not a humiliation but a benefit."

   Imagine that you are W.E.B. DuBois and you are preparing for a conversation with President Wilson. Recall the principles of refutation from book 5 of this series, in which you attacked an idea as unbelievable, improbable, unclear, or improper. Which of those categories would you use to refute segregation? What would you say to Wilson's idea that "segregation is not a humiliation"? Use evidence to support your position.

8. Woodrow Wilson (1856–1924): the twenty-eighth president of the United States. He was criticized for being slow to help the cause of women's suffrage

3. "Hypocrisy" is an English word that comes from the Greek word *hypokrisis*, which means "acting on the stage." Actors were called *hypokrites*. Over time the word "hypocrite" began to be used as a negative term that referred to people who were pretenders or who were fake. After World War I, Garvey and DuBois called the leaders of the United States hypocrites because they claimed to be fighting for freedom around the world but were not concerned about ensuring liberty and equality for African Americans in their own country. Discuss a time in your life when you have seen someone act like a hypocrite. What emotions did this hypocrisy cause you to feel?
4. Garvey argued for separation of the races, while DuBois was convinced that white and black people could coexist peacefully and equally. In 1963, Dr. Martin Luther King Jr. said in his "I Have a Dream" speech, "I have a dream that little black boys and black girls will be able to join hands with little white boys and white girls as sisters and brothers." Imagine if King were to meet with Garvey and DuBois. Which of them do you think he would agree with the most? Explain your answer.

Harlem

—Langston Hughes

What happens to a dream deferred?

Does it dry up
like a raisin in the sun?
Or fester like a sore—
And then run?
Does it stink like rotten meat?
Or crust and sugar over—
like a syrupy swcct?

Maybe it just sags
like a heavy load.

Or does it explode?

1. After reading this poem by Langston Hughes, an African American poet who was a major contributor to the **Harlem Renaissance**[9] of the 1920s, define any words you may not know. Then discuss which comparison to a dream deferred (for example, a raisin in the sun or rotten meat) you like best. Make sure to explain why you like it.

9. Harlem Renaissance: a revival of the arts (music, dance, literature, poetry, and theatre) that took place in the black community of Harlem, NY, during the 1920s

2. How does this poem relate to the speeches of Marcus Garvey and W.E.B. DuBois, or even to the quote from Dr. King found in the Talk About It section?
3. Memorize this poem and be prepared to recite it during your next class.
4. Write this poem in your commonplace book, along with any thoughts you have about it.

Go Deeper—

1. As you make comparisons, you may, without realizing it, explain your observations by using comparative or superlative adjectives. **Comparative adjectives**—such as "larger," "smaller," "faster," or "higher"—are used to compare, or show the differences between one person and another person, or one thing and another thing. For example, "That piece of cake is *larger than the other one.*" Comparative adjectives can be used when showing a minor difference ("Today was hotter than yesterday") or a major difference ("Today was way hotter than yesterday!") **Superlative adjectives**—such as "tallest," "smallest," "fastest," or "highest"—are used to describe a person or thing as having more of a quality than all of the other people or things in a group. For example, "China has the largest population in the world." In this sentence, China's population is being compared to the populations of all other countries.

   In the space provided, write either "comparative" or "superlative" to identify the adjectives in each of the following sentences.

   a. ____________________ New York City has a smaller population than Sao Paulo, Brazil.

   b. ____________________ Driving a car is harder than riding a bike.

   c. ____________________ The cheetah is the fastest animal in the world.

   d. ____________________ The tallest building in the world is the Burj Khalifa in Dubai.

   e. ____________________ The Amazon is the world's largest river.

   f. ____________________ Rhode Island is a smaller state than Iowa, but Michigan is bigger than both of them.

   g. ____________________ World War II was deadlier than World War I.

   h. ____________________ Planes can travel faster than ships.

   i. ____________________ Golden retrievers are furrier than elephants.

   j. ____________________ The oldest college in the United States is Harvard University.

2. From your math studies, you probably already know about Venn diagrams and how they can help you to make comparisons between sets. This tool can be just as useful in writing comparison essays. With Venn diagrams, similarities and differences can be listed in a form that is easy to see.

For the comparisons in this book, a Venn diagram would be made up of two or more overlapping circles, one for each subject you are comparing. In the outer part of a circle, characteristics that are unique to the subject are listed. These unique qualities are the differences between the two things. In the overlapping space of both circles, shared characteristics (similarities) are listed. For example, say you want to compare two desserts, ice cream and cake. Here is a possible Venn diagram for the comparison:

Here's another example using Marcus Garvey and W.E.B. DuBois:

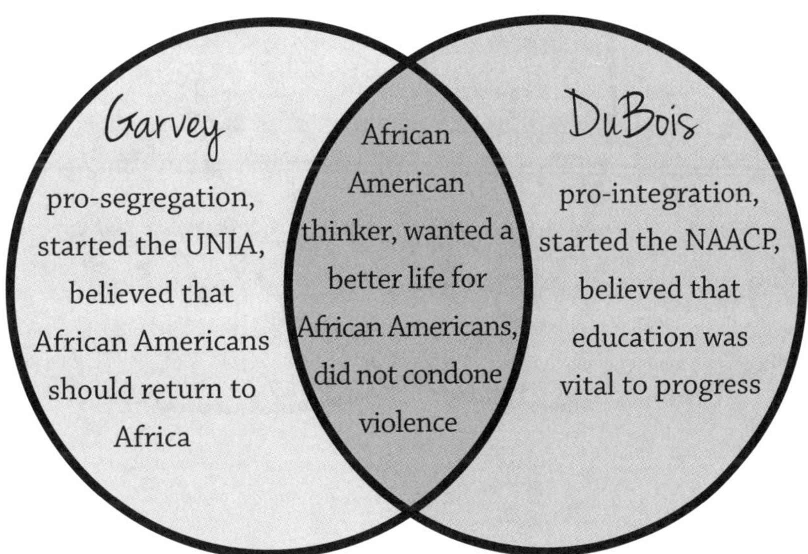

For each of the following sets, create a Venn diagram that shows the similarities and differences between the subjects. List at least three items in each circle and at least three items in the overlapping area.

a. Africa and North America

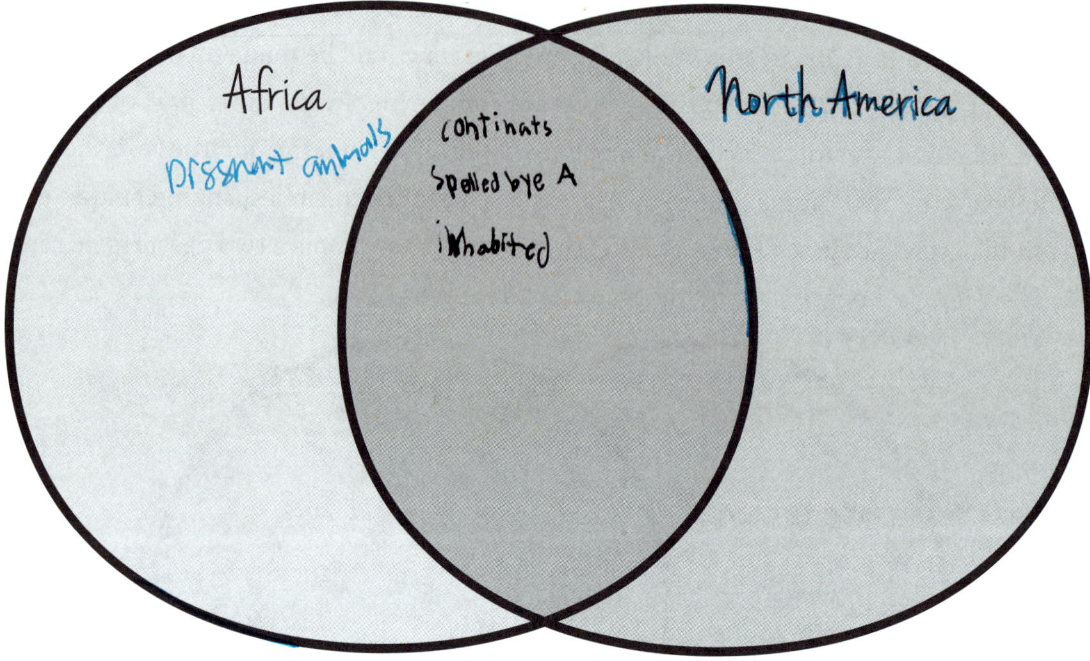

b. trucks and passenger jets

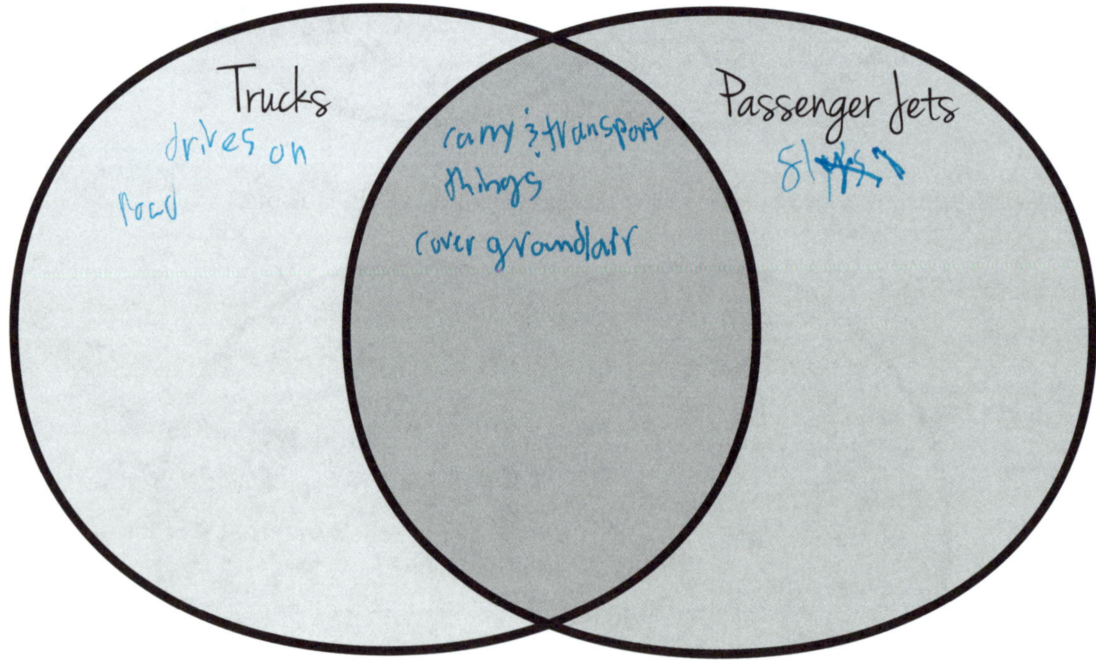

c. dogs and cats

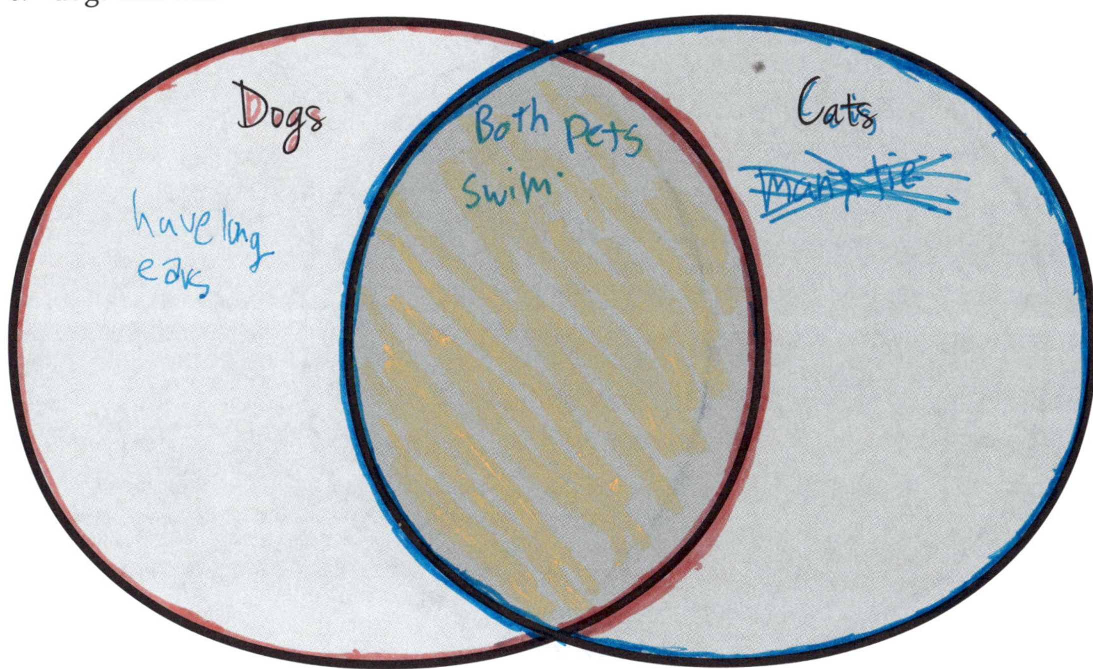

d. classical music and rock music

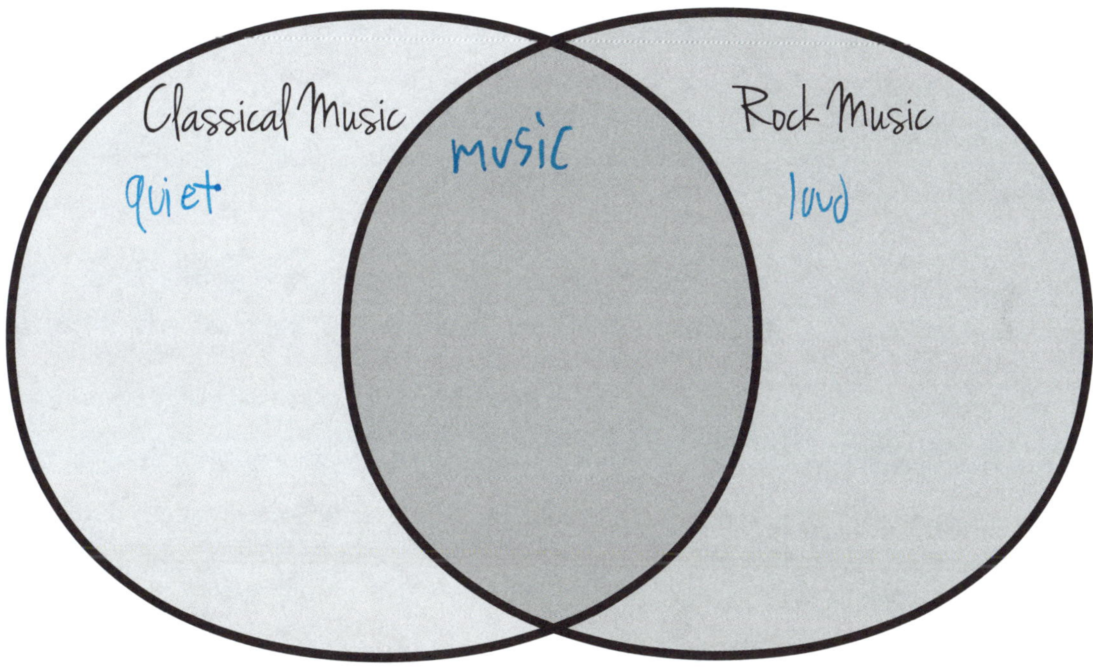

e. pizza and spaghetti

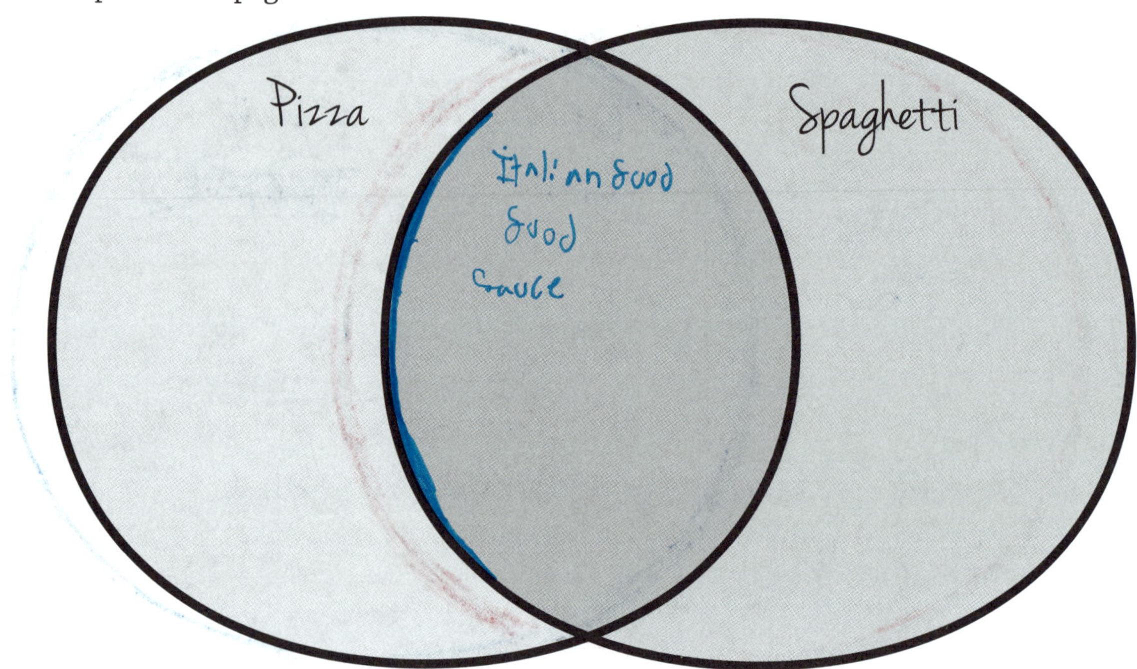

Lesson 3

The Tools of Metaphor & Simile

Say your friend says to you, "I am a fish when I get into the swimming pool." Or "I run like a cheetah on the soccer field." Wait a minute! Is your friend saying that she actually turns into a fish when she gets into water? Or that he can really run as fast as a cheetah? Of course not! "I am a fish" is just a creative way of saying, "I swim really well," and "I run like a cheetah" is a way of saying, "I'm a fast runner." Your friends are comparing themselves to something in order to describe themselves. Comparisons like these are called analogies.

Analogy is a broad term for a comparison between two ideas, events, or objects that is used to describe or explain one of those things. An analogy focuses on similarities. The two things may look very different from each other, but when you look closer you will find that they have some things in common. For example, you may not think your friend has anything in common with a fish or a cheetah, but when you look closer, you can see that she has swimming in common with a fish or that he has running fast in common with a cheetah.

The word "metaphor" comes from two Greek words: *meta* meaning "across" or "transport" or "transfer," and *pherein*, which means "to bear" or "to carry." When you put the two words together they mean "to carry across." So a metaphor "carries across" the meaning of one object to another.

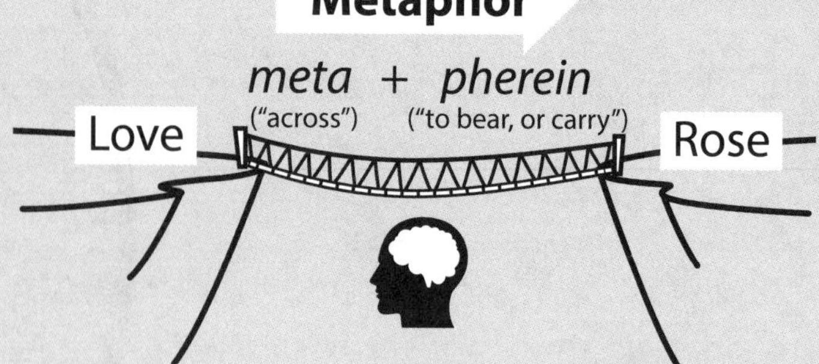

Using an analogy to describe something can help us to understand it better. For example, I could tell you that the sky is blue, but if I told you that the sky is as blue as a robin's egg, you would have a better idea of just what shade of blue I'm talking about. Analogies also can help to communicate ideas that may otherwise be difficult to explain, and they can help to catch an audience's attention as well.

Two common ways of making an analogy are simile and metaphor, and you will be writing some of your own for the essays in this book. Both simile and metaphor are types of figurative language, which is wording that suggests an imaginative meaning that goes beyond what the actual words say. A simile is a comparison that uses the words "like" or "as." For example, "I run like a cheetah" or "He is as clever as a fox." A metaphor makes a comparison without using the words "like" or "as." For example, "I am a fish when I get into the swimming pool" or "He is a monkey on the rope ladder." We naturally use simile and metaphor all the time to describe our ideas. Try for one day to speak without using any metaphor—I bet you can't!

There are a lot of different ways to make an analogy. Some, such as simile and metaphor, are usually pretty simple and short. Others, such as extended metaphors and allegory, are much longer and more detailed. You may encounter such longer or more complicated analogies as you move forward in your education, but for now you'll be sticking with simile and metaphor.

Figurative language—wording that suggests an imaginative meaning that goes beyond what the actual words say

Analogy—a broad term for a comparison between two ideas, events, or objects that is used to describe or explain one of those things

Metaphor—a comparison in which one thing is used to describe another thing that appears to be different but that actually has some similarities; does not use the words "like" or "as" (e.g., "That test was a breeze," "Love is a rose, a red and thorny flower.")

Simile—a comparison using the words "like" or "as" (e.g., "I'm as silly as a clown with a fire hose.")

Sometimes simile and metaphor are more complicated than "I am a fish" or "I run like a cheetah." Sometimes they don't directly say that one thing is the same as another, but if you look closely, you will see that a comparison is being made. To better understand this more complicated type of metaphor, take a look at an excerpt from one of the great American novels, *Moby-Dick*. *Moby-Dick* was written in 1851 by Herman Melville. It tells the story of Captain Ahab, who is obsessed with tracking down and destroying a giant whale that was responsible for the loss of Ahab's leg. Ahab, who is in charge of a ship called the *Pequod*, pursues the whale **relentlessly** and recklessly, even to the point of endangering his own life and the lives of his sailors. As you read, make note of the passages that are marked with a dotted underline. Those are some of the analogies in this reading.

Moby-Dick

—adapted from *Moby-Dick* by Herman Melville

Please note: This passage from *Moby-Dick* can be found in updated language at the back of the book (see page 224). We recommend that you try to read and understand Melville's original writing first. His use of English is very rich indeed! However, if you find yourself bogged down by the language, if the pictures aren't clear in your head, the updated version may help.

Note also that this is a difficult text, so if you find yourself struggling with challenging words, you can look them up in the glossary or, if you don't find them there, in a dictionary.

For long days and weeks, Ahab and anguish lay stretched together in one hammock. Here his torn body and gashed soul bled into one another, and so interfusing, made him mad.[1] It was only then, on the homeward voyage, after the encounter with the whale, that the final monomania seized him. At intervals during the passage, he was a raving lunatic; and, though unlimbed of a leg,[2] yet such vital strength lurked in his chest, and was moreover intensified by his delirium, that his mates were forced to lace him fast[3] there, as he sailed, raving in his hammock. In a straitjacket, he swung to the mad rockings of the gales. Now and then the ship floated across the tranquil tropics, and, to all appearances, the old man's delirium seemed left behind him with the Cape Horn swells. Ahab came forth from his dark den into the blessed light and air, bearing that firm, collected front,[4] however pale, and issued his calm orders once again; and his mates thanked God the direful[5] madness was now gone. Even then, Ahab, in his hidden self, raved on. Human madness is oftentimes a cunning and most feline thing. When you think it fled, it may have but become transfigured into some still subtler form.

Certain it is, that with the mad secret of his unabated rage bolted up and keyed[6] in him, Ahab had purposely sailed upon the present voyage with the sole and all-engrossing object of hunting the White Whale. Had any one of his old acquaintances on shore but half dreamed of what was lurking in him then, how soon would their aghast and righteous souls have wrenched the ship from such a fiendish man! They were bent on profitable cruises, the profit to be counted down in dollars from the mint. He was intent on an audacious, immitigable, and supernatural revenge.

---

1. Sometimes the word "mad" was used to describe mental illness. Another term that people used and still use is "crazy." Neither term, however, is as accurate as the term "mental illness."
2. unlimbed of a leg: missing one of his legs
3. lace him fast: tie him tightly
4. front: often means "false front." Ahab is putting on a false look of sanity and calm.
5. direful: dreadful, terrible
6. keyed: likely means "locked"

Often he was forced from his hammock by exhausting and intolerably vivid dreams of the night. When he woke, his thoughts would whirl round and round in his blazing brain, till the very throbbing of his lifespot[7] became insufferable anguish. Sometimes these spiritual throes in him heaved his being up from its base, and a chasm seemed to open up in him, from which forked flames and lightnings shot up, and accursed fiends beckoned him to leap down among them. When this hell in himself yawned beneath him, a wild cry would be heard through the ship; and with glaring eyes Ahab would burst from his state room, as though escaping from a bed that was on fire.

Here, then, was this grey-headed, ungodly old man, chasing with curses a Job's whale[8] round the world, at the head of a crew, too, chiefly made up of mongrel renegades, and castaways, and cannibals. Such a crew, so officered, seemed specially picked to help him to his monomaniac revenge. How it was that they so aboundingly responded to the old man's ire—by what evil magic their souls were possessed, that at times his hate seemed almost theirs, the White Whale as much their insufferable foe as his—how all this came to be—what the White Whale was to them, or how to their unconscious understandings, also, in some dim, unsuspected way, he might have seemed the gliding great demon of the seas of life[9]—to explain all this would be to dive deeper than I can go.

There are a number of complicated analogies in this reading, aren't there? Here are explanations of the few that we've marked:

- "Ahab came forth from his dark den" is a metaphor that compares Ahab to a type of animal that would have a den, such as a fox, coyote, cougar, bear, or lion. Many of the animals that live in dens tend to be dangerous and to hibernate (sleep or rest through the winter). Both of these are qualities that Ahab has. He is dangerous in his "madness," and he "hibernates" as he hides away in his room.
- "Human madness is oftentimes a cunning and most feline thing" is a metaphor that compares mental illness to a cat. The word "feline" means "catlike." Cats are known to be tricky and hard to find because they can fit into small spaces. They can take you by surprise when they come out of hiding, and they can lie in wait for a long time. Madness can also be tricky and hard to find. It can take us by surprise when it appears, and it can stay hidden for a long time.
- "With glaring eyes Ahab would burst from his state room, as though escaping from a bed that was on fire" is a simile. It compares the way Ahab comes out of his room to the way a person would move in an emergency situation. It describes the way that Ahab moves and gives us a picture of what he looked like.

7. lifespot: this may be a reference to the heart or the brain
8. Job's whale: a reference to the Hebrew Scriptures. Job's whale is a sea monster or huge fish that is terrifying and impossible to control.
9. the gliding great demon of the seas of life: This is a metaphor. The White Whale, Moby Dick, is like a demon that torments them.

- "To explain all this would be to dive deeper than I can go" is a metaphor that compares the job of trying to explain a difficult subject to diving into the depths of the sea. Diving deep into the sea is very hard to do, and many people could not do it. This comparison emphasizes the idea that the reasons for the crew's behavior are very hard to figure out.

As you can see, analogies can be used in many ways. Some are simple and some are more complicated, but they all have the same goal: to make a piece of writing more interesting or easier to understand. In your comparison essays you will use simile and metaphor to introduce the two subjects you will compare.

Tell It Back—Narration

1. Without looking at the text, give the definitions for the following terms:
    - figurative language
    - analogy
    - metaphor
    - simile
2. What are some reasons a writer might use analogy?

Talk About It—

1. Melville describes Captain Ahab as selfish and vengeful. What are some quotes from the text that show Ahab's desire for revenge?
2. In the previous book, *Encomium & Vituperation*, you learned that encomium is praise and vituperation is blame. Based on the reading selection, would you be more likely to write an encomium or a vituperation about Captain Ahab? Explain your answer. Be sure to include specific quotes from the text in your explanation.
3. Melville uses figurative language throughout his story. There is an imaginative meaning to his descriptions that goes well beyond what the actual words say. For example, when he describes the "gashed soul" of Ahab as bleeding, he means that Ahab's soul is hurt, or wounded. Melville tells us this by comparing Ahab's soul to a body that has been wounded, or cut, and is bleeding. Why do you suppose authors use figurative language like this? Why don't they just say exactly what they mean?

The Noiseless, Patient Spider

—by Walt Whitman

A NOISELESS, patient spider,
I mark'd, where, on a little promontory, it stood, isolated;
Mark'd how, to explore the vacant, vast surrounding,
It launch'd forth filament, filament, filament, out of itself;
Ever unreeling them—ever tirelessly speeding them.

And you, O my Soul, where you stand,
Surrounded, surrounded, in measureless oceans of space,
Ceaselessly musing, venturing, throwing,—seeking the spheres, to connect them;
Till the bridge you will need, be form'd—till the ductile anchor hold;
Till the gossamer thread you fling, catch somewhere, O my Soul.

1. After reading this poem by Walt Whitman, an important American poet from the 1800s, define any words you may not know. Then discuss something particular that you like about this poem. You might choose a specific stanza, line, or phrase, a sound or rhythm, an image or a word. Make sure to explain why you like it.
2. In this poem, Whitman makes a comparison between the spider, in the first stanza, and the soul, in the second stanza. As the spider stands alone in a vast, empty space, so the soul stands surrounded by measureless empty space. As the spider creates threads and throws them out to attach them to something, the soul seeks to build a bridge to connect it to something. Both spider and soul are alone and looking for connection. How is the soul like a spider spinning its web?
3. Memorize the second stanza of the poem and be prepared to recite it during your next class.
4. Write one or two of your favorite comparisons from this poem in your commonplace book, along with any thoughts you have about them.

1. Answer the questions and follow the instructions after each of the provided analogies.

   Examples:

   Human madness is oftentimes a cunning and most feline thing.

   What kind of comparison is it? metaphor

   What is being compared? Mental illness is being compared to a cat.

   What does the comparison mean? Cats are known to be tricky and hard to find because they can fit into small spaces. They can take you by surprise when they come out of hiding, and they can lie in wait for a long time. Madness can also be tricky and hard to find. It can take us by surprise when it appears, and it can stay hidden for a long time.

   Write your own metaphor that compares madness to another type of animal. Madness is a bird that squawks and does a sharp nose dive into the ocean.

   With glaring eyes Ahab would burst from his state room, as though escaping from a bed that was on fire.

   What kind of comparison is it? simile

   What is being compared? The way Ahab comes out of his room is being compared to the way a person would move in an emergency situation.

   What does the comparison mean? In the case of a fire, a person would move very quickly. This comparison means that Ahab was alarmed and moving with speed.

   Write your own simile that compares the way a person leaves a room to another type of action. With sleepy eyes, the girl came slowly out of her room like a turtle emerging from its shell.

   a. The cat stuck like a bur[10] to girl's back.

      What kind of comparison is it? ______

      What is being compared? ______

      What does the comparison mean? ______

      Write your own simile that compares a cat to another object. ______

10. bur: a prickly seed pod

b. The winter wind was a knife, cutting through my coat.

What kind of comparison is it? ________________________________

What is being compared? ________________________________

What does the comparison mean? ________________________________

____

Write your own metaphor that compares the winter wind to another object. ________

____

c. The ripples on the pond hit the shore with a sound like a dog lapping water.

What kind of comparison is it? ________________________________

What is being compared? ________________________________

____

What does the comparison mean? ________________________________

____

Write your own simile or metaphor that compares the sound of water to another sound. ________________________________

____

2. Create one metaphor and one simile from each of the following sets of columns by comparing objects from Column A to objects from Column B. For each analogy choose one object from each column. Notice that the objects are all specific nouns (e.g., oak), which are often more vivid than general words (e.g., tree). Also make sure that your sentences use strong verbs.

It might be fun for you to roll a die to help you choose what words you will use in your analogies. With your first roll, you can use the word in Column A that corresponds to the number you rolled. With your second roll, you can use the word in Column B that corresponds to the number you rolled.

Column A	Column B
1. eye	1. silver bowl
2. moon	2. head of cabbage
3. nightmare	3. rotten egg
4. brat	4. pizza pie
5. kingdom	5. snow globe
6. pimple	6. rose

Example simile: After he awoke, he shook his nightmare away like glitter in a snow globe.
Example metaphor: The moon shone brightly on the surface of a pond, an overturned silver bowl.

Simile: ______________________________

Metaphor: ______________________________

Column A	Column B
1. mustache	1. bronze sword
2. sunlight	2. branch
3. toes	3. banana
4. happiness	4. French fries
5. teeth	5. candle
6. ball gown	6. lion's mane

Simile: ______________________________

Metaphor: ______________________________

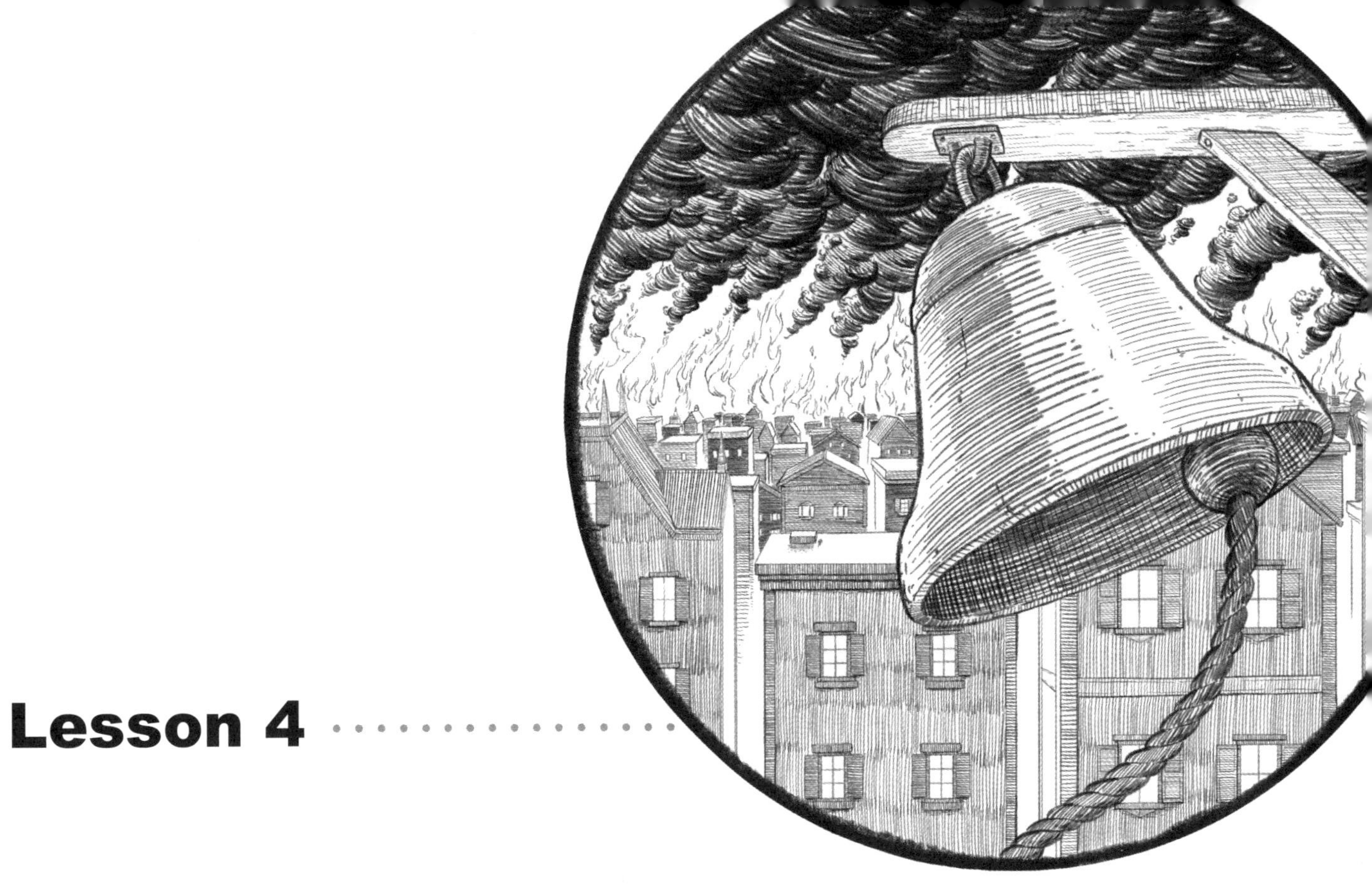

Lesson 4

Two Disasters: Fire & Ice

Have you heard the story about the cow that kicked over a lantern in the barn and started a fire? Um . . . actually, it's not just a joke. It really happened. Sort of. In 1871, there was a massive fire that leveled the city of Chicago, and at first it was rumored that the fire had been started when Mrs. O'Leary's[1] cow knocked over a lantern. How the fire actually began is unknown, but once it had done its work, it was responsible for one of the worst disasters in the nineteenth century. The fire destroyed over 70,000 buildings and 73 miles of streets.

Maybe you've heard the story about the so-called "unsinkable ship" that did precisely that: sink on its **maiden** voyage. The owners and builders of the ship were so confident that they rejected plans that called for as many as sixty-four lifeboats, enough to accommodate all the ship's passengers. In one of history's great ironies,[2] the "unsinkable" *Titanic* sank after colliding with an iceberg off the banks of Newfoundland. More than 1,500 people died in the accident.

---

1. Mrs. Kate O'Leary was an Irish immigrant whose cow supposedly knocked over the lantern that started the Chicago Fire. People blamed her because her house was the first to catch fire.
2. irony: a difference between what is expected and what actually happens. In this case, people expected the *Titanic* to be unsinkable, and yet it sank on its first voyage.

Now, there's a good deal more to the story of the Great Chicago Fire than the rumor about Mrs. O'Leary's cow knocking over a lantern, and there's more to the story of the *Titanic* than what an employee of the ship allegedly said upon its launch: "Not even God himself could sink this ship." In addition, while these two events may seem unrelated at first, if you look more closely, you will find that they have some similarities and some differences. In other words, you will be able to compare them.

In the next lesson you will learn in detail how to write a comparison essay, and the Chicago Fire and the sinking of the *Titanic* will be the topics of the sample essay. First, however, take some time to read the following selections, which will you give you a more complete picture of each event. As you read, make note of both main points and details. Read carefully so that you will be able to identify similarities and differences later.

The Great Chicago Fire

—adapted from *The Great Conflagration* by James W. Sheahan

The Great Chicago Fire began on Sunday, October 8, 1871, and lasted for two days. The fire killed more than 300 people, destroyed roughly 3 square miles of the city, and left more than 100,000 residents homeless. Though the fire was one of the largest US disasters of the nineteenth century and destroyed much of the city's central business district, Chicago was eventually rebuilt and continued to thrive as one of the most populous American cities. This reading vividly captures some of the worst moments of the fire.

At precisely 9:30 p.m. on Sunday, October 8, the fire-bell sounded an alarm, and simultaneously a bright light appeared in the southwest. It was just as church services were letting out and the congregations were returning to their homes. No special attention was given to the fire, and many hundreds of families, after noticing that it was at a great distance, went to their homes and later retired to sleep, all unconscious that the demon was unloosed which would disturb and expel them before many hours.

The fire had originated in a cow shed in the rear of a one-story frame building, on the northeast corner of DeKoven and Jefferson streets. The origin of the fire is a mystery. The story that an attempt to milk a cow by the light of a kerosene lamp had ended in the overturning of the lamp, and the rapid firing of the cow shed, is now known to be untrue.

It must always be borne in mind that for thirty-six hours previously the wind had been blowing with unusual violence from the southwest. The flames, carried away by the wind, immediately spread to the nearby sheds on the block. It seemed as if the fire and the gale had united to mow a breadth of desolation from one place to the other in the shortest possible time.

The firemen posted themselves in front of the fire, struggling to arrest it, but their labors were in vain. They might as well have attempted to arrest the wind itself, because at this time the wind and the fire were the same thing, the blaze often reaching across the streets, and burning brands[3] were carried far in advance of the actual fire. There had been no rain in Chicago, of any account, for nearly six weeks, and the wooden buildings, tenements, lumber piles, and sidewalks were as dry as paper.

Within two hours the fire had reached Van Buren Street, and had there been no more than an ordinary gale, it would have stopped. But the buildings here covered perhaps 150 acres and contained saw mills, dwellings, barns, factories, shops, lumber yards, and coal depots—all of the most combustible character. The fire was, notwithstanding its terrors, a brilliant spectacle. The smoke did not obscure the view. Everywhere was a broad sheet of flame leaping, darting, and sending

3. burning brands: burning pieces of wood

forth, as if from some grand pyrotechnic preparation, the most brilliant, dazzling meteors of living fire. It was sublime, yet terrifying; magnificent, yet appalling.

Here was the grand turning point in the conflagration. Here the fire, under ordinary circumstances, would have stopped; here it had consumed everything that had been in its path. To the north lay the plain that had been laid waste[4] the night before. To the west was the wind; to the east was the river. But far off to the northeast beyond two rivers, beyond the great structures of hotels, banks, and warehouses, beyond the towering walls of marble and of brick—a full two miles distant—were the water works, the only possible agent[5] that could save the city from annihilation, and to that point, this conflagration seemed determined to reach. With a huge head of flying sparks and burning embers, the fire roared and leaped over the Chicago River. It engulfed a railroad car there, a car loaded with kerosene, and blew it to pieces. From that explosion, the fire raged in every direction. It made its way north again, this time on the eastern shore, and destroyed the waterworks, and all of the pipes within, the last hope of the firefighters to drown the fire with water.

Men, women, and children on foot took up their march from the flames. To comprehend the horrors of that flight let the reader imagine a population of 76,000 men, women, and children, suddenly driven from their homes, hemmed in by a roaring blaze on each side. Let her imagine these people shuffling along in a few streets, trying to keep families together, enveloped in clouds of smoke, and covered at every step with blazing cinders. The horrors of the exodus were made more terrible by the wild foray[6] of horses and cattle, terrified by the fire, madly running hither and thither, kicking and trampling, often in herds of a dozen, aimlessly trying to escape or plunging through the human procession. There was no shelter, no refuge, no escape, but to push on through the narrow streets to the north.

Occasionally, above the roar and din, above the shrieks and shouts of the moving mass, above the wild neighing and snorting of the frenzied horses and cattle, would be heard the explosions of drug stores, distilleries, and warehouses, and the crumbling of stone walls. Then would come the shower of fiery projectiles, the horrors of which were often aggravated by the pitiable sight of dismembered portions of human bodies, the victims of explosions.

Anyone who has witnessed the passage of an army of 75,000 men moving through the streets in perfect order and discipline can get a faint picture of this terrible flight of the inhabitants of the city by imagining, instead of a disciplined army, a horde of terrified men, women, and children, most of them half clothed, bearing their sick, their dying, their aged, and their helpless, with the sidewalks on fire, the buildings in a blaze in every direction, the horrible roar behind, the stifling smoke and cinders, and all this fearful procession hastening forward as best it could—going no one knew where. When someone fell it meant almost

4. laid waste: completely destroyed; in this case, completely burned up
5. agent: tool or help; literally "active power"
6. foray: an attack; in this case, a stampede

certain death. The ever-surging crowd could not stop to pick up the exhausted or the feeble, but over the fallen bodies rushed on, away from the monster that was pursuing them.

How many thus perished will never be known; but the next day, when the fire was out, and the scattered families called their rolls,[7] over 2,000 children were missing, most of whom were of an age as to exclude all hope of their safety. The once teeming place became as silent as the graveyard.

The Titanic Disaster

—adapted from *The Sinking of the* Titanic *and Great Sea Disasters* by Logan Marshall

The RMS *Titanic* was a passenger ship that sank in the early morning hours of April 15, 1912. While on its maiden voyage from England to New York City, the ship collided with an iceberg, and it now sits at the bottom of the Atlantic Ocean. More than 1,500 passengers were killed, making the sinking one of the largest peacetime disasters on the sea in history. This selection describes the aftermath of the *Titanic*'s collision, when the ship's passengers had to decide how to act.

There were some terrible scenes. Fathers were parting from their children and giving them an encouraging pat on the shoulders. Men were kissing their wives and telling them that they would be with them shortly. One man continued to insist that there was absolutely no danger, that the boat was the finest ever built, with water-tight compartments, and that it could not sink. That seemed to be the general impression.

A few of the men, however, were panic-stricken even when the first of the lifeboats was being filled. Ten men threw themselves into the boats that were already crowded with women and children. These men were dragged back and hurled sprawling across the deck. Six of them, screaming with fear, struggled to their feet and made a second attempt to rush to the boats. Gunshots sounded in quick succession, and the six cowardly men were stopped in their tracks. They staggered and collapsed one after another. At least two of them vainly attempted to creep toward the boats again. The others lay quite still. This scene of bloodshed served its purpose. In that particular section of the deck there was no further attempt to violate the rule of "women and children first."

Scenes on the sinking vessel grew more tragic as the remaining passengers faced the awful certainty that most would die. In that hour, when cherished illusions of possible safety had all but vanished, manhood and womanhood aboard the *Titanic* rose to their sublimest[8] heights. It was in that crisis of the direst extremity that many brave women deliberately rejected life and chose rather to remain and die with the men whom they loved.

7. called their rolls: called everyone's name to see who was present
8. sublimest: most sublime, or highest

"I will not leave my husband," said Mrs. Ida Straus. "We are old; we can best die together." And she turned from those who would have forced her into one of the boats and clung to the man who had been the partner of her joys and sorrows. Thus they stood hand in hand and heart to heart, comforting each other until the sea claimed them, united in death as they had been through a long life.

Miss Elizabeth Evans of New York was placed in the same boat with many other women. As it was about to be lowered away it was found that the craft contained one more than its full quota of passengers. The grim question arose as to which of them should surrender her place and her chance of safety. Miss Evans, looking at the mothers surrounding her, was the first to volunteer her life. "Your need is greater than mine," said she to the others. "You have children who need you, and I have none." So saying, she arose from the boat and stepped back upon the deck. The twenty-five-year-old woman, beloved by all who knew her, found no later refuge and was one of those who went down with the ship.

Unfortunately, many of the lifeboats left the ship with much room to spare for others. Scarcely any of the lifeboats were properly manned. Two, filled with women and children, capsized immediately, and the collapsible boats[9] were only temporarily useful, as they soon filled with water. In one boat eighteen or twenty persons sat in water above their knees for six hours.

Ida Straus

Ida was married to Isidor Straus, a former US congressman and the co-owner of Macy's department store. He was one of the wealthiest passengers on board the Titanic. When Ida refused to get on a lifeboat without her husband, Isidor was offered a seat in a lifeboat to accompany her. However, he would not go as long as there were still women and children aboard. He refused to be made an exception. Later, a friend asked an officer if Isidor and Ida could both enter a lifeboat together. Isidor was reported to have responded, "I will not go before the other men." Ida even insisted that her English maid, Ellen Bird, get into a lifeboat, and gave Ellen her fur coat, stating that she would not be needing it.

▲ Isidor and Ida Straus

9. Collapsible boats were smaller than the lifeboats and could be folded up and tucked away. They could each hold almost fifty people, while the wooden lifeboats could hold sixty-five. Their canvas sides might have made them more prone to water leaks or more vulnerable to wave action above the waterline.

An Eyewitness to the Sinking of the Titanic

—adapted from *The Loss of the S.S.* Titanic by Lawrence Beesley

This selection describes the weather conditions and the sinking of the great ship from the perspective of an eyewitness rowing away from the ship on a lifeboat. There was a danger that the *Titanic* would suck the lifeboats underwater when its great bulk took its final plunge.

The stars seemed really to be alive and to talk. The complete absence of haze produced a phenomenon I had never seen before: where the sky met the sea, the line was as clear and definite as the edge of a knife. The captain of one of the ships near us that night said the stars were so extraordinarily bright near the horizon that he was deceived into thinking that they were ships' lights: he did not remember seeing such a night before. Those who were afloat will all agree with that statement: we were often deceived into thinking they were lights of a ship.

And next the cold air! Here again was something quite new to us: there was not a breath of wind to blow keenly round us as we stood in the boat, and because of its continued persistence to make us feel cold; it was just a keen, bitter, icy, motionless cold that came from nowhere and yet was there all the time; the stillness of it—if one can imagine "cold" being motionless and still—was what seemed new and strange.

The sky and the air were overhead; and below was the sea. Here again was something uncommon: the surface was like a lake of oil, heaving gently up and down with a quiet motion that rocked our boat dreamily to and fro. The sea slipped away smoothly under the boat, and I think we never heard it lapping on the sides, so oily in appearance was the water. So when one of the stokers said he had been to sea for twenty-six years and never yet seen such a calm night, we accepted it as true without comment. Just as expressive was the remark of another—"It reminds me of a bloomin'[10] picnic!" It was quite true; it did: a picnic on a lake, or a quiet inland river like the Cam, or a backwater on the Thames.[11]

And so in these conditions of sky and air and sea, we gazed upon the *Titanic* from a short distance. She was absolutely still—indeed from the first it seemed as if the blow from the iceberg had taken all the courage out of her and she had just come quietly to rest and was settling down without an effort to save herself, without a murmur of protest against such a foul blow. For the sea could not rock her: the wind was not there to howl noisily round the decks, and make the ropes

10. bloomin': an expression added for emphasis
11. Cam and Thames: two rivers in England

hum; from the first what must have impressed all as they watched was the sense of stillness about her and the slow, insensible way she sank lower and lower in the sea, like a stricken animal.

The mere bulk alone of the ship viewed from the sea below was an awe-inspiring sight. Imagine a ship nearly a sixth of a mile long, seventy-five feet high to the top decks, with four enormous funnels above the decks, and masts again high above the funnels; with her hundreds of portholes, all her saloons and other rooms brilliant with light, and all round her, little boats filled with those who until a few hours before had trod her decks and read in her libraries and listened to the music of her band in happy contentment; and who were now looking up in amazement at the enormous mass above them and rowing away from her because she was sinking.

And before we knew it, in place of the *Titanic*, we had the level sea now stretching in an unbroken expanse to the horizon: heaving gently just as before, with no indication on the surface that the waves had just closed over the most wonderful vessel ever built by man's hand; the stars looked down just the same and the air was just as bitterly cold.

There seemed a great sense of loneliness when we were left on the sea in a small boat without the *Titanic*: not that we were uncomfortable (except for the cold) nor in danger: we did not think we were either, but the *Titanic* was no longer there.

We waited head on[12] for the wave which we thought might come—the wave we had heard so much of from the crew and which they said had been known to travel for miles—and it never came. But although the *Titanic* left us no such legacy of a wave as she went to the bottom, she left us something we would willingly forget forever, something which it is well not to let the imagination dwell on—the cries of many hundreds of our fellow-passengers struggling in the ice-cold water.

I would willingly omit any further mention of this part of the disaster from this book, but for two reasons it is not possible—first, that as a matter of history it should be put on record; and secondly, that these cries were not only an appeal for help in the awful conditions of danger in which the drowning found themselves,—an appeal that could never be answered,—but an appeal to the whole world to make such conditions of danger and hopelessness impossible ever again; a cry that called to the heavens for the very injustice of its own existence; a cry that clamored for its own destruction.

We were utterly surprised to hear this cry go up as the waves closed over the *Titanic*. Unprepared as we were for such a thing, the cries of the drowning floating across the quiet sea filled us with stupefaction: we longed to return and rescue at least some of the drowning, but we knew it was impossible. The boat was filled to standing-room, and to return would mean the swamping of us all, and so the captain told his crew to row away from the cries. We tried to sing to keep from thinking of them; but there was no heart for singing in the boat at that time.

The cries, which were loud and numerous at first, died away gradually one by one, but the night was clear, frosty and still, the water smooth, and the sounds must have carried for miles. I think

12. head on: looking directly at the water

the last of them must have been heard nearly forty minutes after the *Titanic* sank. Life vests would keep the survivors afloat for hours; but the cold water was what stopped the cries.

There must have come to all of us safe in the lifeboats, a deep resolve that, if anything could be done in the future to prevent the repetition of such sounds, we would do it. And not only to them are those cries an imperative call, but to every man and woman who has known of them. It is not possible that ever again can such conditions exist; but it is a duty imperative on one and all to see that they do not. Think of it! a few more boats, a few more planks of wood nailed together in a particular way at a trifling cost, and all those men and women whom the world can so ill afford to lose would be with us today, there would be no mourning in thousands of homes which now are desolate, and these words need not have been written.

Tell It Back—Narration

1. **MARK UP THE TEXT—Annotation:** Read through the passages about the Great Chicago Fire and the sinking of the *Titanic* again. As you read, write in the margin of the text symbols that will help you understand it better and find important details later. The following are some symbols you might use:
   - Underline the main idea of the story or any important point.
   - Put a question mark in the margin to mark any part of the story you don't understand.
   - Write any questions or thoughts you have in the margin.
   - Put an exclamation point in the margin to mark any part of the story you find surprising or particularly interesting.
   - Circle any important or unfamiliar vocabulary words or proper nouns when they are first introduced. Remember, a proper noun is the name for any specific person, place, thing, or idea. How do you know which words to circle? Circle words that appear repeatedly, or words you can't understand from the context of the sentence alone. Look up any unfamiliar words in the glossary, or, if they aren't there, in a dictionary.

2. **ORAL NARRATION:** Look over the annotations you made for *An Eyewitness to the Sinking of the* Titanic. Then, without looking at the text, retell the story as best you remember it using your own words. Try not to leave out any important details.

Here are the first few sentences to help you get started:

> The stars seemed really to be alive and to talk. The complete absence of haze produced a phenomenon I had never seen before: where the sky met the sea, the line was as clear and definite as the edge of a knife. The captain of one of the ships near us that night said the stars were so extraordinarily bright near the horizon that he was deceived into thinking that they were ships' lights: he did not remember seeing such a night before.

3. **OUTLINE:** Create an outline for *The* Titanic *Disaster* using Roman numerals (*I*, *II*, *III*) for the most important events and capital letters (*A*, *B*, *C*) for less important events. Use standard numbers (*1*, *2*, *3*) for minor points.

This icon points to more tips on outlining on page 205.

Talk About It—

1. Comb through *The Great Chicago Fire* for any use of simile or metaphor. Then share one of the examples you find with your class and describe or explain the comparison using your own words.
2. Most experts believe that the Great Chicago Fire was made worse by three factors: flammable building materials, poor weather conditions, and an inadequate response by the fire department. More than two-thirds of the structures in Chicago at that time were made entirely of wood, and most houses and buildings were topped with highly flammable tar or shingle roofs. All of the city's sidewalks and many roads were made of wood. There had also been a severe **drought** the summer before the fire, with only an inch of rain in the span of three months. That night, strong winds carried flying embers toward the heart of the city. The response by the fire department was quick, but the firefighters were accidentally sent to the wrong place, allowing the fire to grow in the meantime. In addition, in 1871 the Chicago Fire Department had only 185 firefighters with just 17 horse-drawn steam engines to protect the entire city. Based on these factors, what do you think can be learned from this disaster?
3. As with the Chicago Fire, many factors contributed to the sinking of the *Titanic*. Prior to launch, the owners and builders of the *Titanic* rejected plans that called for as many as sixty-four lifeboats. Although the number of lifeboats on the *Titanic*—twenty—was enough by government standards, that number would only accommodate about half of the 2,228 people onboard. Also, reports suggest that Captain Edward J. Smith was driving the ship too fast in an attempt to beat the Atlantic crossing time of another ship in the *Titanic*'s fleet. Finally, the captain and crew ignored iceberg warnings from other ships, with the last and most specific warning not even being passed along to the captain. As a result, more than 1,500 people died in the accident. Based on these factors, what can be learned from this disaster?
4. Disasters tend to bring out both the good and the bad in people. Many men and women in dire circumstances demonstrate acts of great courage and heroism, while others show cowardice or carelessness toward others. In the *Titanic* accounts, the authors mention several examples of chivalry, such as when most of the people on the ship insisted upon getting women and children into the lifeboats first, or when some people gave their lives to save others. Disastrous circumstances certainly give people the opportunity to be brave. Why do you think some show bravery while others do not?

Memoria—

Thou shalt respect the weak and constitute thyself the defender of them.

1. After reading this quotation taken from the Chivalric Code and Measure of the Middle Ages, a set of rules guiding the behavior of knights, define any words you may not know. Then discuss the meaning of the quotation.
2. How does this quote relate to the stories of the Great Chicago Fire and the *Titanic*?
3. Memorize this quotation and be prepared to recite it during your next class.
4. Write this quotation in your commonplace book, along with any thoughts you have about it.

Go Deeper—

1. In the last lesson you learned about the importance of analogies in helping to communicate ideas, and you're going to use analogies when writing your comparison essays. You can practice for this by composing some similes and metaphors. Remember, both similes and metaphors describe one thing by comparing it to a second, seemingly unlike thing and showing how they are similar. A simile uses the words "like" or "as" to make a comparison, whereas a metaphor does not.

   For each of the following emotions, write one simile and one metaphor to describe a person who is feeling that emotion.

   Example:

   Emotion: surprise
   Simile: I was as shocked as a finger in an electric outlet.
   Metaphor: I was a bowling pin that had been suddenly knocked over.

   a. Emotion: embarrassed

   Simile: ______________________________

   Metaphor: ______________________________

   b. Emotion: excited

   Simile: ______________________________

   Metaphor: ______________________________

c. Emotion: angry

Simile: ____________________

Metaphor: ____________________

d. Emotion: fear

Simile: ____________________

Metaphor: ____________________

e. Emotion: sad

Simile: ____________________

Metaphor: ____________________

2. Now turn your focus on the Chicago Fire and the sinking of the *Titanic*. Use the information from this lesson to help you write two statements—one a simile and one a metaphor—about each disaster. Use your imagination to describe what each event might have been like.

   Examples:

   Simile about the Great Chicago Fire: The people scurried from their burning homes like ants running from a magnifying glass.
   Metaphor about the *Titanic* disaster: The lifeboat was a brown leaf floating on a pond.

Simile about the Great Chicago Fire: ____________________

____

Metaphor about the Great Chicago Fire: ____________________

____

Simile about the *Titanic* disaster: ____________________

____

Metaphor about the *Titanic* disaster: ____________________

____

3. An extended metaphor is another way of making an analogy. Can you guess what an "extended metaphor" is? If you guessed "a longer metaphor," then you're correct! Making a metaphor longer—by adding detail, description, or explanation—makes your comparison more interesting. It captures the imaginations of your readers and makes them think about the imagery of your metaphor for more than just a sentence.

   Try writing an extended metaphor. Take one of the metaphors you wrote in the previous exercise and expand it into two or three sentences by adding detail, description, or explanation to it.

   Example: The lifeboat was a brown leaf floating on a pond. Thin and fragile, it was tossed about by the little ripples of the water. At times, it seemed as though it could crumple and sink, but somehow its edges remained above the water.

Lesson 5

Writing the Comparison Essay

You've been doing a lot of preparation, haven't you? The good news is that it's almost time to start writing!

The main goal of a comparison essay is to describe some of the similarities and differences between two people, events, things, or ideas. Sometimes you may find that two subjects are more alike than they are different, or vice versa. As you write your essay, however, you should aim for a balanced discussion that equally considers both types of comparison. For the essays in this book, you will achieve balance by writing about the same number of similarities and differences. You will have two body paragraphs that explain similarities and two body paragraphs that explain differences.

Similarities x 2

Differences x 2

In this lesson you will take a walk through the entire essay and see how it's done. Before you get started, take a minute to look back at the readings in the previous lesson and review your annotations. The sample essay in this lesson will be about the Chicago Fire and the sinking of the *Titanic*, so a quick review of the readings will keep the information fresh in your mind. Once you've done your review, dig in to the following step-by-step guide to writing a comparison essay.

Prewriting

Before you compose your essay, you will need to do some prewriting to help you organize your thoughts. To start, you should make a list of as many similarities and differences between your subjects as you can. This will give you a list of ideas to pick from as you decide what to write about.

Begin by making a list of all the similarities between your two subjects. For example, in the case of the Chicago Fire and the sinking of the *Titanic*:

- They were both disasters on a large scale.
- They both had many deaths.
- There were moments of heroism in each.
- They both showed a failure of preparation or forethought.
- They both had instances of human error (starting a fire, colliding with an iceberg).
- They both happened in the same period of history.
- They both are worthy of retelling because of what we learned from them.

Now list their differences. For example:

- The sinking of the *Titanic* caused the loss of more lives than the Chicago Fire did (1,500 vs. 300).
- The Chicago Fire resulted in more destroyed property than the sinking of the *Titanic* did.
- The sinking of the *Titanic* was more likely to have been caused by pride, while the Chicago Fire was caused by circumstances and mistakes.
- The fire left hundreds of thousands homeless, but the sinking of the *Titanic* did not destroy any homes.
- One disaster was a fire, the other a shipwreck.

After making your lists, you will need to narrow your ideas down to two significant similarities and two key differences. Don't just go with the obvious, but look for important points of comparison. What would your audience think if you wrote something such as, "The Great Chicago Fire and the *Titanic* disaster had many things in common. For example, they both happened. And they both involved people. Finally, they both occurred when the United States was a country"? You would seem like an amateur writer who didn't have anything worthwhile to say! Instead, focus on more meaningful observations: They both had many casualties. They both made headlines around the world. In both events, some people involved were praised for heroism. The *Titanic* disaster involved the loss of more lives than the Chicago Fire. The Chicago Fire was the result of circumstances, whereas the sinking of the *Titanic* was a result of human pride. You get the idea.

Once you have made your lists and chosen the similarities and differences that you will include in your essay, you are ready to start working on your paragraphs.

Paragraph 1 (Introduction)

You will begin your essay with the introduction paragraph, which should start with an analogy. The following example compares epic disasters to wild animals.

> An epic disaster is like a wild animal. Both are hard to control and nearly impossible to tame.

Next comes a short narrative overview of the two subjects. You will be sprinkling narrative details throughout your essay, so there is no need to give a lot of detail here. What you want to do for the introduction is stick to the basic facts. Consider the questions who, what, when, and where (avoid why and how for now), and tell about each subject in one or two sentences. The following example gives a short overview of both the Chicago Fire and the sinking of the *Titanic*:

> On the evening of October 8, 1871, a deadly fire began to scorch its way through Chicago, consuming everything in its path. After blazing for two days, this great fire would end up destroying much of the city's downtown area. Roughly forty years later, another disaster would make headlines. The sinking of the *Titanic* on April 15, 1912, caused the deaths of 1,500 passengers and would become one of the greatest tragedies of the twentieth century.

Finally, you will write your topic sentence, which simply states the main idea of your essay. In this case, the essay compares and contrasts the Great Chicago Fire and the sinking of the *Titanic*, so a topic sentence might read like this:

> The Great Chicago Fire of 1871 and the sinking of the *Titanic* have many similarities and differences, some of which are considered here.

Note that in the previous book in this series, your introduction paragraph included both a thesis statement and a transition sentence. A topic sentence is simpler than a thesis, because it doesn't argue a point but instead simply states a main idea. By stating what the rest of the essay's paragraphs will be about, the topic sentence creates a bridge between the introduction and the next paragraph. This means that your topic sentence ends up serving as the transition sentence as well. It gives the reader an idea of what is to come in the paragraphs that follow.

Paragraph 2 (Similarity #1)

In the first body paragraph, you will write about one major similarity between the two subjects. Start by identifying the similarity you will be describing. Then tell more about the similarity by adding facts, examples, or details from the readings for both subjects. For inspiration, look back at the reading selections, your annotations, and the Talk About It section in lesson 4. Here's an example:

> One similarity between these disasters is that they were both deadly misfortunes involving the loss of lives and property. The Great Chicago Fire began on Sunday, October 8, 1871, and lasted for two days. The fire killed 300 people, destroyed 3 square miles of the city, and left more than 100,000 residents homeless. Legend has it that the fire began when a cow tipped over a lantern in the barn of one Mrs. O'Leary, but that was later proven to be false. There had been a severe drought all summer before the fire, and once the fire started, strong winds carried flying embers toward the heart of the city. The *Titanic* was a luxury steamship that sank in the Atlantic Ocean on April 15, 1912, during its maiden voyage. In general, people thought this gigantic ship was unsinkable, but at approximately 11:30 p.m. on April 14, the ship hit an iceberg and began to capsize. Lifeboats were loaded up with women and children first, but they were often under-filled. Even worse, there were only twenty lifeboats on board—enough to accommodate only half of the passengers. Only 705 of the more than 2,200 passengers survived.

Paragraph 3 (Similarity #2)

In the second body paragraph, you will write about another major similarity between the two subjects. Start again by identifying the similarity you will be describing. Then tell more about the similarity by adding facts, examples, or details from the readings for both subjects. For inspiration, look back at the reading selections, your annotations, and the Talk About It section in lesson 4. In addition, look in the readings for a quote that gives a supportive fact, example, or detail and include it in your description.

> These disasters also share a common thread in that people were able to learn from them. The fire taught people not to rely so heavily upon wood as a building material. At the time, more than two-thirds of the structures in Chicago were made entirely of wood, including sidewalks and roads. Nowadays, brick, steel, concrete, and aluminum, which are less flammable, are commonly used when constructing buildings. From the *Titanic* people learned to be more prepared for disaster. The engineers and designers of the ship only included enough lifeboats to save half the passengers onboard. This is because, in general, people thought the ship was unsinkable. According to Lawrence Beesley, "the boat was the finest ever built, with water-tight compartments, and . . . it could not sink." Beesley, like so many

others, believed the *Titanic* to be an unsinkable ship. Now, we know that to not be true. Today all ships are equipped with enough lifeboats to make sure that all of the passengers can make it safely off the boat in the event of a disaster.

Paragraph 4 (Difference #1)

In this body paragraph, you will write about a major difference between the two subjects. Start by identifying the difference you will be describing. Then tell more about the difference by adding facts, examples, or details from the readings for both subjects. For inspiration, look back at the reading selections, your annotations, and the Talk About It section in lesson 4. Here's an example:

> One major difference between these events is the nature of the disasters: One was a fire, and the other was a shipwreck. As a result, the devastating effects of the Great Chicago Fire and the sinking of the *Titanic* were much different. Fire reduces things to ashes. This meant that much of downtown Chicago was consumed by the blaze, and Chicagoans had to rebuild their city from the ground up. The *Titanic*, on the other hand, was not completely destroyed. In fact, its ruins still lie at the bottom of the Atlantic, where scientists can explore the remains. Yet despite the fact that the Chicago Fire destroyed more property, the *Titanic* caused the loss of more lives. Over 1,500 perished in the shipwreck, compared to 300 in the fire.

Paragraph 5 (Difference #2)

In the final body paragraph, you will write about another major difference between the two subjects. Start again by identifying the difference you will be describing. Then tell more about the difference by adding facts, examples, or details from the readings for both subjects. For inspiration, look back at the reading selections, your annotations, and the Talk About It section in lesson 4. In addition, look in the readings for a quote that gives a supportive fact, example, or detail and include it in your description.

> However, the greatest distinction between these disasters is what caused them. The Chicago Fire was caused by a combination of natural disaster, ignorance, and bad circumstances. James Sheahan says, "There had been no rain in Chicago . . . for nearly six weeks, and the wooden buildings, tenements, lumber piles, and sidewalks, were as dry as paper." The city's lack of rain and overall dryness was the perfect environment for a huge fire. It's no surprise that things burned up so quickly! In some ways, the fire was unavoidable, given the drought conditions. In contrast, the *Titanic* tragedy involved arrogance. People foolishly thought they had constructed an unsinkable ship, so they chose not to carry enough lifeboats for all the crew and passengers to survive. Reports also suggest that the captain and crew ignored

iceberg warnings from other ships, and that they were traveling too fast through icy waters. It seems that the *Titanic* disaster could have been avoided.

Paragraph 6 (Conclusion)

Finally, you will write an epilogue, or concluding paragraph. Often, young writers look at their conclusion as an afterthought—just a couple of throwaway sentences to wrap things up. Far from it! The conclusion is the last thing your audience will read. The words you choose to end your essay with will ring in their ears and influence the way they think about the comparison. You should always strive to make your concluding paragraph as memorable as possible.

For this essay, your conclusion should first recap the main point of your essay. It will then reflect on something important that can be learned from making the comparison. Finally, it will contain an observation or question about your subjects that would be interesting to learn more about in the future. For example:

Restatement of main point

In conclusion, these disasters had a number of similarities and differences. In comparing them, it is interesting to see that both events, while tragic, resulted in the improvement of human life. In the future it would be interesting to learn more about the heroes and their actions from both disasters.

Reflection on something learned

Question for future study

Think of the introduction as the head of the essay, the four supporting paragraphs as the body, and the conclusion (epilogue) as the feet. Head, body, and feet make a complete essay.

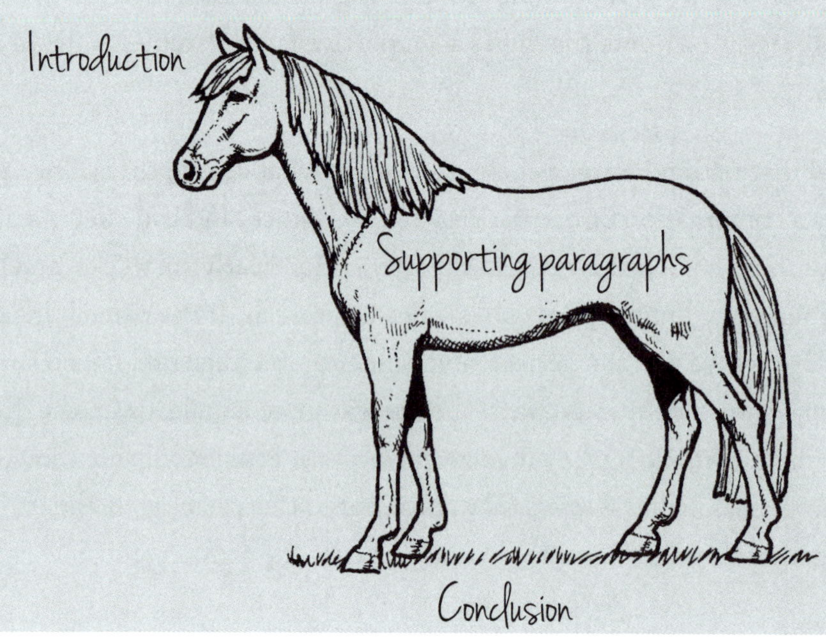

Now look at the entire essay all put together:

Paragraph 1 (Introduction)

An epic disaster is like a wild animal. Both are hard to control and nearly impossible to tame. On the evening of October 8, 1871, a deadly fire began to scorch its way through Chicago, consuming everything in its path. After blazing for two days, this great fire would end up destroying much of the city's downtown area. Roughly forty years later, another disaster would make headlines. The sinking of the *Titanic* on April 15, 1912, caused the deaths of 1,500 passengers and would become one of the greatest tragedies of the twentieth century. The Great Chicago Fire of 1871 and the sinking of the *Titanic* have many similarities and differences, some of which are considered here.

Paragraph 2 (Similarity #1)

One similarity between these disasters is that they were both deadly misfortunes involving the loss of lives and property. The Great Chicago Fire began on Sunday, October 8, 1871, and lasted for two days. The fire killed 300 people, destroyed 3 square miles of the city, and left more than 100,000 residents homeless. Legend has it that the fire began when a cow tipped over a lantern in the barn of one Mrs. O'Leary, but that was later proven to be false. There had been a severe drought all summer before the fire, and once the fire started, strong winds carried flying embers toward the heart of the city. The *Titanic* was a luxury steamship that sank in the Atlantic Ocean on April 15, 1912, during its maiden voyage. In general, people thought this gigantic ship was unsinkable, but at approximately 11:30 p.m. on April 14, the ship hit an iceberg and began to capsize. Lifeboats were loaded up with women and children first, but they were often under-filled. Even worse, there were only twenty lifeboats on board—enough to accommodate only half of the passengers. Only 705 of the more than 2,200 passengers survived.

Paragraph 3 (Similarity #2)

These disasters also share a common thread in that people were able to learn from them. The fire taught people not to rely so heavily upon wood as a building material. At the time, more than two-thirds of the structures in Chicago were made entirely of wood, including sidewalks and roads. Nowadays, brick, steel, concrete, and aluminum, which are less flammable, are commonly used when constructing buildings. From the *Titanic* people learned to be more prepared for disaster. The engineers and designers of the ship only included enough lifeboats to save half the passengers onboard. This is because, in general, people thought the ship was unsinkable. According to Lawrence Beesley, "the boat was the finest ever built, with water-tight compartments, and . . . it could not sink." Beesley, like so many others, believed the *Titanic* to be an unsinkable ship. Now, we know that to not be true. Today all ships are equipped with enough lifeboats to make sure that all of the passengers can make it safely off the boat in the event of a disaster.

Paragraph 4 (Difference #1)

One major difference between these events is the nature of the disasters: One was a fire, and the other was a shipwreck. As a result, the devastating effects of the Great Chicago Fire and the sinking of the *Titanic* were much different. Fire reduces things to ashes. This meant that much of downtown Chicago was consumed by the blaze, and Chicagoans had to rebuild their city from the ground up. The *Titanic*, on the other hand, was not completely destroyed. In fact, its ruins still lie at the bottom of the Atlantic, where scientists can explore the remains. Yet despite the fact that the Chicago Fire destroyed more property, the *Titanic* caused the loss of more lives. Over 1,500 perished in the shipwreck, compared to 300 in the fire.

Paragraph 5 (Difference #2)

However, the greatest distinction between these disasters is what caused them. The Chicago Fire was caused by a combination of natural disaster, ignorance, and bad circumstances. James Sheahan says, "There had been no rain in Chicago . . . for nearly six weeks, and the wooden buildings, tenements, lumber piles, and sidewalks, were as dry as paper." The city's lack of rain and overall dryness was the perfect environment for a huge fire. It's no surprise that things burned up so quickly! In some ways, the fire was unavoidable, given the drought conditions. In contrast, the *Titanic* tragedy involved arrogance. People foolishly thought they had constructed an unsinkable ship, so they chose not to carry enough lifeboats for all the crew and passengers to survive. Reports also suggest that the captain and crew ignored iceberg warnings from other ships, and that they were traveling too fast through icy waters. It seems that the *Titanic* disaster could have been avoided.

Paragraph 6 (Conclusion)

Restatement of main point

In conclusion, these disasters had a number of similarities and differences. In comparing them, it is interesting to see that both events, while tragic, resulted in the improvement of human life. In the future it would be interesting to learn more about the heroes and their actions from both disasters.

Reflection on something learned

Question for future study

Tell It Back—Narration

WRITTEN NARRATION: For each paragraph of the previous sample essay, write down a summary statement—one sentence that captures the main idea of the paragraph.

Example:

Paragraph 1: The Great Chicago Fire of 1871 and the sinking of the *Titanic* in 1912 have many similarities and differences.

Paragraph 2:

Paragraph 3:

Paragraph 4:

Paragraph 5:

Paragraph 6:

▲ Photo of an etching of the city of Chicago after the Great Chicago Fire.

Talk About It—

1. Take a look at the image of the city of Chicago after the fire devastated its downtown. After you've studied the picture for a few minutes, turn the book over and describe the picture. How would you feel if you were one of the residents of Chicago at the time?

2. History teaches us valuable lessons, if we are willing to learn from the past. Based on the selections you read in lesson 4 about the Great Chicago Fire and the sinking of the *Titanic*, think about some of the possible conclusions you can draw or lessons you can learn from these two tragedies. What do these events teach us about disasters? About human nature? With a partner, come up with a list and then share your ideas with the class.

3. Throughout this book you will be asked to carefully and thoroughly compare two subjects without judging them. At times it may be difficult to avoid making claims about which one is better or worse than the other. Give some examples of situations in which it would be better to withhold judgment, and other situations in which it would be better to take a position.

Memoria—

> Noble souls, through dust and heat, rise from disaster and defeat the stronger.
> —Henry Wadsworth Longfellow

1. After reading this quotation by Henry Wadsworth Longfellow, a poet who lived in the nineteenth century, define any words you may not know. Then discuss the meaning of the quotation.
2. How does this quotation relate to the comparison of the Great Chicago Fire and the sinking of the *Titanic*?

3. Memorize this quotation and be prepared to recite it during your next class.
4. Write this quotation in your commonplace book, along with any thoughts you have about it.

Go Deeper—

1. **IMAGINATIVE FICTION:** Look back at the readings about the *Titanic* in lesson 4. Then, on a separate sheet of paper, write a response to the following prompt: "Imagine that you are on board the *Titanic* the evening that it sinks. Using your senses (sight, hearing, smell, taste, and touch), describe what it felt like to be on the ship while the disaster was happening."

2. My siblings and I used to quarrel a lot when we were younger. Surprising, right? Sometimes in the middle of an argument one of them would run to tell my mom. Then he would come back and say, "Mom said you have to . . . ". Those words, "Mom said," gave weight and authority to what followed. The fact that Mom or Dad said something to support him made my brother's argument more convincing.

   In a similar way, our ideas can be made stronger when we use the **testimony** of others to support them. The words "testimony" and "testify" both have a root in the Latin word *testis*, which refers to the notion of a third person, a witness. Testimony is the expert opinion or evidence of a credible witness. In essay-writing, using testimony means using a quotation from a trusted source that helps to support the idea you are writing about. You're going to be required to use testimony in the form of a quote in your comparison essay, and knowing how to use testimony is also something that will be useful for you in your future academic career.

   Using testimony is more complicated than just finding a quote and sticking it in your essay, however.

There's an art to smoothly adding a quote into your text. Think of it like a burger: The meat is sandwiched between a bun on the top and the bottom. Each time you use a quote, you want to sandwich it between your own ideas and comments. The top bun will be a sentence that leads in to the quote. You do this by mentioning the important idea that the quote is about. If your quote is about courage, for example, you would want to lead in to the quote by introducing the idea of courage. You could write: "All of us at one time or another will be required to demonstrate courage." Next, you have the meat. You will insert the quote itself using quotation marks, and be sure to cite the name of the author or speaker if it is known. For example: "Nelson Mandela said, 'Courage is not the absence of fear but the triumph over it.'" Finally, you have the bottom bun, which is a sentence that comments on the quote by summarizing it in your own words or giving additional explanation. For example: "So even when we are afraid, we can still show courage."

Now that you understand how to smoothly add testimony into your writing, take some time to practice doing it. For each of the following quotes, write a sentence leading in to the quote, then write down the quote, and finally, follow it with a sentence commenting on the quote.

Example:
"It is better to light a candle than curse the darkness." —Eleanor Roosevelt

We all face dark or difficult circumstances. Eleanor Roosevelt said, "It is better to light a candle than curse the darkness." In other words, complaining doesn't do much when you're in a difficult place, and it's better to look for solutions to the problem instead.

a. "Twenty years from now you will be more disappointed by the things that you didn't do than by the ones you did do." —Mark Twain

____

____

____

b. "Whether you think you can or you think you can't, you're right." —Henry Ford

you can do what you think you can :)

____

____

c. "There is only one way to avoid criticism: do nothing, say nothing, and be nothing."
—Aristotle

d. "Despite everything, I believe that people really are good at heart." —Anne Frank

e. "Hate cannot drive out hate; only love can do that." —Martin Luther King Jr.

3. In your comparison essay, you will include quotes from the readings in some of your body paragraphs. In this kind of writing, your first sentence should lead in to the quote by providing a little narrative background for the quote. In other words, it should explain what is happening, what is going on in the story that the quote will describe. Then you will add the quote, being sure to identify the speaker of the quote. Your third sentence will again simply comment on the quote by summarizing it in your own words or providing further explanation.

The following are quotes from the *Titanic* and Chicago Fire readings in lesson 4. For each quote, write a sentence leading in to the quote, then write down the quote, and finally, follow it with a sentence commenting on the quote.

Example: "The smoke did not obscure the view; everywhere was a broad sheet of flame leaping, darting, and sending forth, as if from some grand pyrotechnic preparation, the most brilliant, dazzling meteors of living fire." —James Sheahan

The fire began to spread quickly and violently across the city. According to James Sheahan, "The smoke did not obscure the view; everywhere was a broad sheet of flame leaping, darting, and sending forth, as if from some grand pyrotechnic preparation, the most brilliant, dazzling meteors of living fire." Though absolutely terrifying and deadly, the fire was also marvelous to behold.

a. "The horrors of the exodus were made more terrible by the wild foray of horses and cattle, terrified by the fire, madly running hither and thither, kicking and trampling, aimlessly trying to escape or plunging through the human procession." —James Sheahan

During the sire, it was pure cause, "Quote" James Sheahan Stated, Not only were the people asraid, but the animals too, which made it even more caotic.

b. "It was in that crisis of the direst extremity that many brave women deliberately rejected life and chose rather to remain and die with the men whom they loved." —Logan Marshall

The Titanic Sank to the ground, Many waman had stayed behind, "Quote" These woman should be honored sor there bravery, Not only did others live because of them, but they also died with there husband.

c. "There seemed a great sense of loneliness when we were left on the sea in a small boat without the *Titanic*." —Lawrence Beesley

only sisty lise boats escaped, "quote" the boats had to senr sor themselves, there was no turning back.

Lesson 6

First Comparison: Roald Amundsen's Journey to the South Pole & Charles Lindbergh's Solo Transatlantic Flight

When I was thirteen years old, some of my friends and I discovered an abandoned **quarry** in the woods that had become a secret swimming hole. On summer nights, under cover of dark, we would head there in our swimming trunks and swing like monkeys from a rope that had been tied to one of the nearby trees. It was exhilarating—running and grabbing hold of the rope, swinging far out over the water, making a giant splash as I hit the surface. But it was also a bit dangerous. There were no lifeguards; no one had tested the rope to make sure it was secure. One of us could have gotten hurt, and we would have had a hard time finding him in the dark. Thankfully, that never happened—but it just goes to show that adventure always comes with an element of danger.

The desire for adventure is a part of who we are as human beings. From the time we are able to crawl, we seek out adventure. We explore the kitchen cupboards and find endless fascination with the pots and pans. We find crumbs of leftover food on the floor and put them in our mouths. As we learn to walk, we take our adventures outside and explore the great outdoors. In our imaginary world of play, we become captains of pirate ships, explorers discovering new lands, cowboys rounding up outlaws, and archaeologists digging for dinosaur bones or discovering new Egyptian tombs. We just love adventure.

This has been true since long before you or I were even born. Throughout history people have gone on adventures big and small. The early 1900s, for example, were a time of great adventure and exploration. Parts of our world had not yet been discovered or reached. Men were seeking to be the first to reach the North and South Poles, each one hoping to gain glory for himself and his country. With the invention of the airplane in 1903, new possibilities were opening up for exploration in the sky. Along with these opportunities came many risks, but there were many who were bold enough to accept the challenge.

In this lesson you're going to compare two historical events that were filled with adventure. The following selections will give you a good idea of just how exciting—and risky—those adventures were.

Journey to the South Pole

—adapted from *The South Pole* by Roald Amundsen

▲ Roald Amundsen

Roald Amundsen, born in Norway in 1872, was one of the great figures in polar exploration. In 1897, he was first mate[1] on an expedition that was the first ever to winter[2] in the Antarctic. In 1903, he became the first navigator to traverse the Northwest Passage.[3]

Amundsen dreamed of being the first man to reach the North Pole, and he was about to embark in 1909, when he learned that the American Robert Peary had already achieved the feat. (That claim was later disputed, but that's beside the point.) Amundsen changed his plans and secretly prepared for a different journey. In June of 1910 he set sail for Antarctica, where the English explorer Robert F. Scott was also headed, with the aim of reaching the South Pole. That winter, Amundsen sailed his ship into Antarctica's Bay of Whales and set up base camp sixty miles closer to the Pole than Scott. In October of 1911, both explorers set off across the continent—Amundsen driving sled dogs, and Scott using motor sledges, Siberian ponies, and dogs. On December 14, 1911, Amundsen's expedition won the race to the Pole and returned safely to base camp in late January.

Scott's expedition did not fare so well. The sleds broke down, the exhausted and freezing ponies had to be shot, and the dog teams were sent back, but Scott and four companions continued on foot. They reached the pole on January 18, 1912, only to find that Amundsen had beaten them by over a month. As they returned to camp, the weather took a turn for the worse. Two members of their party perished, and a storm later trapped Scott and the other two survivors in their tent only eleven miles from their base camp. Scott's frozen body was found later that year.

The following selection gives Amundsen's account of the end of his journey to the Pole.

December 1 was a very fatiguing one for us all. From early morning a blinding blizzard raged from the southeast, with a heavy fall of snow. The going was of the very worst kind—polished ice. I stumbled forward on ski, and had comparatively easy work. The drivers had been obliged to take off their skis so as to walk by the side, support the sledges, and give the dogs help when they came to a difficult place; and that was pretty often, for on this smooth ice surface there were a number of small scattered sastrugi (ridges in the snow), and these consisted of a kind of snow that reminded

1. first mate: second in command after the commander of the expedition
2. winter: spend a winter
3. Northwest Passage: a sea route in the Arctic Ocean between the Atlantic and Pacific Oceans

one more of fish-glue[4] than of anything else. The dogs could get no hold with their claws on the smooth ice, and when the sledge came on to one of these tough little waves, they could not manage to haul it over, try as they might. The driver then had to put all his strength into it to push the sledge over. Thus in most cases the combined efforts of men and dogs carried the sledge on.

If this part of the journey was trying for the dogs, it was certainly no less so for the men. If the weather had even been fine, so that we could have looked about us, we should not have minded it so much, but in this vile weather it was, indeed, no pleasure. Our time was also a good deal taken up with thawing noses and cheeks as they froze—not that we stopped; we had no time for that. We simply took off a mitt, and laid the warm hand on the frozen spot as we went; when we thought we had restored sensation, we put the hand back into the mitt. By this time it would want warming. One does not keep one's hands bare for long with the thermometer several degrees below zero and a storm blowing. In spite of the unfavorable conditions we had been working in, the sledge-meters that evening showed a distance of fifteen and a half miles. We were well satisfied with the day's work when we camped.

Let us cast a glance into the tent this evening. . . . Hanssen is cook, and will not turn in until the food is ready and served. . . . He evidently does not like to burn the food, and his spoon stirs the contents of the pot incessantly. "Soup!" The effect of the word is instantaneous. Everyone sits up at once with a cup in one hand and a spoon in the other. . . . Scalding hot it is, as one can see by the faces, but for all that it disappears with surprising rapidity. Again the cups are filled, this time with more solid stuff—pemmican.[5] The cups are carefully scraped, and the enjoyment of bread and water begins. It is easy to see, too, that it is an enjoyment—greater, to judge by the pleasure on their faces, than the most skillfully devised menu could afford.

When the meal is over, one of them calls for scissors and looking glass,[6] and then one may see the polar explorers dressing their hair for the approaching Sunday. The beard is cut quite short with the clipper every Saturday evening; this is done not so much from motives of vanity as from considerations of utility and comfort. The beard invites an accumulation of ice, which may often be

4. fish-glue: an adhesive taken from the tissue and skeleton of fish, often used in woodwork or for artistic purposes
5. pemmican: dried meat pounded into powder and mixed with fat, fruits, or berries, then shaped into a loaf or a cake; originally prepared by Native Americans
6. looking glass: a small mirror

very embarrassing. A beard in the polar regions seems to me to be just as awkward and unpractical as—well, let us say, walking with a tall hat on each foot. As the beard clipper and the mirror make their round, one man after the other disappears into his sleeping bag, and with five "Good-nights," silence falls upon the tent. . . . The dogs have curled themselves up and do not seem to trouble themselves about the weather.

December 5 there was a gale from the north, and once more the whole plain was a mass of drifting snow. In addition to this there was thick falling snow, which blinded us and made things worse, but a feeling of security had come over us and helped us to advance rapidly and without hesitation, although we could see nothing. That day we encountered new surface conditions—big, hard snow waves (sastrugi). These were anything but pleasant to work among, especially when one could not see them. It is a difficult matter to drive Eskimo dogs forward when they cannot see, but we managed it well. In spite of all hindrances, and of being able to see nothing, we traveled nearly twenty-five miles.

December 6 brought the same weather: thick snow, sky and plain all one, nothing to be seen. . . . These irregularities that one was constantly falling over were a nuisance. If we had met with them in our usual surroundings it would not have mattered so much, but up here on the high ground, where we had to stand and gasp for breath every time we rolled over, it was certainly not pleasant.

That day we passed 88°S, and camped in 88° 9'S.[7] A great surprise awaited us in the tent that evening. I expected to find, as on the previous evening, that the boiling point had fallen somewhat;[8] in other words, that it would show a continued rise of the ground, but to our astonishment this was not so. The water boiled at exactly the same temperature as on the preceding day. . . . There was great rejoicing among us all when I was able to announce that we had arrived on the top of the plateau.

All the sledges had stopped, and from the foremost of them the Norwegian flag was flying. It shook itself out, waved and flapped so that the silk rustled; it looked wonderfully well in the pure, clear air and the shining white surroundings. 88° 23' was past; we were farther south than any human being had been. No other moment of the whole trip affected me like this. The tears forced their way to my eyes; by no effort of will could I keep them back. It was the flag yonder that conquered me and my will. Luckily I was some way in advance of the others, so that I had time to pull myself together and master my feelings before reaching my comrades. We all shook hands,

7. 88°S and 88° 9'S: These are latitudinal coordinates. They tell how far south the expedition has come.
8. The South Pole is at an elevation of about 2,800 meters. The boiling point, the temperature at which water boils, goes down as elevation gets higher. Therefore, the higher up the explorers climbed, the lower the boiling point would be. The fact that the boiling point didn't decrease proved that they were no longer climbing higher, which meant that they had reached the plateau and were close to the Pole.

with mutual congratulations; we had won our way far by holding together, and we would go farther yet—to the end.

We did not pass that spot without according our highest tribute of admiration to the man who—together with his gallant companions—had planted his country's flag so infinitely nearer to the goal than any of his precursors. Sir Ernest Shackleton's[9] name will always be written in the annals of Antarctic exploration in letters of fire. Pluck and grit can work wonders, and I know of no better example of this than what that man has accomplished.

Every step we now took in advance brought us rapidly nearer the goal; we could feel fairly certain of reaching it on the afternoon of the 14th. . . . What should we see when we got there? A vast, endless plain, that no eye had yet seen and no foot yet trodden; or no, it was an impossibility; with the speed at which we had traveled, we must reach the goal first, there could be no doubt about that. And yet—wherever there is the smallest loophole, doubt creeps in and gnaws and gnaws and never leaves a poor wretch in peace. . . . It was quite extraordinary to see how [the dogs] raised their heads, with every sign of curiosity, put their noses in the air, and sniffed due south. One would really have thought there was something remarkable to be found there.

On the morning of December 14 the weather was of the finest, just as if it had been made for arriving at the Pole. I am not quite sure, but I believe we dispatched our breakfast rather more quickly than usual and were out of the tent sooner, though I must admit that we always accomplished this with all reasonable haste. . . . We advanced that day in the same mechanical way as before; not much was said, but eyes were used all the more.

At three in the afternoon a simultaneous "Halt" rang out from the drivers. They had carefully examined their sledge meters, and they all showed the full distance—our Pole by reckoning. The goal was reached, the journey ended. I cannot say—though I know it would sound much more effective—that the object of my life was attained. That would be romancing rather too barefacedly.[10] I had better be honest and admit straight out that I have never known any man to be placed in such

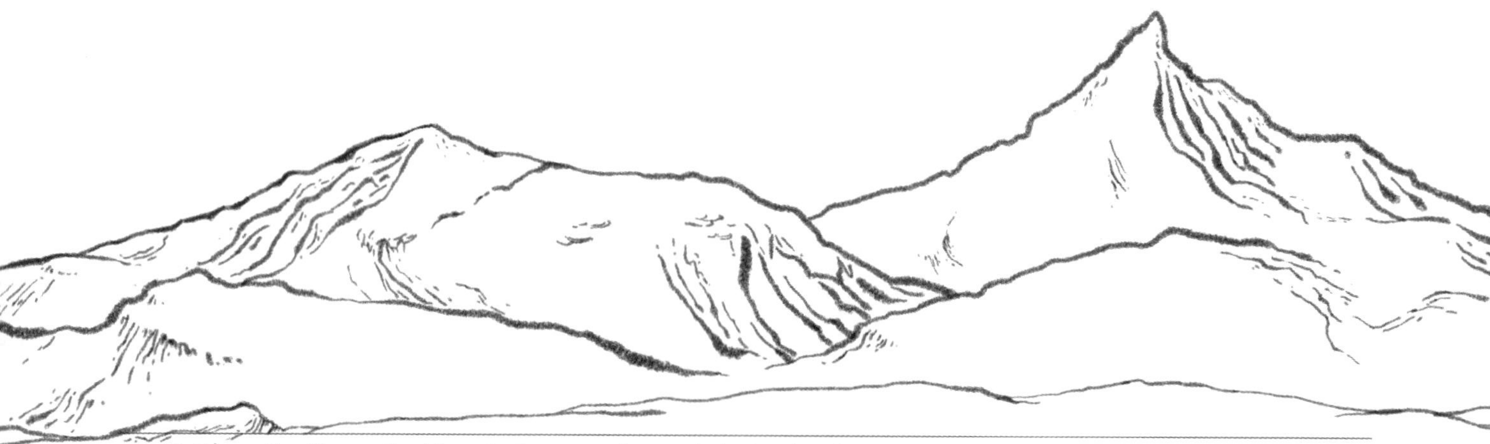

9. Sir Ernest Shackleton: Shackleton had attempted to reach the South Pole prior to Roald Amundsen but was unsuccessful. Later, he sought to become the first man to travel all the way across Antarctica, but he and his crew on the Endurance encountered lots of bad luck and never even set foot on the continent. It is a miraculous story, however, how they survived.
10. "romancing rather too barefacedly": This expression means that Amundsen would be putting too "romantic" or fairy-tale-like a spin on what happened and how he actually felt.

a diametrically opposite position[11] to the goal of his desires as I was at that moment. The regions around the North Pole—well, yes, the North Pole itself—had attracted me from childhood, and here I was at the South Pole. Can anything more topsy-turvy be imagined? . . .

After we had halted we collected and congratulated each other. . . . After this we proceeded to the greatest and most solemn act of the whole journey—the planting of our flag. I had determined that the act of planting it—the historic event—should be equally divided among us all. It was not for one man to do this; it was for all who had staked their lives in the struggle, and held together through thick and thin. . . . I could see that they understood and accepted it in the spirit in which it was offered. Five weather-beaten, frostbitten fists they were that grasped the pole, raised the waving flag in the air, and planted it as the first at the geographical South Pole. "Thus we plant thee, beloved flag, at the South Pole, and give to the plain on which it lies the name of King Haakon VII's Plateau."[12] That moment will certainly be remembered by all of us who stood there.

Of course, there was a festivity in the tent that evening—not that champagne corks were popping and wine flowing—no, we contented ourselves with a little piece of seal meat each, and it tasted well and did us good. There was no other sign of festival indoors. Outside we heard the flag flapping in the breeze. Conversation was lively in the tent that evening, and we talked of many things.

11. "diametrically opposed position": Amundsen is saying that his desire and his goal were exact opposites. Amundsen had always wanted to reach the North Pole, yet he instead had reached the South Pole—at the exact opposite end of the earth.
12. King Haakon VII's Plateau: King Haakon was king of Norway from 1905–1957. King Haakon VII's Plateau is a large area in the Antarctic that surrounds the South Pole.

The Spirit of St. Louis

—adapted from *The Spirit of St. Louis* by Charles A. Lindbergh[13]

▲ Charles Lindbergh

In 1903 the Wright brothers conducted the first successful airplane flight in Kitty Hawk, North Carolina. Within a decade much progress had been made in the field of aviation, and World War I ushered humanity into a new era in which aircraft were used in battle. Some of the most dashing young men were flying aces who lit up the skies. And yet there was still a lot of aerial exploration to do.

In 1919 a hotel owner in New York City offered a prize of $25,000 to the first pilot who could successfully fly nonstop from New York to Paris, a 3,600-mile journey. By 1927, four men had died, three were seriously injured, and two others went missing in the attempt. The prize still remained tantalizingly out of reach.

Charles Lindbergh, an ordinary twenty-five-year-old mail pilot known as "Slim," convinced some St. Louis businessmen to finance his attempt. He used their funds to build a special plane, the *Spirit of St. Louis*, which he helped to design. Its single-engine design led many to doubt its ability to cross the vast Atlantic, because previous attempts had all been made with multi-engine planes. Lindbergh intended to fly alone, dismissing the notion of a co-pilot. He also omitted a parachute and a radio from his gear, choosing instead to include more gasoline. Newspapers called him "the flying fool."

On May 20, 1927, at 7:52 a.m., a crowd of 500 gathered to watch the *Spirit of St. Louis* lift off from Long Island, barely clearing the telephone wires at the end of the runway strip. Lindbergh flew over Cape Cod and Nova Scotia, reaching the Atlantic just as the sun set. The night brought thick fog, and sleet formed on his plane as he tried to pass through the clouds. As the hours wore on, he became drowsy, fighting hard to stay awake. Sometimes he flew only ten feet above the ocean. Eventually he reached Europe, passing over Ireland and England, headed toward Paris. Darkness fell again as he reached the coast of France. Finally, after traveling more than 3,600 miles in 33½ hours, Lindbergh landed safely in Paris. A frenzied crowd of 100,000 swarmed around the plane, hoisting the pilot on their shoulders and cheering his achievement. Henceforth he was known as "Lucky Lindy."

The following selection is some of Lindbergh's account of his famous flight.

---

13. Reprinted with the permission of Scribner, a Division of Simon & Schuster, Inc., from *The Spirit of St. Louis* by Charles A. Lindbergh.

The Ninth Hour

Over Nova Scotia and Cape Breton Island, I hadn't noticed being tired. There was too much to think about, too much to see—the storms, the wind, the lakes and clearings. Before that, sleep would have been pleasant, like dozing off for an extra hour on a Sunday morning; but not too difficult to overcome. Now, it's getting really serious.

Why does the desire to sleep come over water so much more than over land? Is it because there's nothing to look at, no point different from all others to rivet one's attention to—nothing but waves, ever changing and yet changeless: no two alike, yet monotonous in their uniformity? Hold the compass needle on its mark, glance at the instruments occasionally; there's nothing else to do.

If I could throw myself down on a bed, I'd be asleep in an instant. In fact, if I didn't know the result, I'd fall asleep just as I am, sitting up in the cockpit—I'm beyond the stage where I need a bed, or even to lie down. My eyes feel dry and hard as stones. The lids pull down with pounds of weight against their muscles. Keeping them open is like holding arms outstretched without support. After a minute or two of effort, I have to let them close. Then, I press them tightly together, forcing my mind to think about what I'm doing so I won't forget to open them again; trying not to move stick[14] or rudder,[15] so the plane will still be flying level and on course when I lift them heavily.

It works at first; but soon I notice that the minute hand of the clock moves several divisions forward while I think only seconds pass. My mind clicks on and off, as though attached to an electric switch with which some outside force is tampering. I try letting one eyelid close at a time while I prop the other open with my will. But the effort's too much. Sleep is winning. My whole body argues dully that nothing, nothing life can attain, is quite so desirable as sleep. My mind is losing resolution and control.

I pull the *Spirit of St. Louis* up two or three hundred feet above the water, shake my head and body roughly, flex muscles of my arms and legs, stamp my feet on the floor boards. Shaking clarifies my mind a little—enough to make new resolutions. I will force my body to remain alert. I will force my mind to concentrate—never let it get dull again. I simply can't think of sleep. I have an ocean yet to cross, and Paris to find.

The Fifteenth Hour

I'd almost forgotten the moon. Now, like a neglected ally, it's coming to my aid. Every minute will bring improving sight. As the moon climbs higher in the sky, its light will brighten, until finally it ushers in the sun. The stars ahead are already fading. The time is 10:20. There have been only two hours of solid darkness.

Gradually, as light improves, the night's black masses turn into a realm of form and texture. Silhouettes give way to shadings. Clouds open their secret details to the eyes. In the moon's reflect-

14. stick: the main control device of early airplanes, held between the pilot's legs
15. rudder: a flap at the rear of the airplane used to control the plane's direction

ed light, they seem more akin to it than to the earth over which they hover. They form a perfect setting for that strange foreign surface one sees through a telescope trained on the satellite of the world. Formations of the moon, they are—volcanoes and flat plateaus; great towers and bottomless pits; crevasses and canyons; ledges no earthly mountains ever knew—reality combined with the fantasy of a dream. There are shapes like growths of coral on the bed of a tropical sea, or the grotesque canyons of sandstone and lava at the edge of Arizona deserts—first black, then grey, now greenish hue in cold, mystical light.

I weave in and out, eastward, toward Europe, hidden away in my plane's tiny cockpit, submerged, alone, in the magnitude of this weird, unhuman space, venturing where man has never been, irretrievably launched on a flight through this sacred garden of the sky, this inner shrine of higher spirits. Am I myself a living, breathing, earth-bound body, or is this a dream of death I'm passing through? Am I alive, or am I really dead, a spirit in a spirit world? Am I actually in a plane boring through the air, over the Atlantic, toward Paris, or have I crashed on some worldly mountain, and is this the afterlife?

The Eighteenth Hour

I've lost command of my eyelids. When they start to close, I can't restrain them. They shut, and I shake myself, and lift them with my fingers. I stare at the instruments, wrinkle forehead muscles tense. Lids close again regardless, stick tight as though with glue. My body has revolted from the rule of its mind. . . . Every cell of my being is on strike, sulking in protest, claiming that nothing, nothing in the world, could be worth such effort; that man's tissue was never made for such abuse. My back is stiff; my shoulders ache; my face burns; my eyes smart. It seems impossible to go on longer.

I've got to find some way to keep alert. There's no alternative but death and failure. No alternative but death and failure, I keep repeating, using the thought as a whip on my lagging mind; trying to make my senses realize the importance of what I'm saying. I kick rudder over sharply, skid back into position. But there's no use taking it out on the plane; that's unfair; it's not the plane's fault; it's mine. I try running fast on the floorboards with my feet for as many seconds as the *Spirit of St. Louis* will hold to course. Then, I clamp the stick between my knees while I simulate running with my hands. I push first one wing low and then the other, to blow fresh air through the cockpit and change pressures on my body. I shake my head until it hurts; rub the muscles of my face to regain feeling. I pull the cotton[16] from my ears, fluff it out, and wad it in again.

I'll set my mind on the sunrise—think about that—watch the clouds brighten—the hands of the clock—count the minutes till it comes. It will be better when the full light of day has broken. It's always better after the sun comes up.

16. cotton: Pilots had to place fluffy cotton balls in their ears because the noise of the plane engine could damage their hearing. The cotton balls may also have relieved some of the painful pressure caused by changes in altitude.

The Thirty-Third Hour

The *Spirit of St. Louis* is a wonderful plane. It's like a living creature, gliding along smoothly, happily, as though a successful flight means as much to it as to me, as though we shared our experiences together, each feeling beauty, life, and death as keenly, each dependent on the other's loyalty. *We* have made this flight across the ocean, not *I* or *it*.

I'm leveled off at four thousand feet, watching for the luminosity in the sky ahead that will mark the city of Paris. Within the hour, I'll land. The dot on my map will become Paris itself, with its airport, hangars, and floodlights, and mechanics running out to guide me in. All over the ground below there are clusters of lights. Large clusters are cities; small ones, towns and villages; pin points are buildings on a farm. I can imagine that I'm looking through the earth to the heavens on the other side. Paris will be a great galaxy lighting up the night.

Within the hour I'll land, and strangely enough I'm in no hurry to have it pass. I haven't the slightest desire to sleep. My eyes are no longer salted stones. There's not an ache in my body. The night is cool and safe. I want to sit quietly in this cockpit and let the realization of my completed flight sink in. Europe is below; Paris, just over the earth's curve in the night ahead—a few minutes more of flight. It's like struggling up a mountain after a rare flower, and then, when you have it within arm's reach, realizing that satisfaction and happiness lie more in the finding than the plucking. Plucking and withering are inseparable. I want to prolong this culminating experience of my flight. I almost wish Paris were a few more hours away. It's a shame to land with the night so clear and so much fuel in my tanks.

Afterword

My reception by the French people, in 1927, cannot be compressed into a final chapter of this book. After the warnings I had been given in America, I was completely unprepared for the wel-

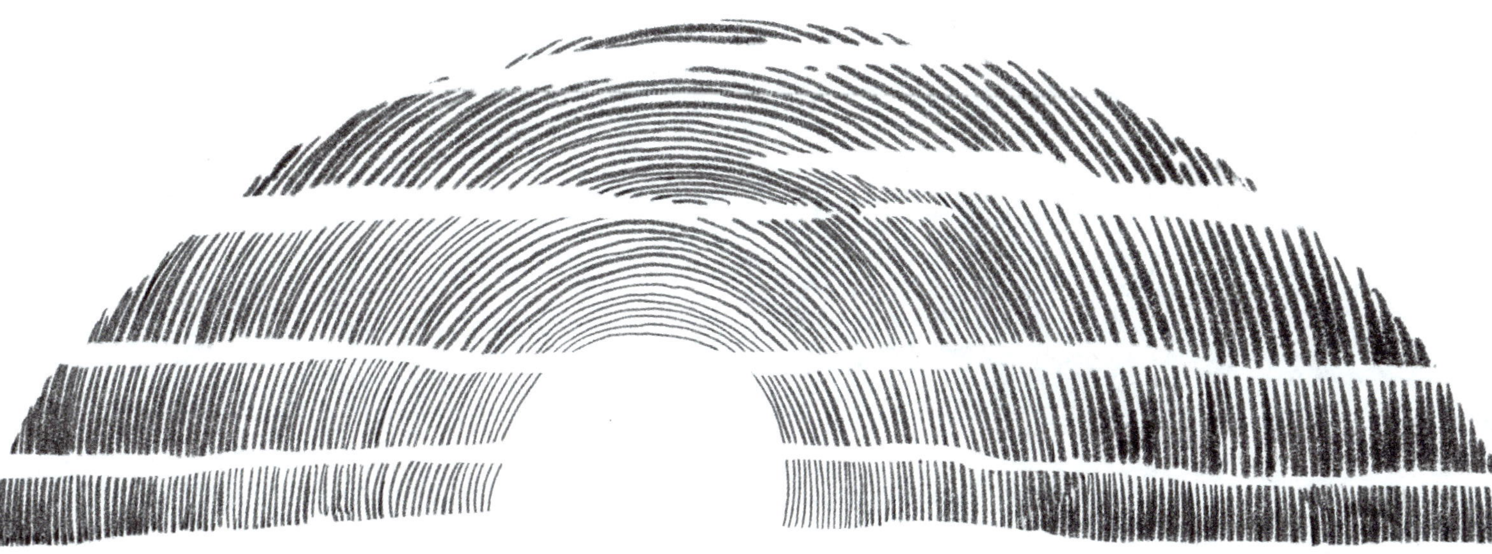

come which awaited me on Le Bourget.[17] I had no idea that my plane had been so accurately reported along its route between Ireland and the capital of France—over Dingle Bay, over Plymouth, over Cherbourg. When I circled the aerodrome it did not occur to me that any connection existed between my arrival and the cars stalled in traffic along the roads. When my wheels touched earth, I had no way of knowing that tens of thousands of men and women were breaking down fences and flooding past guards.

I had barely cut the engine switch when the first people reached my cockpit. Within seconds my open windows were blocked with faces. My name was called out over and over again, in accents strange to my ears—on this side of the plane—on that side—in front—in the distance. I could feel the *Spirit of St. Louis* tremble with the pressure of the crowd. I heard the crack of wood behind me when someone leaned too heavily against a fairing strip. Then a second strip snapped, and a third, and there was the sound of tearing fabric. That meant souvenir hunters were going wild. It was essential to get a guard stationed around my plane before more damage was done.

There were rips of fabric every few seconds, and I could feel my tail skid inching back and forth across the ground. I was afraid the *Spirit of St. Louis* might be seriously injured. The thought entered my mind that the longerons[18] would buckle if enough men climbed on top; and I knew the elevators[19] wouldn't stand much of any pressure without bending. I decided to get out of the cockpit and try to find some English-speaking person who would help me organize a guard to hold back the crowd.

I opened the door, and started to put my foot down on the ground. But dozens of hands took hold of me—my legs, my arms, my body. No one heard the sentences I spoke. I found myself lying in a prostrate position, up on top of the crowd, in the center of an ocean of heads that extended as far out into the darkness as I could see. Then I started to sink down into that ocean, and was buoyed up again. Thousands of voices mingled in a roar. Men were shouting, stumbling. My head and shoulders went down, and up, and down again, and up once more. It was like drowning in a human sea.

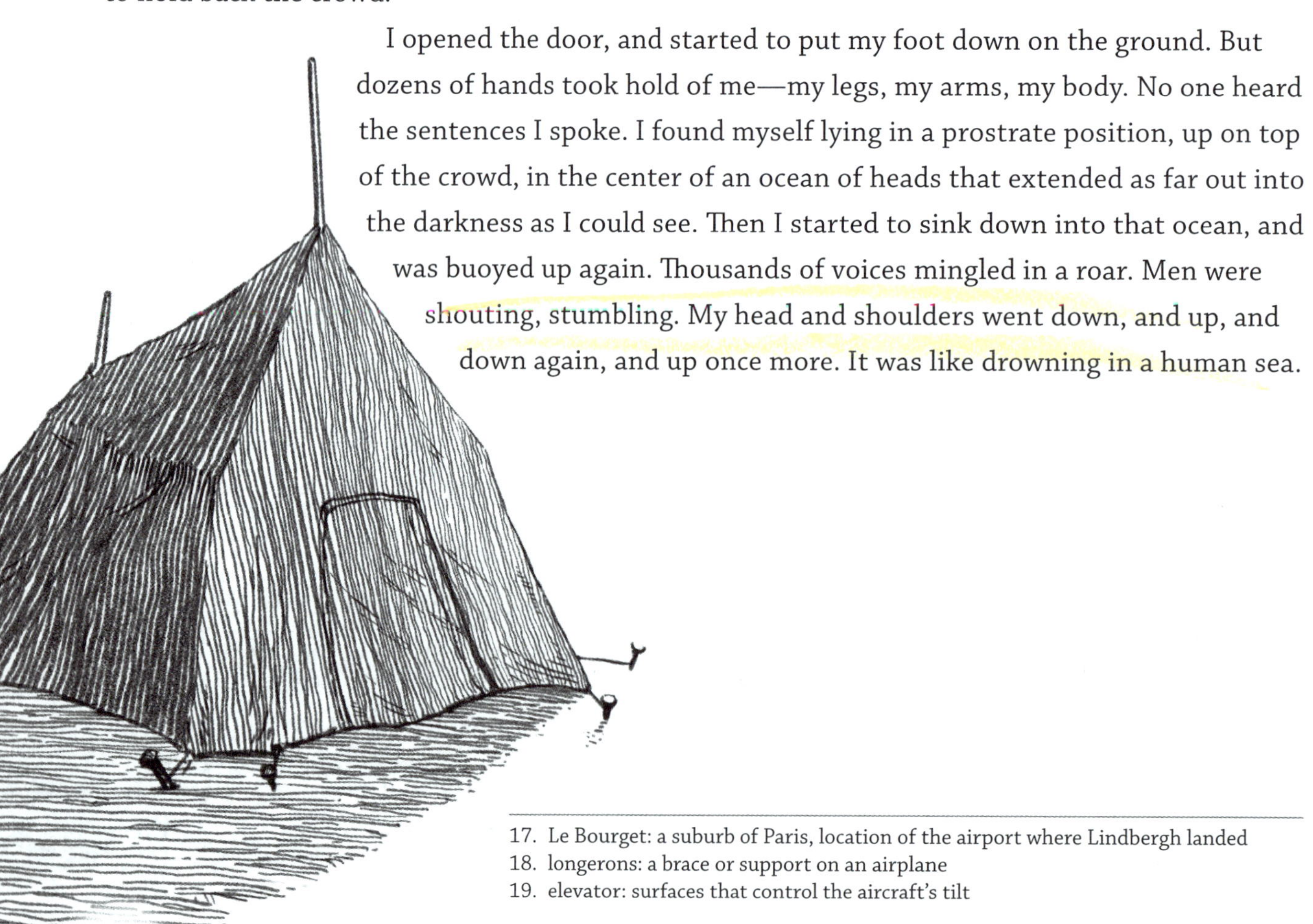

17. Le Bourget: a suburb of Paris, location of the airport where Lindbergh landed
18. longerons: a brace or support on an airplane
19. elevator: surfaces that control the aircraft's tilt

Tell It Back—Narration

1. **MARK UP THE TEXT—Annotation:** Read through the reading selections again. As you read, write in the margin of the text symbols that will help you understand it better and find important details later. The following are some symbols you might use:
   - Underline the main idea of the story or any important point.
   - Put a question mark in the margin to mark any part of the story you don't understand.
   - Write any questions or thoughts you have in the margin.
   - Put an exclamation point in the margin to mark any part of the story you find surprising or particularly interesting.
   - Circle any important or unfamiliar vocabulary words or proper nouns when they are first introduced. Remember, a proper noun is the name for any specific person, place, thing, or idea. How do you know which words to circle? Circle words that appear repeatedly, or words you can't understand from the context of the sentence alone. Look up any unfamiliar words in the glossary, or, if they aren't there, in a dictionary.

2. **ORAL NARRATION:** Look over the annotations you made for *The Spirit of St. Louis*. Then, without looking at the text, retell the story as best you remember it using your own words. Try not to leave out any important details.

   Here's the first sentence to help you get started:

   Over Nova Scotia and Cape Breton Island, I hadn't noticed being tired.

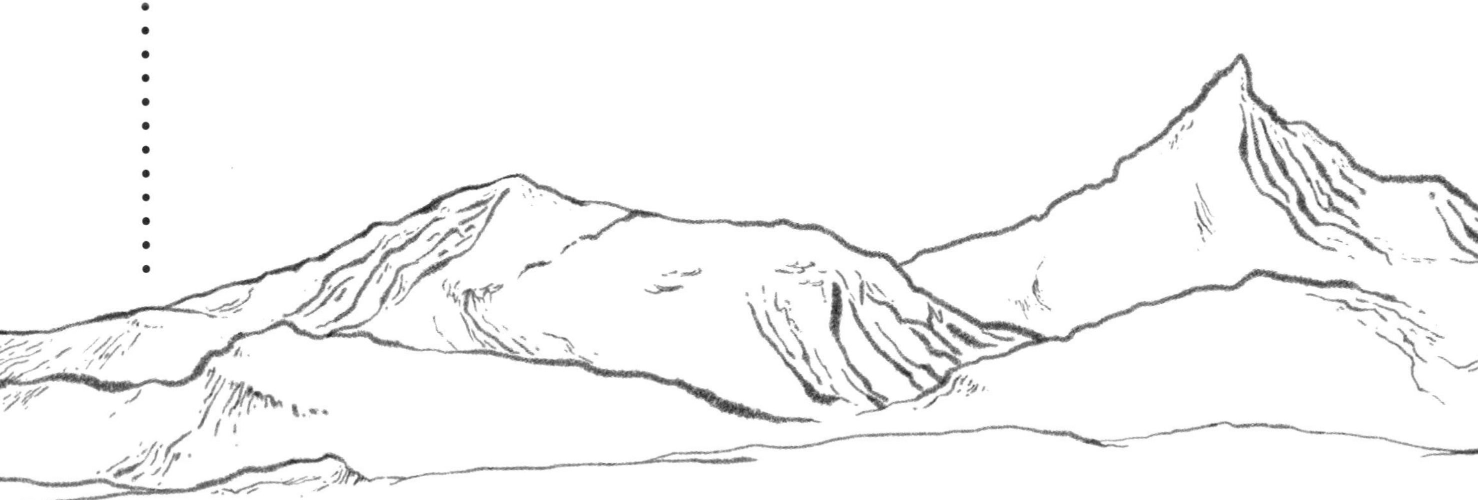

3. **OUTLINE:** Create an outline for *Journey to the South Pole* using Roman numerals (*I*, *II*, *III*) for the most important events and capital letters (*A*, *B*, *C*) for less important events. Use standard numbers (*1*, *2*, *3*) for minor points.

Talk About It—

1. Charles Lindbergh made a beautiful analogy for his flight when he said, "It's like struggling up a mountain after a rare flower, and then, when you have it within arm's reach, realizing that satisfaction and happiness lie more in the finding than the plucking." What does he mean by this? How is it an analogy for Lindbergh's flight? Have you ever felt something similar to what Lindbergh is expressing?

2. Both of the journeys you read about in this lesson involved a high amount of risk. In fact, it was just as possible that each explorer would die on his adventure as that he would reach his goal. What are some reasons you think that a person would take that kind of risk? Can you find any passages in the readings that reveal the explorers' reasons?

3. In the 1960s, another type of exploration—space exploration—became a major focus. America put the first man on the moon in 1969, and now, as I'm writing this, an astronaut is just about to complete an entire year of space travel. There are even those who believe that at some point in the future people could be living on Mars! In your opinion, what other parts of our world or even the universe are still left to be explored? Do you have any desire to explore unknown places, and if so, where?

Memoria—

> We should come home from adventures, and perils, and discoveries every day with new experience and character. —Henry David Thoreau

1. After reading this quotation by Henry David Thoreau, an American philosopher and essayist who was especially famous for living alone in a small cabin in the woods for several years, define any words you may not know. Then discuss the meaning of the quotation.

2. How does this quotation relate to the stories of Amundsen and Lindbergh?

3. Memorize the quotation and be prepared to recite it during your next class.

4. Write the quotation in your commonplace book, along with any thoughts you have about it.

Writing Time—

1. **SENTENCE PLAY**—In his record of his flight, Lindbergh writes, "Why does the desire to sleep come over water so much more than over land? Is it because there's nothing to look at, no point different from all others to rivet one's attention to—nothing but waves, ever changing and yet changeless?" In the previous book in this series, you practiced a rhetorical device called hypophora, in which the author asks a question and then immediately supplies an answer. In this quotation, Lindbergh "answers" his question with another question, which is also a wonderful rhetorical device. A single question can cause your audience to stay alert, to stay on its toes. When a second question follows, that can create even higher interest.

   In the following sentences, do what Charles Lindbergh does: Answer the question by posing another question.

   Example: Why am I always so much hungrier in the evening than I am in the morning?
   Answer: Is it because my stomach is fully awake, because I've run ten laps around the track—always with a cheeseburger in mind?

   A. Why are spiders so much creepier than butterflies? Is it because ____________________

   ____

   ____?

   B. Why is it that most people prefer fall over winter? Is it because ____________________

   ____

   ____?

   C. What is the best way to greet a friend? Should I ______________________________

   ____

   ____?

   D. Why do some people dislike going to the dentist? Is it because ____________________

   ____

   ____?

   E. How do I build a fire? Do I ____

   ____

   ____?

2. **COPIOUSNESS**—From time to time in this series, you will be revisiting the rhetorical devices you have learned so that, by practice, they will become tools that are easy for you to use. Remember that hypophora is a rhetorical device that asks a question and then immediately provides an answer in the form of a statement. Writers and speakers use hypophora for dramatic effect. Two of the most famous examples of hypophora are found in Winston Churchill's "Blood, Toil, Tears and Sweat" speech, given in 1940 as Great Britain was going to war with Nazi Germany. Here is an excerpt from that speech:

> You ask, what is our policy? I will say: It is to wage war, by sea, land and air, with all our might and with all the strength that God can give us; to wage war against a monstrous tyranny, never surpassed in the dark and lamentable catalogue of human crime. That is our policy. You ask, what is our aim? I can answer in one word: victory; victory at all costs, victory in spite of all terror, victory, however long and hard the road may be.

Roald Amundsen uses hypophora when he says this:

> Every step we now took in advance brought us rapidly nearer the goal; we could feel fairly certain of reaching it on the afternoon of the 14th. . . . What should we see when we got there? A vast, endless plain, that no eye had yet seen and no foot yet trodden.

Use the information in each of the following short paragraphs to create an example of hypophora. These paragraphs are adapted from *South! The Story of Shackleton's Last Expedition, 1914–1917*. Like Amundsen, Ernest Shackleton explored Antarctica, where his ship, the *Endurance*, became stuck fast as the ocean froze around it. The ice shifted slowly and the ship was crushed and swallowed under the water. Shackleton and his crew were forced to travel over ice and sea in lifeboats to reach safety.

Example: Four dogs which had been ailing were shot. Some of the dogs were suffering badly from worms, and the remedies at our disposal, unfortunately, were not effective.

Hypophora: What did we do with our ailing dogs? We shot them.

A. Monday, December 21, was beautifully fine, with a gentle west-north-westerly breeze. Seabirds of several species, penguins, and seals were plentiful, and we saw four small blue whales.

____

____

Does hypophora make your writing much stronger and more interesting? It sure does! If you feel confident using hypophora, feel free to include it in one of your comparison essays.

B. Just at daybreak I went over to the *Endurance* in order to retrieve some tins of petrol that could be used to boil up milk for the rest of the men. The ship presented a painful spectacle of chaos and wreck.

____

____

____

C. We could only cook seal or penguin or stews on this stove. On one occasion a wonderful stew made from seal meat fell into the fire through the bottom of the saucepan, becoming burnt out on account of the sudden intense heat of the fire below. We lunched that day on one biscuit and a quarter of a tin of corned beef each, frozen hard.

____

____

D. Enormous blocks of ice weighing many tons would break off and fall into the sea and the disturbance would cause great waves. One day Marston was outside the hut digging up the frozen seal for lunch with a pick, when a noise "like an artillery barrage" startled him. Looking up he saw that one of these tremendous waves, over thirty feet high, was advancing rapidly across the bay, threatening to sweep hut and inhabitants into the sea. A hastily shouted warning brought the men tumbling out. It was a narrow escape, though, as had they been washed into the sea nothing could have saved them.

____

____

E. We were dreadfully thirsty now. We found that we could get momentary relief by chewing pieces of raw seal meat and swallowing the blood, but thirst came back with redoubled force owing to the saltiness of the flesh. I gave orders, therefore, that meat was to be served out only at stated intervals during the day or when thirst was driving someone crazy.

____

____

3. **COMPARISON**—The purpose of this lesson's essay is to compare Roald Amundsen's journey to the South Pole with Charles Lindbergh's solo flight across the Atlantic Ocean. Before you start writing, use the following prompts for each paragraph to help you sketch out your ideas. You can use lists, phrases, or complete sentences for your answers. Then compose your full essay on a separate paper or on a computer. Remember that each paragraph has its own job to do.

   The paragraphs you write after going through these steps will be your first draft, or your first version of the essay. Assume that your first draft will need some rewriting to make it the best essay it can be.

   Prewriting: Begin by making a list of as many similarities and differences between your subjects as you can think of.

   Similarities between the two events:

This icon indicates where you will be doing prewriting.

   Differences between the two events:

Now select two of the most important similarities from your list.

Similarity #1: ______________________________

____

____

Similarity #2: ______________________________

____

____

Select two of the most important differences from your list.

Difference #1: ______________________________

____

____

Difference #2: ______________________________

____

____

Paragraph 1 (Introduction): Start with an introduction that includes an analogy, a narrative overview of each subject, and a topic sentence.

Begin your introduction with an analogy about adventure, exploration, or discovery. Remember, a simile uses "like" or "as" to make a comparison, and a metaphor uses one thing to describe another, but without using the words "like" or "as." Include a second sentence that explains your analogy if needed.

Analogy: ______________________________

____

____

Next write a short narrative overview of the two subjects. Consider the questions who, what, when, and where, and tell about each subject in one or two sentences.

Amundsen:

Who: ______________________

What: ______________________

____

When: ______________________

____

Where: ______________________

____

Lindbergh:

Who: ______________________

____

What: ______________________

____

When: ______________________

____

Where: ______________________

____

Finally, write your topic sentence, which simply states the main idea of your essay.

Topic sentence: ______________________

____

____

Paragraph 2 (Similarity #1): Write about one major similarity between the two subjects. Start by identifying the similarity you will be describing. Then tell more about the similarity by adding facts, examples, or details from the readings for both subjects.

Details about similarity #1:

Paragraph 3 (Similarity #2): Write about a second major similarity between the two subjects. Start again by identifying the similarity you will be describing. Then tell more about the similarity by adding facts, examples, or details from the readings for both subjects.

Details about similarity #2:

Look in the readings for a quote that gives a supportive fact, example, or detail and include it in your description.

Quote:

____

____

____

____

____

Paragraph 4 (Difference #1): Write about one major difference between the two subjects. Start by identifying the difference you will be describing. Then tell more about the difference by adding facts, examples, or details from the readings for both subjects.

Details about difference #1:

____

____

____

____

Paragraph 5 (Difference #2): Write about a second major difference between the two subjects. Start again by identifying the difference you will be describing. Then tell more about the difference by adding facts, examples, or details from the readings for both subjects.

Details about difference #2:

____

____

____

____

____

Look in the readings for a quote that gives a supportive fact, example, or detail and include it in your description.

Quote:

____

____

____

____

____

____

Paragraph 6 (Conclusion): Write an epilogue, or concluding paragraph. First, recap the main point of your essay. Then reflect on something important that can be learned from the comparison. Finally, write an observation or question about your subjects that would be interesting to learn more about in the future.

Something that can be learned from the comparison:

____

____

____

Something to learn more about:

____

____

____

Once you have completed your prewriting, go through these instructions again and write your paragraphs based on the prompts.

This icon means that you can also use a recording device for this exercise.

This icon points to more tips on elocution at the back of the book.

1. **FORMAL DISCUSSION:** Your teacher may instruct you to have a formal discussion. This sort of discussion is not a debate. Rather, it is an opportunity for your class to have a conversation around an open question or a controversial topic. Discussion is a great way to hear other people's ideas and to learn to express your own thoughts well. You can take sides as in a debate, but you are also free to agree with one another, enhancing each other's arguments. Usually a teacher will not participate in a formal discussion; instead she stands aside and listens in.

   Here's how it works: Your teacher will assign you a question or a topic. She might allow you to prepare for the discussion as homework, or she may give you time in class to jot down your thoughts. Either way, you will probably be permitted to keep your notes with you as you discuss. You will then have a conversation about the topic; this conversation usually lasts for fifteen to twenty minutes. Be sure to let everyone have a chance to speak, and if some people are being quiet, feel free to draw them into the conversation by asking them direct questions. If you can support your ideas by quoting a text, so much the better! In the end, your teacher may assign you a score based on the scoring guidelines included with this exercise.

Formal Discussion Scoring Guidelines

Award points based on the following criteria:

- taking a stand by clearly stating an argument (thesis) +2
- providing evidence for the argument +2
- making an analogy +2
- making a relevant comment +1
- asking a clarifying question +1
- inviting another student to participate +1
- interrupting -1
- monopolizing the conversation -2
- making personal attacks -2
- distracting the audience -2

1. Partner Feedback: With a student partner (or your teacher), take turns reading the rough drafts of your comparison essays. You and your partner should give each other comments about what is more or less effective about your writing. Use the following rubric to help you get ideas for your comments. (A rubric is a guide to evaluating and grading writing, and your teacher may use this particular rubric to grade your essay.) Try to say two positive things about your partner's essay, and then come up with at least two suggestions for editing the essay.

Comparison Essay Rubric

Name: ______________________________ Date of Assignment: ______________

Content __________/80

Introduction (15 points)

Does the paragraph begin with an analogy? (5 points) ______

Does the writer include short narrative overviews of each subject? (5 points) ______

Is there a topic sentence that states the main idea of the essay? (5 points) ______

Body Paragraphs (50 points)

Do the four body paragraphs, and the information they present, clearly and strongly expand on the topic sentence found in the introduction? (10 points) ______

Does the first body paragraph identify a major similarity between the two subjects? Does it provide additional facts, examples, or details? (10 points) ______

Does the second body paragraph identify a second major similarity between the two subjects? Does it provide additional facts, examples, or details? Does it use a quote from the readings? (10 points) ______

Does the third body paragraph identify a major difference between the two subjects? Does it provide additional facts, examples, or details? (10 points) ______

Does the fourth body paragraph identify a second major difference between the two subjects? Does it provide additional facts, examples, or details? Does it use a quote from the readings? (10 points) ______

Epilogue (15 points)

Does the conclusion—the epilogue—clearly restate the topic using different words? (5 points) ______

Does it state something important that can be learned from the comparison? (5 points) ______

Does it state something that would be interesting to learn more about? (5 points) ______

Style & Form __________/20

Style (12 points)

Are the sentences varied? (4 points) ______

Do the paragraphs follow each other in a way that makes sense? In other words, do they flow together? (4 points) ______

Does the writer use strong and specific words (vocabulary)? (4 points) ______

Form (8 points)

Number of spelling, punctuation, capitalization errors ______

- 2 or fewer per page: 4 points
- 3–4 per page: 3 points
- 5–6 per page: 2 points
- More than 6 per page: 0 points

Number of sentence errors (run-ons or fragments) ______

- 1 or fewer per page: 2 points
- 2–3 per page: 1 point
- More than 3 per page: 0 points

Is the handwriting neat and legible? Or, is the paper typed according to the teacher's requirements? ______

- Yes: 2 points
- No: 0 points

Total: __________/100

Revise It—

Here is what you must do to effectively revise your work:

1. Get feedback. Use comments from your student partners (or from your teacher) to strengthen and improve your paper.
2. Wait a day or two before you rewrite your paper. The time away from it will help you to see its problems more clearly.
3. Read the paper aloud to yourself. This is often the best way to catch mistakes—grammatical errors, as well as words that don't work well—because you will be using two senses—seeing and hearing—instead of one. If something sounds wrong, it probably is.

Once you are ready to rewrite, use the following steps to aid with your revision:

1. *Find your topic sentence and underline it.* There should be one sentence that states the main idea of your essay. Make sure your paper expresses that idea throughout.
2. *Make sure each paragraph gets the job done.* Remember that each paragraph has a special purpose according to the demands of the prompts. Revisit the goal of each paragraph and compare it to what you've written. Does each paragraph successfully accomplish its goal?
3. *Find and fix grammar mistakes.* Make sure all your nouns and verbs agree and that your writing is clear. Fix any fragments or run-ons. In other words, make sure you are writing complete sentences.
4. *Strengthen phrasing.* Are your word choices specific instead of vague? Do you use strong nouns and verbs? Do you vary your sentences and occasionally begin them with a prepositional phrase or a participial phrase? Weed out passive voice and excess adjectives. Use compound sentences, appositives, adverb phrases, and questions to make your writing more interesting. Transition smoothly between ideas and paragraphs using transition words.
5. *Proofread.* Look for any punctuation, spelling, or capitalization errors. Then fix them!
6. *Retype* the draft with the corrections you have made.

Lesson 7

Second Comparison: Helen Keller & Alice Paul

There is an old proverb that says, "You don't know a man until you walk a mile in his shoes." This means that if you really want to understand people, you have to think about their joys and sorrows, their triumphs and hardships, the experiences that make them different from you and everyone else. People are amazingly complex. No two of the billions of people on the planet are exactly alike. Let that sink in for a moment. Nearly eight billion people and no two alike!

The great diversity of humanity makes it a challenge for us to compare individuals. When we compare people, we can take any number of angles. We can refer to their physical appearance, moral character, actions, words, emotions, spiritual life, or intellect. This makes them like diamonds that can be examined from many different sides. How do we even begin to figure out what sides or angles to write about?

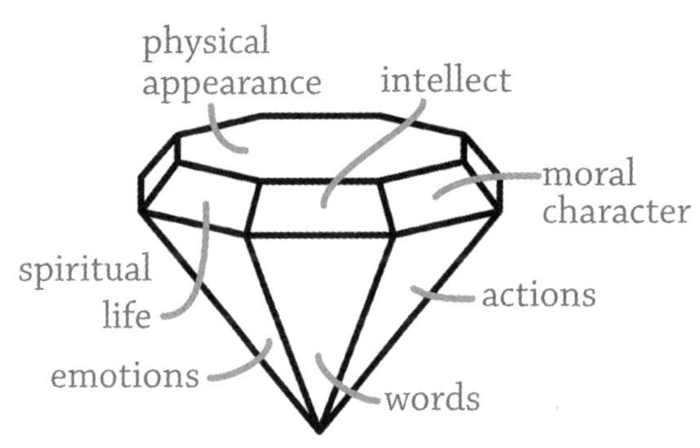

It's helpful, when examining or comparing people, to ask lots of questions: Where are they from? What are they known for? Do they have any relationship to each other? What are they like? What did they do? What do they believe? What struggles or difficulties did they face? Why are they interesting? What stands out most about each of them? The more questions you ask, the better your comparison will be.

In this lesson you will read about and compare two important women, Helen Keller and Alice Paul. Both women were born in the late nineteenth century and lived well into the twentieth century. Both women had an enormous effect on American society that still reverberates through our lives today.

Helen Keller: Overcomer of Disability

—adapted from *The Story of My Life* and *The World I Live In* by Helen Keller

Helen Keller was an American author and humanitarian who lived from 1880–1968. She was born with the ability to see and hear, but when she was a toddler, an illness deprived her of both of these senses. Thanks to careful teaching, Keller learned how to communicate with her hands and also to read and write and even speak. She went on to become the first deaf and blind person to graduate from college. She was a prolific author, and she helped to change negative attitudes toward people with disabilities. For forty years she gave her time and energy in support of the American Foundation for the Blind.

Parts of this reading are taken from the third part of Helen Keller's autobiography, which contains an account of Keller's life and education written by John Macy. His account is based for the most part on the records and observations of Anne Sullivan,[1] Keller's teacher.

Mark Twain has said that the two most interesting characters of the nineteenth century are Napoleon[2] and Helen Keller. The admiration with which the world has regarded her is more than justified by what she has done. No one can tell any great truth about her which has not already been written, and all that I can do is to give a few more facts about Miss Keller's work and add a little to what is known of her personality.

Miss Keller is tall and strongly built, and has always had good health except for the dread disease that visited her when she was nineteen months old. Of that time she writes:

> In the dreary month of February, came the illness which closed my eyes and ears and plunged me into the unconsciousness of a new-born baby. They called it acute congestion of the stomach and brain. The doctor thought I could not live. Early one morning, however, the fever left me as suddenly and mysteriously as it had come. There was great rejoicing in the family that morning, but no one, not even the doctor, knew that I should never see or hear again.

1. Anne Sullivan (1866–1936): Helen Keller's governess, teacher, and lifelong companion
2. Napoleon: French military commander who declared himself emperor of France

> I fancy I still have confused recollections of that illness. I especially remember the tenderness with which my mother tried to soothe me in my wailing hours of fret and pain, and the agony and bewilderment with which I awoke after a tossing half sleep, and turned my eyes, so dry and hot, to the wall away from the once-loved light, which came to me dim and yet more dim each day. But, except for these fleeting memories, if, indeed, they be memories, it all seems very unreal, like a nightmare. Gradually I got used to the silence and darkness that surrounded me and forgot that it had ever been different, until she came—my teacher—who was to set my spirit free. . . .
>
> I cannot recall what happened during the first months after my illness. I only know that I sat in my mother's lap or clung to her dress as she went about her household duties. My hands felt every object and observed every motion, and in this way I learned to know many things. Soon I felt the need of some communication with others and began to make crude signs. A shake of the head meant "No" and a nod, "Yes," a pull meant "Come" and a push, "Go." Was it bread that I wanted? Then I would imitate the acts of cutting the slices and buttering them. If I wanted my mother to make ice-cream for dinner I made the sign for working the freezer and shivered, indicating cold. My mother, moreover, succeeded in making me understand a good deal. I always knew when she wished me to bring her something, and I would run upstairs or anywhere else she indicated. Indeed, I owe to her loving wisdom all that was bright and good in my long night.

Miss Keller seems to be more nervous than she really is, because she expresses more with her hands than do most English-speaking people. One reason for this habit of gesture is that her hands have been so long her instruments of communication that they have taken to themselves the quick shiftings of the eye, and express some of the things that we say in a glance. All deaf people naturally gesticulate.

For someone who is deaf and blind, the sense of touch is vitally important. Here is Miss Keller describing a romp with her dog: "I have just touched my dog. He was rolling on the grass, with pleasure in every muscle and limb. I wanted to catch a picture of him in my fingers, and I touched him as lightly as I would cobwebs; but lo, his fat body revolved, stiffened and solidified into an upright position, and his tongue gave my hand a lick! He pressed close to me, as if he were fain to crowd himself into my hand. He loved it with his tail, with his paw, with his tongue. If he could speak, I believe he would say with me that paradise is attained by touch; for in touch is all love and intelligence." Touch is the way Miss Keller learned to take in the world and to express her inner thoughts.

When she speaks, her face is animated and expresses all the modes of her thought—the expressions that make the features eloquent and give speech half its meaning. On the other hand she does not know another's expression. When she is talking with an intimate friend, however, her hand goes quickly to her friend's face to see, as she says, "the twist of the mouth." In this way she is able to get the meaning of those half sentences which we complete unconsciously from the tone of the voice or the twinkle of the eye.

Her memory of people is remarkable. She remembers the grasp of fingers she has held before, all the characteristic tightening of the muscles that makes one person's handshake different from that of another.

Miss Keller can also "listen" with her feet. Here is a story she tells from a visit to a restaurant: "Often footsteps reveal in some measure the character and the mood of the walker. I found that two waiters were walking back and forth in the restaurant, but not with the same gait. A band was playing, and I could feel the music-waves along the floor. One of the waiters walked in time to the band, graceful and light, while the other disregarded the music and rushed from table to table to the beat of some discord in his own mind. Their steps reminded me of a spirited war-steed harnessed with a cart-horse."

The trait most characteristic, perhaps, of Miss Keller is humor. Skill in the use of words and her habit of playing with them make her ready with metaphors and analogies. Someone asked her if she liked to study. "Yes," she replied, "but I like to play also, and I feel sometimes as if I were a music box with all the play shut up inside me."

When she met Dr. Furness, the Shakespearean scholar, he warned her not to let the college professors tell her too many assumed facts about the life of Shakespeare; all we know, he said, is that Shakespeare was baptized, married, and died. "Well," she replied, "he seems to have done all the essential things."

Some time ago she made up her mind to learn to speak, and she gave her teacher no rest until she was allowed to take lessons, although wise people, even Miss Sullivan, the wisest of them all, regarded it as an experiment unlikely to succeed and almost sure to make her unhappy. It was this same perseverance that made her go to college. After she had passed her examinations and received her certificate of admission, she was advised by the dean of Radcliffe[3] and others not to go on. She accordingly delayed a year. But she was not satisfied until she had carried out her purpose and entered college.

Her life has been a series of attempts to do whatever other people do, and to do it as well. Her success has been complete, for in trying to be like other people she has come most fully to be herself. Her unwillingness to be beaten has developed her courage. Where another can go, she can go. She tramps in the woods, plunging through the underbrush, where she is scratched and bruised; yet you could not get her to admit that she is hurt, and you certainly could not persuade her to stay at home next time. So when people try experiments with her, she displays a sportsmanlike determination to win in any test, however unreasonable, that one may wish to put her to.

Miss Keller likes to be part of the company. If anyone whom she is touching laughs at a joke, she laughs, too, just as if she had heard it. If others are aglow with music, a responding glow shines in her face. Indeed, she feels the movements of Miss Sullivan so minutely that she responds to her

3. dean: the head of a college; in this case the head of Radcliffe College, a school for women in Cambridge, Massachusetts

moods, and so she seems to know what is going on, even though the conversation has not been spelled to her for some time. In the same way her response to music is in part sympathetic, although she enjoys it for its own sake.

Music probably can mean little to her but beat and pulsation. She cannot sing and she cannot play the piano. Her enjoyment of music, however, is very genuine, for she has a tactile recognition of sound when the waves of air beat against her. Part of her experience of the rhythm of music comes, no doubt, from the vibration of solid objects which she is touching: the floor, or, what is more evident, the case of the piano, on which her hand rests. But she seems to feel the pulsation of the air itself. When the organ was played for her in St. Bartholomew's,[4] the whole building shook with the great pedal notes, but that does not altogether account for what she felt and enjoyed. The vibration of the air as the organ notes swelled made her sway in answer. Sometimes she puts her hand on a singer's throat to feel the muscular thrill and contraction, and from this she gets genuine pleasure.

Much of her knowledge comes to her directly. When she is out walking she often stops suddenly, attracted by the odor of a bit of shrubbery. She reaches out and touches the leaves, and the world of growing things is hers, as truly as it is ours, to enjoy while she holds the leaves in her fingers and smells the blossoms, and to remember when the walk is done.

When she is in a new place, especially an interesting place like Niagara, whoever accompanies her is kept busy giving her an idea of visible details. If her companion does not give her enough details, Miss Keller asks questions until she has completed the view to her satisfaction.

She does not see with her eyes, but "sees" through her other senses: touch, taste, and smell. When she returns from a walk and tells someone about it, her descriptions are accurate and vivid, though occasionally she astonishes you by ignorance of some fact which no one happens to have told her; for instance, she did not know, until her first plunge into the sea, that it is salt.

Miss Keller reads by means of embossed print or the various kinds of braille. The ordinary embossed book is made with roman letters, both small letters and capitals. These letters are of simple, square, angular design. The small letters are

4. St. Bartholomew's: likely refers to an Episcopal church in New York City

about three-sixteenths of an inch high, and are raised from the page the thickness of the thumbnail. The books are not heavy, because the leaves with the raised type do not lie close. The time that one of Miss Keller's friends realizes most strongly that she is blind is when he comes on her suddenly in the dark and hears the rustle of her fingers across the page. Miss Keller does not as a rule read very fast, but she reads deliberately, not so much because she feels the words less quickly than we see them, but because it is one of her habits of mind to do things thoroughly and well.

Like every deaf or blind person, Miss Keller depends on her sense of smell to an unusual degree. When she was a little girl she smelled everything and knew where she was, what neighbor's house she was passing, by the distinctive odors.

As for her character, let us see what others have to say. Her friend Charles Dudley Warner[5] wrote about her in 1896. What he said was true then, and it remains true now:

"I believe she is the purest-minded human ever in existence. . . . The world to her is what her own mind is. She has not even learned that exhibition on which so many pride themselves, of 'righteous indignation.' Some time ago, when a policeman shot dead her dog, a dearly loved daily companion, she found in her forgiving heart no condemnation for the man; she only said, 'If he had only known what a good dog she was, he wouldn't have shot her.'

"Her mind is not only vigorous, but it is pure. She is in love with noble things, with noble thoughts, and with the characters of noble men and women."

She is logical and tolerant, most trustful of a world that has treated her kindly. "Toleration," she said once, when she was visiting her friend Mrs. Laurence Hutton, "is the greatest gift of the mind; it requires the same effort of the brain that it takes to balance oneself on a bicycle." It is this message of toleration that makes her so popular with American presidents. She has met every president from Grover Cleveland to Lyndon Johnson, thirteen presidents in all. She even gave some of them advice on how to stop discrimination against people with disabilities.

She has a large, generous sympathy and absolute fairness of temper. She always says exactly what she thinks, without fear of the plain truth; yet no one is more tactful and adroit than she in turning an unpleasant truth so that it will do the least possible hurt to the feelings of others.

She is an optimist and an idealist. In the diary that she kept at the Wright-Humason School in New York she wrote on October 18, 1894, "I find that I have four things to learn in my school life here, and indeed, in life—to think clearly without hurry or confusion, to love everybody sincerely, to act in everything with the highest motives, and to trust in dear God unhesitatingly."

5. Charles Dudley Warner (1829–1900): American novelist

Alice Paul: Fighter for Women's Votes

—adapted from *Jailed for Freedom* by Doris Stevens

Alice Paul, who lived from 1885–1977, was a leader in the women's suffrage movement in both England and the United States. She was a key figure in the fight for the passage of the nineteenth amendment, which gave women the right to vote.

Most people conjure up a menacing picture when a person is called not only a general, but a militant one. In appearance Alice Paul is anything but menacing. Quiet, almost mouse-like, this frail young woman sits in silence and baffles you with her contradictions. Large, soft, gray eyes that strike you with a positive impact make you feel the indescribable force and power behind them. A mass of soft brown hair, caught easily at the neck, makes the contour of her head strong and graceful. Tiny, fragile hands, that look more like an X-ray picture of hands, rest in her lap. Her whole atmosphere when she is not in action is one of strength and quiet determination. In action she is swift, alert, almost panther-like in her movements. Dressed always in simple frocks, preferably soft shades of purple, she conforms to an individual style and taste of her own rather than to the prevailing vogue.[6]

Alice Paul brought back to the fight for women's suffrage[7] that note of immediacy which had gone with the passing of Miss Anthony's[8] leadership. She called a halt on further pleading, wheedling, proving, praying. It was as if she had bidden women to stand erect, with confidence in themselves and in their own judgments, and compelled them to be self-respecting enough to dare to put their freedom first, and so determine for themselves the day when they should be free. Alice Paul gave to thousands of women the essence of freedom. Her attack was so direct, so clear, so simple and unafraid. And her resistance had such a fine quality of strength.

On the very day and hour when Congress, in 1917, left the Capitol building after agreeing to enter the Great War,[9] Alice Paul led eleven women to the White House gates to protest against the Administration's allowing its lawmakers to go home without action on the suffrage amendment. These women[10] carried banners and stood quietly at the White House gates "picketing" the president; they wanted President Wilson to put his power behind the suffrage amendment in Congress. That did not seem so shocking at first. When, however, the women went back on the picket line the

6. "prevailing vogue": This term is a reference to what is popular or fashionable at a given time. For example, one year the "prevailing vogue" for males might be to have a buzz cut, while the next year it will be fashionable to grow your hair long. Girls' fashion trends might include bright colors one year, then earthy tones the next.
7. women's suffrage: "Suffrage" is a term that refers to the right to vote. The women's suffrage movement began in the nineteenth century with key leaders such as Elizabeth Cady Stanton and Susan B. Anthony. The movement was not successful in gaining women's right to vote until 1919, with the nineteenth amendment.
8. Miss Anthony: Susan B. Anthony
9. the Great War: also known as World War I
10. These women are known to history as the Silent Sentinels.

next day and the next and the next, it began to dawn upon the excited press that such persistence was "undesirable" . . . "unwomanly" . . . "dangerous."

"Silly women" . . . "Pathological" . . . "They must be crazy." . . . "Don't they know anything about politics?" . . . "What can Wilson do? He does not have to sign the constitutional amendment." . . . So ran the comment from the wise elderly gentlemen sitting buried in their cushioned chairs at the gentlemen's club across the Park, watching eagerly the "shocking," "shameless" women at the gates of the White House. No wonder these gentlemen found the pickets irritating! This absorbing topic of conversation, we are told, shattered many an otherwise quiet afternoon and broke up many a quiet game. Here were American women before their very eyes daring to shock them into having to think about liberty. And what was worse—liberty for women. Ah well, this could not go on, this insult to the president. They could with impunity condemn him and gossip about his affairs. But that women should stand at his gates asking for liberty—that was a sin without mitigation.

But the intrepid women stood their long vigils, day by day, at the White House gates, through biting wind and driving rain, through sleet and snow as well as sunshine, waiting for the president to act. Eventually Alice Paul and her colleagues were arrested on the trumped-up charge of obstructing traffic. They were put on trial and thrown into prison for their protests. Let her tell the story in her own words:

> It was late afternoon when we arrived at the jail. There we found the suffragists who had preceded us, locked in cells. The first thing I remember was the distress of the prisoners about the lack of fresh air. Evening was approaching, and every window was closed tight. The air in which we would be obliged to sleep was foul. I went to a window and tried to open it. Instantly a group of men, prison guards, appeared, picked me up bodily, threw me into a cell, and locked the door.
>
> There is absolutely no privacy allowed a prisoner in a cell. You are suddenly peered at by curious strangers, who look in at you all hours of the day and night, by officials, by attendants, by interested philanthropic visitors, and by prison reformers, until one's sense of privacy is so outraged that one rises in rebellion. We set out to secure privacy, but we did not succeed, for to allow privacy in prison is against all institutional thought and habit.
>
> Our meals consisted of a little almost raw salt pork, some sort of liquid—I am not sure whether it was coffee or soup—bread, and occasionally molasses. How we cherished the bread and molasses! We saved it from meal to meal so as to try to distribute the nourishment over a longer period, as almost everyone was unable to eat the raw pork. Lucy Branham, who was more valiant than the rest of us, called out from her cell one day, "Shut your eyes tight, close your mouth over the pork, and swallow it without chewing it. Then you

can do it." This heroic practice kept Miss Branham in fairly good health, but to the rest it seemed impossible, even with our eyes closed, to crunch our teeth into the raw pork.

At the end of two weeks of solitary confinement, without any exercise, without going outside of our cells, some of the prisoners were released, having finished their terms, but five of us were left serving seven months' sentences, and two, one-month sentences. With our number thus diminished to seven, the authorities felt able to cope with us. The doors were unlocked and we were permitted to take exercise. Rose Winslow fainted as soon as she got into the yard and was carried back to her cell. I was too weak to move from my bed. Rose and I were taken on stretchers that night to the hospital. Here we decided to wage a hunger strike,[11] as the ultimate form of protest left us—the strongest weapon left with which to continue within the prison our battle against the Administration. One authority after another, high and low, in and out of prison, came to attempt to force me to break the hunger strike, threatening that I would be taken to a "very unpleasant place" or force-fed.

After about three days of the hunger strike a man entered my room in the hospital and announced himself as Dr. White. He said that he had been asked by District Commissioner Gardner[12] to make an investigation. Coming close to my bedside and addressing the attendant, who stood at a few respectful paces from him, Dr. White said: "Does this case talk?"

"Why wouldn't I talk?" I answered quickly.

"Oh, these cases frequently will not talk, you know," he continued in explanation.

"Indeed I'll talk," I said gaily, not having the faintest idea that this was an investigation of my sanity. "Talking is our business," I continued. "We talk to anyone on earth who is willing to listen to our suffrage speeches."

"Please talk," said Dr. White. "Tell me about suffrage; why you have opposed the president; the whole history of your campaign, why you picket, what you hope to accomplish by it. Just talk freely."

I drew myself together, sat upright in bed, propped myself up for a discourse of some length, and

11. hunger strike: a form of protest in which a prisoner refrains from eating food. At this time, Alice Paul weighed only about ninety pounds, and death by starvation was a very serious possibility for her. Not only was she protesting her imprisonment, she was protesting the prison food as well. She wrote, "If we are to be starved, I prefer to be starved all at once." (*New York Times*, November 7, 1917)

12. District Commissioner Gardner: Gwynne Gardner, the commissioner in charge of the District of Columbia prisons at the time

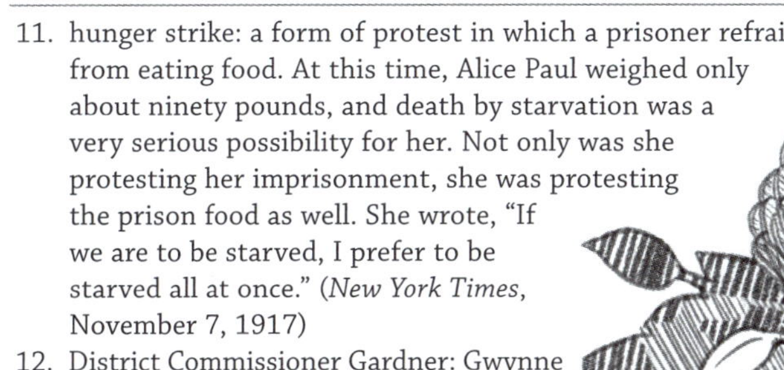

began to talk. The stenographer whom Dr. White brought with him took down in shorthand everything that was said.

I may say it was one of the best speeches I ever made. I recited the long history and struggle of the suffrage movement from its early beginning up to the present moment, outlining the status of the suffrage amendment in Congress at that time. In short, I told him everything. He listened attentively, interrupting only occasionally to say, "But, has not President Wilson treated you women very badly?" Whereupon, I, still unaware that I was being examined, launched forth into an explanation of Mr. Wilson's political situation and the difficulties he had confronting him. I continued to explain why we felt our relief lay with him; I cited his extraordinary power, his influence over his party, his undisputed leadership in the country, always painstakingly explaining that we opposed President Wilson merely because he happened to be president, not because of who he was. Again came an interruption from Dr. White, "But isn't President Wilson directly responsible for the abuses and indignities which have been heaped upon you? You are suffering now as a result of his brutality, are you not?"

Presently Dr. White took out a small light and held it up to my eyes. Suddenly it dawned upon me that he was examining me personally, that his interest in the suffrage agitation and the jail conditions did not exist, and that he was merely interested in my reactions to the agitation and to jail. Even then I was reluctant to believe that I was the subject of mental investigation and I continued to talk.

But he continued in what I realized, with a sudden shock, was an attempt to discover in me symptoms of the persecution mania.[13] How simple he had apparently thought it would be to prove that I had an obsession on the subject of President Wilson!

The day following he came again, this time bringing with him the district commissioner, Mr. Gardner, to whom he asked me to repeat everything that had been said the day before. When the narrative touched upon the president and his responsibility for the obstruction of the suffrage amendment, Dr. White would turn to his associate with the remark: "Note the reaction." It appeared clear that it was their intention either to discredit me, as the leader of the agitation, by casting doubt upon my sanity, or else to intimidate us into retreating from the hunger strike.

I told the commissioner that the hunger strike would not be abandoned. But they had by no means exhausted every possible facility for breaking down our resistance. I overheard the commissioner say to Dr. Gannon[14] on leaving, "Go ahead, take her and feed her." I was thereupon put upon a stretcher and carried into the psychopathic ward.

13. persecution mania: an irrational fear that other people are plotting one's downfall and that they are responsible for one's failures
14. Dr. Gannon was the chief of the hospital.

There were two windows in the room. Dr. Gannon immediately ordered one window nailed shut from top to bottom. He then ordered the door leading into the hallway taken down and an iron-barred cell door put in its place. He departed with the command to a nurse to "observe her." Following this direction, all through the day, once every hour, the nurse came to "observe" me. All through the night, once every hour, she came in, turned on an electric light sharp in my face, and "observed" me. This ordeal was the most terrible torture, as it prevented my sleeping for more than a few minutes at a time. And if I did finally get to sleep it was only to be shocked immediately into wide-awakeness with the pitiless light. Other officials came continually to peer through my barred door.

It is scarcely possible to convey to you one's reaction to such an atmosphere. Here I was surrounded by people on their way to the insane asylum. Some were waiting for their commitment papers.[15] Others had just gotten them. And all the while everything possible was done to attempt to make me feel that I too was a "mental patient."

At this time, forcible feeding[16] with raw eggs began in the district jail. Miss Paul and Miss Winslow, the first two suffragists to undertake the hunger strike, went through the operation of forcible feeding this day and three times a day on each succeeding day until their release from prison three weeks later.

15. commitment papers: papers that officially order someone to be kept in an asylum
16. forcible feeding: feeding against the will of the patient through a tube that goes from the mouth down into the stomach

Tell It Back—Narration

1. **MARK UP THE TEXT—Annotation:** Read through the reading selections again. As you read, write in the margin of the text symbols that will help you understand it better and find important details later. The following are some symbols you might use:
   - Underline the main idea of the story or any important point.
   - Put a question mark in the margin to mark any part of the story you don't understand.
   - Write any questions or thoughts you have in the margin.
   - Put an exclamation point in the margin to mark any part of the story you find surprising or particularly interesting.
   - Circle any important or unfamiliar vocabulary words or proper nouns when they are first introduced. Remember, a proper noun is the name for any specific person, place, thing, or idea. How do you know which words to circle? Circle words that appear repeatedly, or words you can't understand from the context of the sentence alone. Look up any unfamiliar words in the glossary, or, if they aren't there, in a dictionary.

2. **ORAL NARRATION:** Look over the annotations you made for *Helen Keller: Overcomer of Disability*. Then, without looking at the text, retell the information as best you remember it using your own words. Try not to leave out any important details.

   Here's the first sentence to help you get started:

   Mark Twain has said that the two most interesting characters of the nineteenth century are Napoleon and Helen Keller.

3. **OUTLINE:** Create an outline for *Alice Paul: Fighter for Women's Votes* using Roman numerals (*I*, *II*, *III*) for the most important events and capital letters (*A*, *B*, *C*) for less important events. Use standard numbers (*1*, *2*, *3*) for minor points.

Talk About It—

1. Comb through the reading selections for any use of analogy, simile, or metaphor. Then share one of the examples that you find with your class and describe or explain the comparison using your own words.

2. Both Helen Keller and Alice Paul persevered through tremendous difficulty. Think about a time in your life when you or someone close to you went through something very hard. What things helped you (or this person) to endure that difficulty? What qualities did Helen Keller and Alice Paul demonstrate that probably helped them to persevere?

3. "Mark Twain has said that the two most interesting characters of the nineteenth century are Napoleon and Helen Keller." This is a fascinating statement because Napolean and Helen Keller were very different people. Napoleon was a military and political genius, but also one whom history portrays as a borderline tyrant, obsessed with ambitions of greatness and a thirst for power. Keller was afflicted with disabilities that would make it difficult for her to achieve the same kind of power that Napoleon strove toward. However, it could be argued that, in the end, Keller's legacy was equally as memorable as Napoleon's. How is it that someone with Keller's challenges could have such a lasting effect?

4. Alice Paul and her fellow suffragettes had to endure a tremendous amount of hypocrisy and unequal treatment from men. We see in her writing that men could insult the president, condemn him, and gossip about his affairs, and they could do it without penalty. On the other hand, when women stood silently at the gates of the White House and demanded liberty, that was considered a crime that needed to be stopped. Why do you think so many men were opposed to women gaining equal rights, specifically the right to vote?

> Let me not pray to be sheltered from dangers,
> but to be fearless in facing them.
>
> Let me not beg for the stilling of my pain, but
> for the heart to conquer it.
>
> —Rabindranath Tagore

1. After reading this poem by Rabindranath Tagore, a writer, musician, poet, and painter from Kolkata, India, define any words you may not know. Then discuss something particular that you like about this poem. You might choose a specific stanza, line, or phrase, a sound or rhythm, an image or a word. Make sure to explain why you like it.
2. How does this poem relate to the stories of Helen Keller and Alice Paul?
3. Memorize the poem and be prepared to recite it during your next class.
4. Write the poem in your commonplace book, along with any thoughts you have about it.

Writing Time—

1. **SENTENCE PLAY**—Some people are connoisseurs of food, and some are connoisseurs of music. A connoisseur is an expert judge in a matter of taste. An olive oil connoisseur, for instance, can taste the difference between a very good "extra virgin, first cold press" oil and oils of lesser quality. I am a sentence connoisseur, and you can be too!

   A sentence does not have to be complicated to be beautiful. Some of the most famous sentences in the world are short and brilliant. Here are a few of my favorites:
   - "What are men to rocks and mountains?" —from *Pride and Prejudice* by Jane Austen
   - "Let the wild rumpus start!" —from *Where the Wild Things Are* by Maurice Sendak
   - "Journeys end in lovers meeting." —from *Twelfth Night* by William Shakespeare

   The best writing contains a variety of sentences: some short, some long; some simple, some complex. Here is an interesting longer sentence:

   > She reaches out and touches the leaves, and the world of growing things is hers, as truly as it is ours, to enjoy while she holds the leaves in her fingers and smells the blossoms, and to remember when the walk is done.

   It's my opinion, though some people may not agree, that this sentence would be more effective divided into two like this:

   > She reaches out and touches the leaves, and the world of growing things is hers! She enjoys it while she holds the leaves in her fingers and smells the blossoms, and she remembers it when the walk is done.

Whether you like the original version or my version better, the point is that you should feel free to savor and enjoy words, like a connoisseur, and play with them until you create sentences that delight you and that communicate your ideas clearly.

Divide the following longer sentences into at least two shorter sentences. Feel free to add or subtract a few words to achieve the effect you want.

A. It was as if Alice had bidden women to stand erect, with confidence in themselves and in their own judgments, and compelled them to be self-respecting enough to dare to put their freedom first, and so determine for themselves the day when they should be free.

____

____

____

____

B. One reason for this habit of gesture is that Helen's hands have been so long her instruments of communication that they have taken to themselves the quick shiftings of the eye, and express some of the things that we say in a glance.

____

____

____

____

C. At the end of two weeks of solitary confinement, without any exercise, without going outside of our cells, some of the prisoners were released, having finished their terms, but five of us were left serving seven months' sentences, and two, one-month sentences.

____

____

____

____

Now do the opposite. Take the very short sentences in the following two paragraphs and join them together to form one long, well-written sentence. Feel free to add conjunctions and other words, delete a word or two, rearrange clauses, and change verb forms as needed. However, you must still include the important information from each sentence.

Example: I walked up the snowy lane. I saw my home at the far end. It was half a mile distant. The windows were bright with candlelight. Icicles sparkled on the eaves. Mama was baking gingerbread cookies.

Change to: As I walked up the snowy lane, I saw my home at the far end, half a mile distant, the windows bright with candlelight, icicles sparkling on the eaves, and Mama was baking gingerbread cookies.

A. The two cats sat in the café by an open window. They enjoyed the breeze. They quietly sipped coffee. People gave them quick, sideways glances. The cats ignored them.

____

____

____

____

B. K2 is the second tallest mountain in the world. It is considered the hardest mountain to climb. Terrible weather surrounds the peak. Rockslides and avalanches happen frequently. There are many sheer rock faces.

____

____

____

____

____

2. **COPIOUSNESS**—

A. As you learned in the previous book in this series, parallelism is a rhetorical strategy in which words, phrases, clauses, verb forms, and even sounds form a pattern. The term "parallelism" comes from the Greek word *parallelos*, which means "side-by-side." The use of patterns and repetition will give your writing more clarity and power. For example:

- Parallelism of words: She tried to make her pastry fluffy, sweet, and delicate. (pattern of adjectives)
- Parallelism of phrases: Singing a song or writing a poem is joyous. (verb form repeats)
- Parallelism of clauses: Perch are inexpensive; cod are cheap; trout are abundant; but salmon are best. (clause structure repeats)

In each of these examples, the reader consciously or unconsciously recognizes a pattern. Our brains love patterns! They help us to understand what we're reading more easily, and they keep our minds alert.

Finish each of the following sentences so that the pattern is preserved.

Example: Birds chirp, cats meow, lions roar, and ____donkeys bray____.

a. He praised her for her beauty, grace, and ____________________________.

b. I came, I saw, ____________________________.

c. Happy is the man, happy is the woman, and ____________________________ whose heart knows no jealousy.

d. Her stew was full of vegetables, ____________________________, and spices.

e. Silent night, holy night, all is calm, ____________________________.

f. The year revolves around summer and winter, springtime and

____________________________.

g. Banging drums, tooting horns, and ____________________________ woke me from my sleep.

Now write your own examples of parallelism:

h. ____

____

i. ____

____

B. **Chiasmus** is a pattern in which the words in the first half of a sentence are reversed in the second half of the sentence. This comes from the Greek letter word *chi* (X) and means "turning about in the opposite direction." As with parallelism, the repetition of chiasmus causes the brain to perk up and creates a pleasing balance of words. For example:

- "Fair is foul, and foul is fair." —from *Macbeth* by William Shakespeare
- "I flee who chases me, and chase who flees me." —Ovid

Sometimes the chiasmus is a little more complicated because other words are blended in:

- "If black men have no rights in the eyes of the white men, of course the whites can have none in the eyes of the blacks." —from "An Appeal to Congress for Impartial Suffrage" by Frederick Douglass
- "Your manuscript is both good and original; but the part that is good is not original, and the part that is original is not good." —attributed to Samuel Johnson

Fill in the rest of the following sentences by reversing the words and thereby creating chiasmus.

Example: Hear me, men of Ithaca; ___men of Ithaca, hear me___.

a. Ask not what your country can do for you, but ____________________.

b. One should work to live, not ____________________.

c. Beauty is truth; ____________________—that is all Ye know on earth, and all ye need to know.

d. Many that are first, shall be last; And many ____________________.

e. Bad men live that they may eat and drink, whereas good men

____________________.

Now create your own examples of chiasmus:

a. ______________________________

____

____

b. ______________________________

____

____

3. **COMPARISON**—The purpose of this lesson's essay is to compare Helen Keller to Alice Paul. Before you start writing, use the following prompts for each paragraph to help you sketch out your ideas. You can use lists, phrases, or complete sentences for your answers. Then compose your full essay on a separate paper or on a computer. Remember that each paragraph has its own job to do.

   The paragraphs you write after going through these steps will be your first draft, or your first version of the essay. Assume that your first draft will need some rewriting to make it the best essay it can be.

   Prewriting: Begin by making a list of as many similarities and differences between your subjects as you can think of.

   Similarities between the two subjects:

____

____

____

____

____

____

____

____

Differences between the two subjects:

Now select two of the most important similarities from your list.

Similarity #1:

Similarity #2:

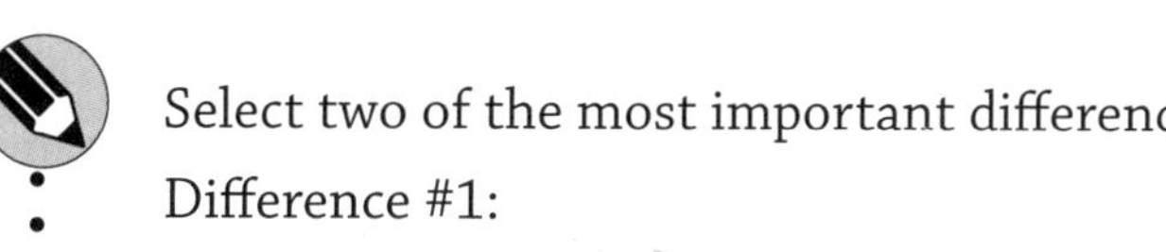

Select two of the most important differences from your list.

Difference #1:

____

____

____

Difference #2:

____

____

____

Paragraph 1 (Introduction): Start with an introduction that includes an analogy, a narrative overview of each subject, and a topic sentence.

Begin your introduction with an analogy about overcoming adversity, doing good for the sake of others, standing up for those who are mistreated, or the strength of Alice Paul and Helen Keller. Remember, a simile uses "like" or "as" to make a comparison, and a metaphor uses one thing to describe another, but without using the words "like" or "as." Include a second sentence that explains your analogy if needed.

Analogy:

____

____

____

____

Next write a short narrative overview of the two subjects. Consider the questions who, what, when, and where, and tell about each subject in one or two sentences.

Keller:

Who: ______________________________

What: ______________________________

____

When: ______________________________

____

Where: ______________________________

____

Paul:

Who: ______________________________

What: ______________________________

____

When: ______________________________

____

Where: ______________________________

____

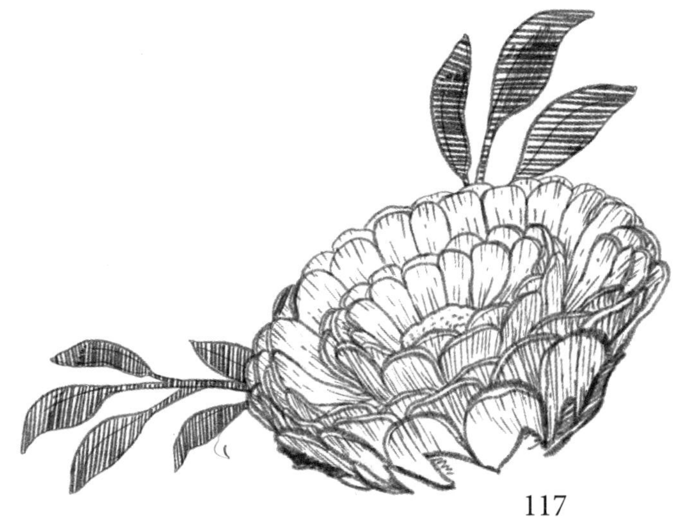

Finally, write your topic sentence, which simply states the main idea of your essay.

Topic sentence:

____

____

____

Paragraph 2 (Similarity #1): Write about one major similarity between the two subjects. Start by identifying the similarity you will be describing. Then tell more about the similarity by adding facts, examples, or details from the readings for both subjects.

Details about similarity #1:

____

____

____

____

____

____

Paragraph 3 (Similarity #2): Write about a second major similarity between the two subjects. Start again by identifying the similarity you will be describing. Then tell more about the similarity by adding facts, examples, or details from the readings for both subjects.

Details about similarity #2:

____

____

____

____

____

____

Look in the readings for a quote that gives a supportive fact, example, or detail and include it in your description.

Quote:

Paragraph 4 (Difference #1): Write about one major difference between the two subjects. Start by identifying the difference you will be describing. Then tell more about the difference by adding facts, examples, or details from the readings for both subjects.

Details about difference #1:

Paragraph 5 (Difference #2): Write about a second major difference between the two subjects. Start again by identifying the difference you will be describing. Then tell more about the difference by adding facts, examples, or details from the readings for both subjects.

Details about difference #2:

Look in the readings for a quote that gives a supportive fact, example, or detail and include it in your description.

Quote:

___

___

___

Paragraph 6 (Conclusion): Write an epilogue, or concluding paragraph. First, recap the main point of your essay. Then reflect on something important that can be learned from the comparison. Finally, write an observation or question about your subjects that would be interesting to learn more about in the future.

Something that can be learned from the comparison:

___

___

Something to learn more about:

___

___

Once you have completed your prewriting, go through these instructions again and write your paragraphs based on the prompts.

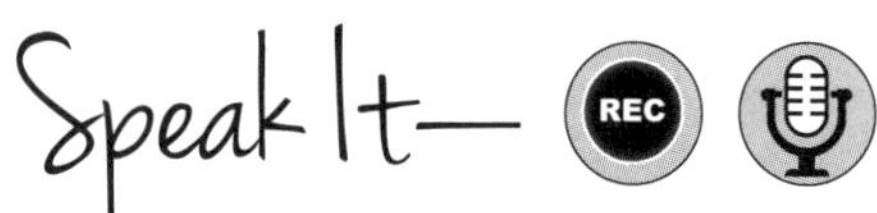

1. **FORMAL DISCUSSION:** Your teacher may instruct you to have a formal discussion. This sort of discussion is not a debate. Rather, it is an opportunity for your class to have a conversation around an open question or a controversial topic. Discussion is a great way to hear other people's ideas and to learn to express your own thoughts well. You can take sides as in a debate, but you are also free to agree with one another, enhancing each other's arguments. Usually a teacher will not participate in a formal discussion; instead she stands aside and listens in.

Here's how it works: Your teacher will assign you a question or a topic. She might allow you to prepare for the discussion as homework, or she may give you time in class to jot down your thoughts. Either way, you will probably be permitted to keep your notes with you as you discuss. You will then have a conversation about the topic; this conversation usually lasts for fifteen to twenty minutes. Be sure to let everyone have a chance to speak, and if some people are being quiet, feel free to draw them into the conversation by asking them direct questions. If you can support your ideas by quoting a text, so much the better! In the end, your teacher may assign you a score based on the scoring guidelines included with this exercise.

Formal Discussion Scoring Guidelines

Award points based on the following criteria:

- taking a stand by clearly stating an argument (thesis) +2
- providing evidence for the argument +2
- making an analogy +2
- making a relevant comment +1
- asking a clarifying question +1
- inviting another student to participate +1
- interrupting -1
- monopolizing the conversation -2
- making personal attacks -2
- distracting the audience -2

2. Partner Feedback: With a student partner (or your teacher), take turns reading the rough drafts of your comparison essays. You and your partner should give each other comments about what is more or less effective about your writing. Use the rubric at the back of the book to help you get ideas for your comments. (A rubric is a guide to evaluating and grading writing, and your teacher may use this particular rubric to grade your essay.) Try to say two positive things about your partner's essay, and then come up with at least two suggestions for editing the essay.

Revise It—

Here again is what you must do to effectively revise your work:

1. Get feedback. Use comments from your student partners (or from your teacher) to strengthen and improve your paper.
2. Wait a day or two before you rewrite your paper. The time away from it will help you to see its problems more clearly.
3. Read the paper aloud to yourself. This is often the best way to catch mistakes—grammatical errors, as well as words that don't work well—because you will be using two senses—seeing and hearing—instead of one. If something sounds wrong, it probably is.

Once you are ready to rewrite, use the following steps to aid with your revision:

1. *Find your topic sentence and underline it.* There should be one sentence that states the main idea of your essay. Make sure your paper expresses that idea throughout.
2. *Make sure each paragraph gets the job done.* Remember that each paragraph has a special purpose according to the demands of the prompts. Revisit the goal of each paragraph and compare it to what you've written. Does each paragraph successfully accomplish its goal?
3. *Find and fix grammar mistakes.* Make sure all your nouns and verbs agree and that your writing is clear. Fix any fragments or run-ons. In other words, make sure you are writing complete sentences.
4. *Strengthen phrasing.* Are your word choices specific instead of vague? Do you use strong nouns and verbs? Do you vary your sentences and occasionally begin them with a prepositional phrase or a participial phrase? Weed out passive voice and excess adjectives. Use compound sentences, appositives, adverb phrases, and questions to make your writing more interesting. Transition smoothly between ideas and paragraphs using transition words.
5. *Proofread.* Look for any punctuation, spelling, or capitalization errors. Then fix them!
6. *Retype* the draft with the corrections you have made.

Lesson 8

Third Comparison: The Telephone & the Phonograph

Recently I overheard someone say, "I'm on my phone 24/7! I couldn't live without it!" That sounds a little extreme, and I doubt most of you would agree. But let's face it: Many of us are pretty attached to some kind of technology.

While too much time using technology can be a bad thing, over the years technology has definitely helped to make life easier or more convenient for people. Think of where we might be today if no one had ever invented the wheel or a compass. We certainly wouldn't be driving around in cars, and without a compass, Columbus might never have found the New World!

The late nineteenth and early twentieth centuries witnessed an explosion of new technology. Arguably the most important and famous of the **inventors** during this time were Alexander Graham Bell and Thomas Edison. Two of their most popular and significant inventions were the telephone and the phonograph.[1] In this lesson, you will learn about and compare those two inventions. Your purpose is not to compare Bell and Edison as inventors, though you will read and learn some about their personal background, but to compare the technology they created that changed the world.

1. phonograph: a machine that reproduces sound

Alexander Graham Bell and the Invention of the Telephone

—adapted from *Great Inventors and Their Inventions* by Frank P. Bachman

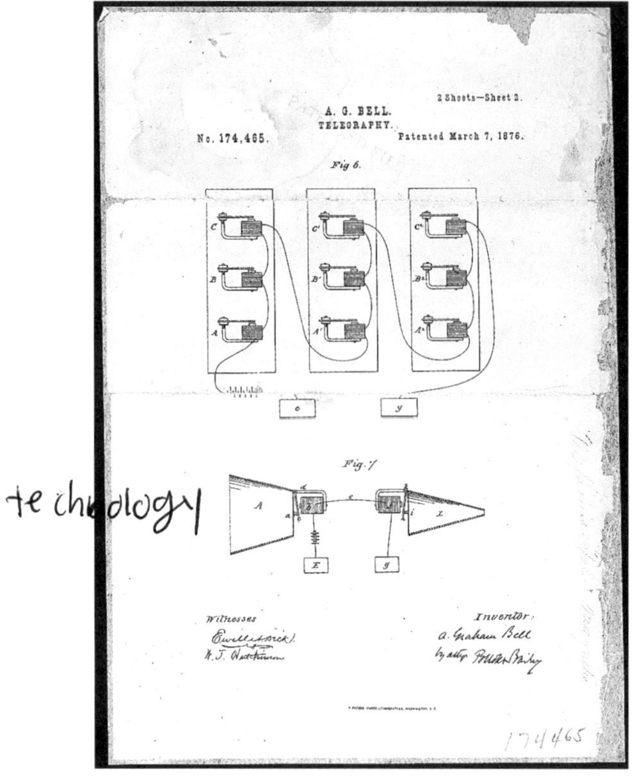

▲ Alexander Graham Bell's Telephone Patent Drawing, 03/07/1876

Alexander Graham Bell was born in Edinburgh, Scotland, in 1847. From boyhood he was taught at home by his father about sound and oral speech, and he also received training in music. When he was more than sixty years old, he wrote the following account of his early experiences.

"I came of a family that had made a study of oral speech for two generations before me. My grandfather, Alexander Bell, a distinguished teacher of elocution in London, was the first. Both of his sons—my father, Alexander Melville Bell, and my uncle, David Charles Bell—took up the same work. They also devoted their attention to the correction of defects of speech. People who lisped, or stammered, or did anything of that sort, came to my father to be taught, for example, how to place the organs of speech[2] in forming sounds.[3]

"In my early boyish days, I had the destructive faculty very fully developed. My toys never remained whole in my hands. I would always pull them to pieces to see how they were made, and one of my earliest studies in that respect was plants. I had a delight in pulling plants to pieces to see how they were made. When I was quite a little fellow, I actually took up the study of botany, and I had my collection of plants. My father encouraged me in it. He always encouraged me in making collections of all sorts, and that is a most important thing in the case of a boy. He taught me to observe, compare, and classify. I passed through the stamp-collecting age, the egg age, and the coin age, but the things I took most interest in were the flowers.

"My father encouraged his boys to study everything relating to the mechanism of speech. He proposed to his boys that they should try to make a speaking machine. . . . The work was

2. organs of speech: In order to form speech, people use the tongue, jaws, lips, throat, teeth, and larynx. Bell probably means the tongue and the lips here.
3. Bell's father and uncle would be called speech therapists today.

parceled out between my brother Melville and myself. He was to make the lungs and the throat, and the vocal chords, and I was to undertake the mouth. . . . I made a mouth modeled from a skull. . . . My brother had finished his larynx about the same time that I had made the mouth, and it was a great day when we put the two together. We did not wait for the wind chest that was to represent the lungs . . . but we stuck the thing together. My brother blew through the tube that was to lead from the wind chest, and I took the lips of my machine and moved them. Out came a sound like a Punch and Judy show,[4] and we were delighted when we moved the lips up and down to hear 'Ma-ma! Ma-ma!' distinctly. . . ."

Over time Bell became infatuated with the idea of speech and planned to spend his career teaching the deaf and dumb to speak. The Board of Education of Boston employed him to teach in the public school for the deaf in April 1871.

"The teachers in the school for the deaf had been trying to teach the children to speak, and had met with good success. But the teachers made a claim that seemed to me to be ridiculous. They claimed not only that deaf children could be taught to speak . . . but that after they had been taught to speak, they could come to understand speech by looking at the mouth of the speaker. . . . I did not dare to say no, but I did not believe it, and out of my skepticism about lip reading grew the telephone."

As time passed, Bell stayed busy instructing teachers how to teach deaf children to talk, and in teaching little deaf children himself. There were many deaf children whose parents were willing to pay almost any sum to have them taught to speak, and Bell was so successful in doing this that he opened a private school of his own. To this school there came deaf-mutes, teachers of the deaf and dumb, and persons with defective speech.

Bell worked to develop a series of "sound pictures," so that deaf children might learn to speak by sight. One of the instruments he worked with was the phonautograph. The phonautograph used by Bell was a large cone, closed at the small end by a stretched animal skin. Speak into the phonautograph, and the skin would vibrate, or move back and forth. A needle made of a pig's bristle was attached to the skin, and when the skin vibrated, the needle scratched zigzag lines on a piece of smoked glass. Each sound, "A," "E," and so on, made its own vibration pattern, or sound picture. Bell's idea was to photograph these sound pictures, then give the deaf child the picture to read. The child would speak into the phonautograph and try to make the same zigzag pattern as the sound picture. In this way the child would learn to sound the different letters.

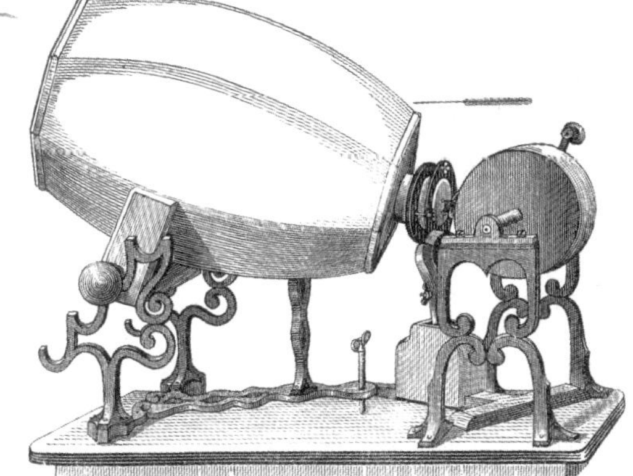

▲ 1859 model of Édouard-Léon Scott de Martinville's phonautograph

4. Punch and Judy show: a puppet show with two silly, combative characters

As Bell worked with the phonautograph, he became struck with the idea of sending the vibrations of the human voice at greater distance. He was well acquainted with another remarkable invention, the telegraph, which carried messages in code along a single wire. Telegraph wires crossed the United States from east coast to west by 1861. What if, somehow, the human voice could also be carried along telegraph wire?

Bell later said, "All I had to do was to attach a steel reed to the center of a stretched membrane, just as in the phonautograph, so that it would vibrate in front of an electromagnet, and put another at the end of a telegraph wire, and we would have a speaking telephone."

The idea of an electric-speaking telephone was thus complete in Bell's mind in the summer of 1874. By trying to enhance the phonoautograph using telegraph wire, he put two ideas together. The skin in the phonoautograph would vibrate with sound, while the telegraph would use electricity to carry the sound over distance.

At first, Bell did not try to make a telephone, for he felt it would not work. At one time he was about ready to give up trying to invent a telephone, but was encouraged to go on by the same great man who helped Samuel Morse,[5] Professor Henry. "I explained the idea of the telephone to him and said: 'What would you advise me to do, publish it and let others work it out, or attempt to solve the problem myself?' He said he thought it was 'the germ of a great invention,' and advised me to work at it myself. . . . I added that I felt that I had not the electrical knowledge necessary to overcome the difficulties. His answer was 'Get it.' "

In June 1875, Bell decided that he had enough electrical knowledge under his belt to build a device that carried sound. This device was now a practical thing, and he instantly gave his assistants instructions to have the first telephone made.

June was a busy and feverish month for Bell. Everything about an electric-speaking telephone had to be learned. Numerous experiments and tests had to be conducted. The different parts were put together now in this way and now in that way. At least two unsuccessful instruments were made. Finally the third instrument was ready for trial. The same instrument was used both as a transmitter and as a receiver. That is, one would speak into the instrument and then place his ear to it to hear what was said in reply.

The trial was made in a noisy electrical workshop. Bell was upstairs with one instrument, and Watson[6] was downstairs with another; the two instruments were connected in an electric circuit. Of this trial Bell says: "I spoke, and shouted, and sang into the instrument upstairs. Presently Mr. Watson came upstairs in a state of great excitement. He said: 'I hear your voice!' "

5. Samuel Morse helped to invent the telegraph as well as the tapping code that bears his name—Morse Code.
6. Watson: Thomas A. Watson was an assistant to Bell in his lab. He is known for being on the receiving end of the first phone call ever made.

Bell was granted a patent on his telephone on March 6, 1876. He was then twenty-nine years of age, and the possessor of what turned out to be the "most valuable single patent ever granted."

A few months later, one of Bell's friends, Mr. Hubbard, persuaded him to exhibit his telephone at the Centennial World Fair[7] in Philadelphia. His telephone instruments were at the Centennial for a month, but no one paid much attention to them, until suddenly the telephone became the most talked-of article at the great exhibition. The wonderful change came about in this way:

On Sunday, June 25, the electrical instruments were to be shown to the judges. Dom Pedro, emperor of Brazil, Sir William Thompson, the greatest electrical scientist in the world at that time, and other famous people were to be there.

"On Sunday I went out to the exhibition. There were a whole lot of electrical exhibits to be shown, and the poor judges were trotted around to see one thing after another until they were fairly ready to drop. I followed the judges around, while they looked at this thing and that thing. They came finally to an exhibit of Elisha Gray, who had a machine for transmitting musical tones like my multiple telegraph. He gave a very interesting talk. It was very interesting to me, because I came next, and he kept on and kept on, until at last, when he got through, the chairman of the judges said they would postpone the further examination of electrical apparatus to another day. That meant that they would never see the telephone. I could only stay that Sunday, and I felt that my whole exhibit was cut out. The judges began to disperse, when suddenly Emperor Dom Pedro saw me, and recognized me as the young man whom he had met in Boston, when he visited the school for the deaf and dumb. He came up to me and said, 'Mr. Bell, how are the deaf-mutes in Boston?' I told him they were very well, and that my exhibit was the next. He said he must go to see it, took my arm, and walked off with me, and of course the judges followed like a flock of sheep. My exhibit was saved."

The instruments were ready for use. Dom Pedro took a seat at a table on which rested the little iron-box receiver, and was asked to hold his ear near the top of the strange little instrument. Bell sat down in another room and spoke slowly and with great distinctness into the tube of the transmitter. Dom Pedro, of course, did not know what to expect, nor did anyone else in the room. Suddenly the emperor raised his head and with a look of utter amazement on his face exclaimed, "It talks!" Then came Sir William Thompson, who knew so much about electricity; he listened, and listened, and listened to that little iron disk talk with a human voice. Then with great emphasis he said, "It does speak. It is the most wonderful thing I have seen in America. . . . It is the greatest marvel hitherto achieved. . . . Before long, friends will whisper their secrets over the electric wire!"

Sure enough, millions upon millions of people have telephones today—wireless phones!—and they use the phones to do much more than whisper secrets. They conduct business meetings, perform surgeries, fly airplanes, supervise battles, talk to people in outer space, and say, "I love you"—all with the help of the amazing telephone.

7. Centennial World Fair: Also known as the Centennial Exhibition, the Centennial World Fair was the first world's fair held in the United States. In addition to the telephone, the sewing machine and the typewriter were introduced at the fair.

Thomas Edison and the Invention of the Phonograph

—adapted from *Men of Achievement: Inventors* by Philip G. Hubert Jr.

Thomas Edison patented over 1,000 inventions, but his favorite was the phonograph. The phonograph is an instrument for mechanically recording and playing back sounds. It was invented by Edison in the spring of 1877, at his Menlo Park laboratory in New Jersey, and came into existence as he was working on improvements to the telegraph and the telephone. Edison figured out a way to record sound on tinfoil-coated cylinders. Then, in 1877, he created a machine with two needles: one for recording and one for playback. When Edison spoke into the mouthpiece of the machine, the sound vibrations of his voice would be indented onto the cylinder by the recording needle. The playback needle of the phonograph was then sent over the indentations (or grooves) in the tinfoil cylinder, and the sounds produced by a vibrating diaphragm were magnified by a large, horn-shaped instrument.

The phonograph became one of the most popular of modern inventions, as it was able to bring the music of the masters within the reach of the home, at small cost. Ever practical and visionary, Edison offered the following possible future uses for the phonograph in *North American Review* in June 1878:

1. Letter writing and all kinds of dictation without the aid of a stenographer.
2. Phonographic books, which will speak to blind people without effort on their part.
3. The teaching of elocution.
4. The reproduction of music.
5. The "Family Record"—a registry of sayings, reminiscences, etc., by members of a family in their own voices, and of the last words of dying persons.
6. Music-boxes and toys.
7. Clocks that should announce in articulate speech the time for going home, going to meals, etc.
8. The preservation of languages by exact reproduction of the manner of pronouncing.
9. Educational purposes, such as preserving the explanations made by a teacher, so that the pupil can refer to them at any moment, and spelling or other lessons placed upon the phonograph for convenience in committing to memory.

Many of the uses Edison suggested for the phonograph have become a reality, but there were others he hadn't imagined. For example, the phonograph allowed soldiers to take music off to war with them. In 1917, when the United States became involved in World War I, the Edison Company created a special model of the phonograph for the US Army. This basic machine sold for $60. Many Army units purchased these phonographs because it meant a lot to the soldiers to have music to cheer them and remind them of home.

There is one great invention for which Edison deserves credit, both as discoverer and practical inventor—the phonograph.

▲ Thomas Edison and his early phonograph, circa 1877.

Thomas Alva Edison was born February 11, 1847, in Milan, Ohio, an obscure canal village. When he was a small boy, his family, a most humble one, moved to Port Huron, Michigan, where Edison's boyhood was passed. There his father was in turn tailor, well-digger, nursery-man,[8] dealer in grain, lumber, and farm lands. His mother, born in Massachusetts, had a good education and at one time taught school in Canada. Of regular schooling, young Edison had but two months in his life. From his father he learned to be useful with his hands, and from his mother he received his book learning in homeschool. There are no records showing extraordinary promise on his part. He was an omnivorous[9] reader, having an intense curiosity about the world and its great men.

Telegraphy became a hobby with the boy. From every operator along the road he picked up something. He strung the basement of his father's house at Port Huron with wires, and constructed a short line, using for the batteries stove-pipe wire, old bottles, nails, and zinc, which urchins of the neighborhood were induced to cut out from under the stoves of their unsuspecting mothers and bring to young Edison at three cents a pound. In order to save time for his experiments, he had the habit of leaping from a train while it was going at the rate of twenty-five miles an hour, landing upon a pile of sand arranged by him for that purpose. An act of personal courage—the saving of the station-master's child at Port Clements from an advancing train—was a turning-point in his career, for the grateful father of the boy, in return, taught Edison telegraphing in the regular way.

Telegraphy was then in its infancy, comparatively speaking; operators were few, and good wages could be earned with even a basic knowledge of the trade. Still, Edison had little time for learning it, so it took him several years to become an expert operator.

At the age of twelve, he took a job selling newspapers and snacks on a train. Because he could gather all the hottest news reports from the telegraph, he started publishing his own paper, and it became popular with the passengers. The corner of the baggage car served him as printing office, laboratory, and business headquarters. One day, during his absence, a bottle of chemicals tipped over and set the old railroad car on fire, whereupon the conductor threw out all the painfully acquired apparatus and thrashed its owner.[10]

Edison's first regular employment as telegraph operator was at Indianapolis when he was eighteen years old. He received a small salary for day-work in the railroad office there, and at night he

8. nursery-man: a worker in a nursery, which is a shop where trees and plants are sold to be transplanted
9. omnivorous: An omnivore eats both plants and meat. When referring to learning or reading, "omnivorous" means taking in everything, "eating it all up."
10. Edison claimed that this beating caused him to go deaf in one ear. He changed the story later and said that a train conductor had caught him by the ears and lifted him onto a moving train, thus damaging his hearing. Historians believe that his partial deafness was most likely a complication of small pox.

continued to receive newspaper reports via the telegraph. Then it was that he worked out his first invention, and necessity was certainly the mother of it. As he later wrote:

"I got two old Morse registers and arranged them in such a way that by running a strip of paper through them the dots and dashes were recorded on it by the first instrument as fast as they were delivered from the Cincinnati end,[11] and were transmitted to us through the other instrument at any desired rate of speed. They would come in on one instrument at the rate of forty words a minute, and would be ground out of our instrument at the rate of twenty-five. Then weren't we proud! Our copy used to be so clean and beautiful that we hung it up on exhibition; and our manager used to come and gaze at it silently with a puzzled expression. He could not understand it, neither could any of the other operators; for we used to hide my impromptu automatic recorder when our toil was over. But the crash came when there was a big night's work—a presidential vote, I think it was—and newspaper stories kept pouring in at the top rate of speed until we fell an hour and a half or two hours behind. The newspapers sent in frantic complaints, an investigation was made, and our little scheme was discovered. We couldn't use it any more.

"It was that same rude[12] automatic recorder that indirectly led me long afterward to invent the phonograph. I'll tell you how this came about. After thinking over the matter a great deal, I came to the point where, in 1877, I had worked out satisfactorily an instrument that would not only record telegraphs by indenting a strip of paper with dots and dashes of the Morse code, but would also repeat a message any number of times at any rate of speed required. I was then experimenting with the telephone also, and my mind was filled with theories of sound vibrations and their transmission by diaphragms.[13]

"Naturally enough, the idea occurred to me: if the indentations on paper could be made to give forth again the click of the instrument, why could not the vibrations of a diaphragm be recorded and similarly reproduced? I rigged up an instrument hastily and pulled a strip of paper through it, at the same time shouting, 'Hallo'! Then the paper was pulled through again, my friend Batchelor and I listening breathlessly. We heard a distinct sound, which a strong imagination might have translated into the original 'Hallo.' That was enough to lead me to a further experiment. But Batchelor was skeptical, and bet me a barrel of apples that I couldn't make the thing go.

"I made a drawing of a model and took it to Mr. Kruesi, who was at that time engaged on piece-work for me, but now is assistant general manager of our machine shop. I told him it was a talking-machine. He grinned, thinking it a joke; but he set to work and soon had the model ready. I arranged some tinfoil on it, and spoke into the machine. Kruesi looked on, still grinning. But when I arranged the machine for transmission and we both heard a distinct sound[14] from it, he nearly

---

11. "Cincinnati end": This refers to the other end of the telegraph line. Edison was in Indianapolis; the message was coming from Cincinnati.
12. rude: This does not mean "impolite," but rather "simple" or "rudimentary."
13. diaphragms: thin sheets of material much like the skin stretched over a drum. This mention of diaphragms refers to the same technology used by the phonoautograph that helped Bell to create "sound pictures" for his deaf students.
14. The first words recorded into Edison's machine were "Mary had a little lamb."

fell down in his fright. I was a little scared myself, I must admit. I won that barrel of apples from Batchelor, though, and was mighty glad to get it."

Edison began using tinfoil instead of paper to reproduce sound, and the phonograph was born. Before long, Alexander Graham Bell improved Edison's device by using wax-covered cardboard cylinders instead of tinfoil. The earliest phonographs were turned by hand, but electric motors soon replaced the hand crank. The sound improved decade by decade.

At first people would visit "phonograph parlors" in busy arcades where they paid a few pennies to listen to music. By World War I, phonographs had become common appliances in wealthy houses. Instead of only hearing music in a symphony hall, people could now listen to great orchestras in the comfort of their own homes. One of the oldest surviving recordings of music is Arthur Sullivan's song "The Lost Chord," on an 1888 wax cylinder, and we even have a recording of the great composer Johannes Brahms playing his Hungarian Dance No. 1 on the piano in 1889.

Tell It Back—Narration

1. **MARK UP THE TEXT—Annotation:** Read through the reading selections again. As you read, write in the margin of the text symbols that will help you understand it better and find important details later. The following are some symbols you might use:
   - Underline the main idea of the story or any important point.
   - Put a question mark in the margin to mark any part of the story you don't understand.
   - Write any questions or thoughts you have in the margin.
   - Put an exclamation point in the margin to mark any part of the story you find surprising or particularly interesting.
   - Circle any important or unfamiliar vocabulary words or proper nouns when they are first introduced. Remember, a proper noun is the name for any specific person, place, thing, or idea. How do you know which words to circle? Circle words that appear repeatedly, or words you can't understand from the context of the sentence alone. Look up any unfamiliar words in the glossary, or, if they aren't there, in a dictionary.

2. **ORAL NARRATION:** Look over the annotations you made for *Thomas Edison and the Invention of the Phonograph*. Then, without looking at the text, retell the story as best you remember it using your own words. Try not to leave out any important details.

Here's the first sentence to help you get started:

There is one great invention for which Edison deserves credit, both as discoverer and practical inventor—the phonograph.

3. **OUTLINE:** Create an outline for *Alexander Graham Bell and the Invention of the Telephone* using Roman numerals (*I*, *II*, *III*) for the most important events and capital letters (*A*, *B*, *C*) for less important events. Use standard numbers (*1*, *2*, *3*) for minor points.

Talk About It—

1. Both Bell and Edison were notoriously hard workers, sometimes at the expense of their personal relationships. Bell would sometimes disappear into his lab for days at a time, and his wife learned not to bother him in such moods. Would you consider that kind of work habit to be a strength or a weakness?

2. Bell and Edison are two of the most famous inventors in history. Of course, there are many others: Leonardo da Vinci (parachute, flying machines), Benjamin Franklin (wood stove, bifocal glasses, lightning rod), Cai Lun (paper), Nikola Tesla (AC electricity), Granville Woods (multiplex telegraph), Leonardo Torres y Quevedo (computer technology), and Johannes Gutenberg (printing press), to name a few. There are many qualities and characteristics that inventors share in common. What do you think are some of the most important of those qualities or characteristics?

3. "An amazing invention—but who would ever want to use one?" It is said that President Rutherford B. Hayes made this comment after he made a call from Washington to Pennsylvania with Alexander Graham Bell's telephone. Of course, he couldn't have known at the time that the telephone would go on to become one of the most important inventions of the century. Often, inventors and innovators are able to grasp a vision for something that the rest of us do not yet see. What modern inventions—or things yet to be invented—do you think will have a big effect on the world in the next hundred years?

Memoria—

> Concentrate all your thoughts upon the work at hand. The sun's rays do not burn until brought to a focus. —Alexander Graham Bell

1. After reading this quotation by Alexander Graham Bell, define any words you may not know. Then discuss the meaning of the quotation.
2. How does this quotation relate to the lives or inventions of Bell and Edison?
3. Memorize the quotation and be prepared to recite it during your next class.
4. Write the quotation in your commonplace book, along with any thoughts you have about it.

Writing Time—

1. **SENTENCE PLAY**—

   A. In lesson 5 you learned how to smoothly add quotations into your writing. You learned that you need a sentence that leads in to the quote so that one thought flows naturally together with the next. Then you write the quote itself—and be sure to use quotation marks and cite the name of the quote's author or speaker if it is known. Finally, you help your readers understand the quote by summarizing it in your own words or giving additional explanation.

   Thomas Edison had a knack for memorable sayings and proverbs. For each of the following quotes by Edison, write a sentence leading in to the quote, then write down the quote, and finally, follow it with a sentence commenting on the quote.

   Example: "I have not failed. I've just found 10,000 ways that won't work."
   People often look at failure in the wrong way. Thomas Edison said, "I have not failed. I've just found 10,000 ways that won't work." In other words, it's better to look at one's failures as opportunities to learn and grow.

a. "Genius is one percent inspiration and ninety-nine percent perspiration."

b. "Our greatest weakness lies in giving up. The most certain way to succeed is always to try just one more time."

c. "If we did all the things we are capable of, we would literally astound ourselves."

d. "Everything comes to him who hustles while he waits."

e. "We don't know a millionth of one percent about anything."

B. Have you ever read an essay in which the writer seemed to keep repeating herself? Sometimes essays get clunky because the writer just has too many words. Good writers are constantly in the habit of trimming down their work to be concise. Clear and precise language is the key to a well-organized paper.

Make each of the following sentences clearer or more direct by fixing the underlined wordy phrases. You will need to cut out words, rephrase the text, or even delete the entire phrase. Rewrite the new sentence in the space provided.

Example: We have <u>a considerable number of</u> worms in our apples.

Change to: We have <u>many</u> worms in our apples.

a. <u>In my opinion,</u>[A] left-handed people are more creative than right-handed people.

____

____

____

[A]It is almost always better to simply state your opinion rather than introduce it with the wordy, stuffy-sounding phrase "in my opinion." "I think that" is another common introduction that can be eliminated. The reader will assume that what you say is your opinion or what you think.

b. <u>I think that</u> limes have a more interesting taste than lemons.

____

____

____

____

____

c. <u>Based on the fact that</u> Kareem Abdul-Jabbar scored the most points in basketball, he should be the number-one player of all time.

____

____

____

d. In the majority of cases, young adults depend too heavily on smartphones to communicate.

e. It is often the case that burglars find the front doors of houses unlocked.

f. In light of the fact that money doesn't grow on trees, I'm not going to give you twenty bucks for a movie.

g. In the event that there's an earthquake, drop to your hands and knees and get under a sturdy table.

h. Everyone is aware of the fact that pepperoni is the most popular pizza topping.

i. Only the wisest and stupidest of men never change in my opinion.

2. **COPIOUSNESS**—During the sixteenth century the Dutch scholar Erasmus used copiousness as a method for training students in rhetoric. His book *De Utraque Verborum ac Rerum Copia* is famous for listing 147 variations of the statement "Your letter pleased me greatly." Examples of these variations include: "Your epistle greatly raised my spirits," "Your missive filled me with much delight," and "What a joy it was to receive your letter." Erasmus's goal was to help his students grow in eloquence and in flexibility as they reworked sentences in a variety of ways.

A. In the space provided, rework the following sentence into six variations:

Sadly, my steak was overcooked.[B]

Feel free to use synonyms, to rearrange words, to add words, to change verbs and verb forms, and to substitute phrases. However, the general idea of the sentence should be maintained.

[B]"Steak" is the common term for various fast-cooking cuts of beef. You can substitute "filet mignon," "rib eye," "strip steak," "sirloin," and "T-bone" for "steak."

Example: Regrettably, my hunk of beef was burnt to a cinder.

a. ______________________________

____

b. ______________________________

____

c. ______________________________

____

d. ______________________________

____

e. ______________________________

____

f. ______________________________

____

B. Now create six variations for this sentence:

I really like you a lot.

Example: Truly, I'm awfully fond of you.

a. ______________________________

____

b. ______________________________

____

c. ______________________________

____

d. ______________________________

____

e. ______________________________

____

f. ______________________________

____

3. **COMPARISON**—The purpose of this lesson's essay is to compare Alexander Graham Bell's invention of the telephone with Thomas Edison's invention of the phonograph. Before you start writing, use the following prompts for each paragraph to help you sketch out your ideas. You can use lists, phrases, or complete sentences for your answers. Then compose your full essay on a separate paper or on a computer. Remember that each paragraph has a job to do in defending the thesis.

   The paragraphs you write after going through these steps will be your first draft, or your first version of the essay. Assume that your first draft will need some rewriting to make it the best essay it can be.

   Prewriting: Begin by making a list of as many similarities and differences between your subjects as you can think of.

   Similarities between the two subjects:

   ____

   ____

   ____

   ____

   ____

   ____

   ____

   Differences between the two subjects:

   ____

   ____

   ____

   ____

   ____

   ____

Now select two of the most important similarities from your list.

Similarity #1:

____

____

Similarity #2:

____

____

Select two of the most important differences from your list.

Difference #1:

____

____

Difference #2:

____

____

Paragraph 1 (Introduction): Start with an introduction that includes an analogy, a narrative overview of each subject, and a topic sentence.

Begin your introduction with an analogy about the inventions and the sensations they caused, or how they bettered the lives of people, or the importance of creativity and the desire to invent. Remember, a simile uses "like" or "as" to make a comparison, and a metaphor uses one thing to describe another, but without using the words "like" or "as." Include a second sentence that explains your analogy if needed.

Analogy:

____

____

____

Next write a short narrative overview of the two subjects. Consider the questions who, what, when, and where, and tell about each subject in one or two sentences.

Telephone:

Who: ______________________________

What: ______________________________

____

When: ______________________________

____

Where: ______________________________

____

Phonograph:

Who: ______________________________

What: ______________________________

____

When: ______________________________

____

Where: ______________________________

____

Finally, write your topic sentence, which simply states the main idea of your essay.

Topic sentence:

____

____

____

Paragraph 2 (Similarity #1): Write about one major similarity between the two subjects. Start by identifying the similarity you will be describing. Then tell more about the similarity by adding facts, examples, or details from the readings for both subjects.

Details about similarity #1:

____

____

____

____

____

____

Paragraph 3 (Similarity #2): Write about a second major similarity between the two subjects. Start again by identifying the similarity you will be describing. Then tell more about the similarity by adding facts, examples, or details from the readings for both subjects.

Details about similarity #2:

____

____

____

____

____

____

Look in the readings for a quote that gives a supportive fact, example, or detail and include it in your description.

Quote:

____

____

____

Paragraph 4 (Difference #1): Write about one major difference between the two subjects. Start by identifying the difference you will be describing. Then tell more about the difference by adding facts, examples, or details from the readings for both subjects.

Details about difference #1:

____

____

____

____

____

____

Paragraph 5 (Difference #2): Write about a second major difference between the two subjects. Start again by identifying the difference you will be describing. Then tell more about the difference by adding facts, examples, or details from the readings for both subjects.

Details about difference #2:

____

____

____

____

____

____

Look in the readings for a quote that gives a supportive fact, example, or detail and include it in your description.

Quote:

____

____

____

Paragraph 6 (Conclusion): Write an epilogue, or concluding paragraph. First, recap the main point of your essay. Then reflect on something important that can be learned from the comparison. Finally, write an observation or question about your subjects that would be interesting to learn more about in the future.

Something that can be learned from the comparison:

____

____

____

____

Something to learn more about:

____

____

____

____

Once you have completed your prewriting, go through these instructions again and write your paragraphs based on the prompts.

Speak It—

REC

1. **TELEGRAPH SPEECH GAME**—This is a variation of the telephone game, in which a secret message is whispered from person to person until it is announced out loud by the last person to hear it. The fun in both versions of the game is to see how the original message changes along the way. The telegraph game is the same as the telephone game except that it is a relay race between two teams.

   Your teacher will start by dividing a group of ten students into two even teams. Two students, one from each team, will be posted in each of the four corners of the room. These students are the telegraph operators. The remaining two students will be the telegraph carriers. They will start the telegraph message going around the room. After the teams are set up, your teacher will whisper a secret telegraph message—a different message for each team—into the ears of the carriers. When your teacher says, "Go!", the two telegraph carriers will run in opposite directions to the telegraph operator in the corner closest to them. In other words, one carrier will start a message going clockwise, and the other will go counterclockwise around the room. After the carrier transmits the telegraph message to the first operator, he then stays in that corner while the first operator runs to tell the message to the second operator in the second corner, and so on. The message gets passed in a whisper from one operator to the next. At the end of the race, the last operators write the messages on the board. If both messages are accurate, the winning team is the one that finishes writing the message first. If both messages are inaccurate, your teacher will decide which message is more accurate than the other.

2. **FORMAL DISCUSSION:** Your teacher may instruct you to have a formal discussion. This sort of discussion is not a debate. Rather, it is an opportunity for your class to have a conversation around an open question or a controversial topic. Discussion is a great way to hear other people's ideas and to learn to express your own thoughts well. You can take sides as in a debate, but you are also free to agree with one another, enhancing each other's arguments. Usually a teacher will not participate in a formal discussion; instead she stands aside and listens in.

   Here's how it works: Your teacher will assign you a question or a topic. She might allow you to prepare for the discussion as homework, or she may give you time in class to jot down your thoughts. Either way, you will probably be permitted to keep your notes with you as you discuss. You will then have a conversation about the topic; this conversation usually lasts for fifteen to twenty minutes. Be sure to let everyone have a chance to speak, and if some people are being quiet, feel free to draw them into the conversation by asking them direct questions. If you can support your ideas by quoting a text, so much the better! In the end, your teacher may assign you a score based on the scoring guidelines included with this exercise.

Formal Discussion Scoring Guidelines

Award points based on the following criteria:

- taking a stand by clearly stating an argument (thesis) +2
- providing evidence for the argument +2
- making an analogy +2
- making a relevant comment +1
- asking a clarifying question +1
- inviting another student to participate +1
- interrupting -1
- monopolizing the conversation -2
- making personal attacks -2
- distracting the audience -2

3. **PARTNER FEEDBACK:** With a student partner (or your teacher), take turns reading the rough drafts of your comparison essays. You and your partner should give each other comments about what is more or less effective about your writing. Use the rubric at the back of the book to help you get ideas for your comments. (A rubric is a guide to evaluating and grading writing, and your teacher may use this particular rubric to grade your essay.) Try to say two positive things about your partner's essay, and then come up with at least two suggestions for editing the essay.

Revise It—

1. Here again is what you must do to effectively revise your work:
   a. Get feedback. Use comments from your student partners (or from your teacher) to strengthen and improve your paper.
   b. Wait a day or two before you rewrite your paper. The time away from it will help you to see its problems more clearly.
   c. Read the paper aloud to yourself. This is often the best way to catch mistakes—grammatical errors, as well as words that don't work well—because you will be using two senses—seeing and hearing—instead of one. If something sounds wrong, it probably is.

   Once you are ready to rewrite, use the following steps to aid with your revision:
   a. *Find your topic sentence and underline it.* There should be one sentence that states the main idea of your essay. Make sure your paper expresses that idea throughout.
   b. *Make sure each paragraph gets the job done.* Remember that each paragraph has a special purpose according to the demands of the prompts. Revisit the goal of each paragraph and compare it to what you've written. Does each paragraph successfully accomplish its goal?

c. *Find and fix grammatical mistakes.* Make sure all your nouns and verbs agree and that your writing is clear. Fix any fragments or run-ons. In other words, make sure you are writing complete sentences.

d. *Strengthen phrasing.* Are your word choices specific instead of vague? Do you use strong nouns and verbs? Do you vary your sentences and occasionally begin them with a prepositional phrase or a participial phrase? Weed out passive voice and excess adjectives. Use compound sentences, appositives, adverb phrases, and questions to make your writing more interesting. Transition smoothly between ideas and paragraphs using transition words.

e. *Proofread.* Look for any punctuation, spelling, or capitalization errors. Then fix them!

f. *Retype* the draft with the corrections you have made.

2. **PROOFREADING PRACTICE**—When it was first invented, the telephone seemed strange and unnecessary to many people. The following paragraph is adapted from *The History of the Telephone* by Herbert N. Casson. The paragraph contains a number of errors, including letters that should be capitalized (2), repeated words that should be deleted (2), words that are missing (2), a lack of proper punctuation (2), and misspellings (2). Use the following proofreader's marks to mark up the text.

≡	capitalize
(delete mark)	delete word
^	insert letter, word, or punctuation
SP.	misspelled word

The very idea of talking into a phone was new and extraordinary, to the average person and the sintist alike. it was too freakish, too bizarre, to be used outside of the laboratory and the the museum. No one, literally, could understand how worked People who talked for the first time into a telephone box had a sort of stage fright They felt foolish. to do so seemed absurd, especially when they had to shout at the top their voices. Plainly, the convenience of the telephone wasn't worth lozing their dignity. The banker said it might do well well enough for grocers, but that it would never be of any value to banking; and the grocer said it might do well enough for bankers, but that it would never be of any value to grocers.

Lesson 9

Fourth Comparison: Boxing & Baseball

Americans love sports. According to a poll taken in 2014, the most popular sport in America is pro football, followed by baseball, men's college football, auto racing, and men's pro basketball.[1] Of course, this ranking will never stay the same because our tastes are constantly changing. For example, soccer and ice hockey have risen in popularity, while baseball and boxing have slowly sunk over the years. Right now, the fastest growing sport among college students is lacrosse.

In the 1920s, boxing and baseball were huge in America. And by huge, I mean *extraordinarily* popular. Back then, if you didn't know the names Jack Dempsey and Babe Ruth, your head was stuck in the sand. In this lesson, you will be reading about these two legends and comparing the sports they played.

1. This information comes from an online survey by The Harris Poll, conducted December 10–15, 2014. It surveyed 2,255 American adults aged eighteen or older.

Boxing: Rock 'Em, Sock 'Em

—adapted from *Ten—and Out! The Complete Story of the Prize Ring in America* by Alexander Johnston

Sport boxing can be traced all the way back to the Greeks, but its modern form started in England. Boxing is an indoor sport and lightning quick. Each round is only three minutes long, but a lot of punches are thrown in that short time. In a boxing match, two people stand in a square "ring" and fight using their fists. They usually wear padded gloves. Boxers are not allowed to hit below the belt or use their heads, feet, mouths, or any other body parts other than their fists. They are allowed to hit the stomach, head, and chest of their opponents, but punching the back is illegal. To win a fight, there must either be a knockout (KO)[2] or a win by punches, which means one boxer lands more punches than the other. The winner of a boxing round receives ten points, while the loser receives nine. Boxing is one of the few games in which the victory is determined by how much physical harm has been done to a player's opponent. Because hurting an opponent is an essential part of the game, some nations have tried to ban the sport.

The most famous boxer in the 1920s was Jack Dempsey. Dempsey lived at the same time as some of America's biggest sports heroes—Babe Ruth (baseball), Red Grange (football), and Bobby Jones (golf). Dempsey was the biggest star in boxing until 1927, when, in his last fight, he lost to Gene Tunney. Americans were enraptured with this Dempsey-Tunney fight, and nearly 105,000 attended it at Soldier Field in Chicago. Millions more listened on the radio. In the seventh round, when Dempsey floored Tunney with a series of rights and lefts, the radio announcer screamed into his mic, "Tunney is down! *Tunney is down!*" with such fervor that listeners all over the country dropped with heart attacks. (Literally. Nine people died of heart attacks while listening to that part of the radio broadcast.) However, Tunney got back on his feet and ended up beating Dempsey.

This selection tells a little about the history of boxing, and then more about Dempsey, who was nicknamed the Manassa Mauler.

Man is a fighting animal. From the teeth and the claws of the caveman to the poison gas of modern warfare, fighting has been one of his principal preoccupations. The lure of the prize ring undoubtedly has its roots deep in this primal human instinct. No other thrill in the world of sports can equal that which comes from watching two men engage in combat with no other weapons of offense or defense but those with which old Mother Nature has provided them.

Back in the days when the Romans held the world in the palms of their hands, they would often encase the hands of their gladiators in gloves of lead and then gloat over the massacres that

2. A knockout occurs when a boxer is hit so hard that he loses consciousness. While the boxer is down on the ground, the referee begins a countdown. If the boxer stays down for a count of ten, he loses the fight.

followed. Virgil in his *Aeneid* described at considerable length a boxing contest as it was waged in those days. He describes with relish the hollow thumps of the leaden mitts as they struck home on the panting chests of the gladiators. Homer chronicled the boxing match held by the Greeks as part of the celebration of the fall of Troy. Of course, in the days when feeding slaves to the eels was considered common, boxing with leaden gloves was probably looked upon as a rather mild branch of sports.

For a great many centuries after the fall of the Roman Empire, boxing appears to have languished. I have been unable to find any record of fighting with the fists during the Dark Ages. The medieval mind rather ran to poison and poniard[3] than to knuckles or gloves. It was not until the beginning of the eighteenth century that boxing again gained a place in the field of sports. To avoid the deaths of boxers in the ring, the sport was reformed through new rules. Officials created three weight classes: lightweight, middleweight, and heavyweight. Also, to reduce the risk of serious injury, the thirty-second count[4] was reduced to a ten-second count. Henceforth, boxing's popularity increased and reached a fever pitch in the 1920s with Jack Dempsey.

During his reign of nearly seven years, Jack Dempsey fought a number of battles. In some of them his showing was disappointing, while in others it was magnificent. But always he proved perfectly able to take care of his opponent.

Dempsey lacked some qualities of the supreme fighter. He did not box with strategy as much as with sheer muscle power. Some boxers tire out their opponents by jabbing and getting away, so that endurance wins the bout. Some boxers play a ducking game to avoid taking shots, and many study their opponents' best punches to know how to block them. Instead, Dempsey believed thoroughly in Knute Rockne's[5] dictum that the best defense is a good offense. Dempsey wasted little time in developing defensive skill. From the moment the first gong rang, he was at his man. He seemed to burn in the ring with a cold white fighting rage. His one idea was to get at his man and knock him horizontal. He plunged in almost wide open, leaving innumerable chances for a really skillful opponent to hit him. He had, though, excellent recuperative powers and he was a vicious hitter. For this reason, in his youth and strength, it was good tactics to take a blow or so from the enemy in order to land the sleep-producer.[6]

3. poniard: a small dagger
4. thirty-second count: Originally, boxers who were hit hard enough could spend thirty seconds recuperating. They could lie on the mat or remain on one knee. If the injured boxer could not fight again after thirty seconds, the win was awarded to the other boxer. A ten-second count ended fights sooner and kept a seriously concussed boxer from returning to the match.
5. Knute Rockne: football coach for the University of Notre Dame during the '20s and '30s
6. sleep-producer: a knockout (KO)

Dempsey's most outstanding quality as a boxer was his fighting spirit. He carried more than his share of the "killer instinct," learned probably on the streets as a youth, where defeat meant death. Given this terrific lust for battle, he could land a violent punch with either hand and had a physique able to stand up under any punishment. In Dempsey was a very formidable lead-fisted gladiator, indeed.

It was Tex Rickard[7] who staged the battle between Dempsey and Luis Firpo, on the night of September 14, 1923. Firpo was an Argentinian boxing champ, a huge bulk of a man, hairy as an ape, with gigantic shoulders which justified the nickname that had been given him by the sports writers, "the Wild Bull of the Pampas." Against Firpo, Jack Dempsey appeared small, with his 193 pounds, but his condition was magnificent and it sufficed.

When the first bell rang, Dempsey bobbed across the ring and launched into one of his accustomed offensives immediately. The champion missed a left to the body, and Firpo promptly sent in a short right uppercut to the jaw, which dropped Dempsey to his knees while the crowd gasped. But before the surprise had time to sink in, Dempsey was up and going again. He held Firpo for a moment, and the latter dug in two short, half-smothered rights to the champion's body. Then Dempsey shot out his left. It landed on Firpo's jaw and the big man went down for a count of "Three." The moment he was up, Dempsey dropped him again, this time for a count of "Two." Again Firpo rose, and a left to the body sent him back to the floor for a count of "Three." When he crawled up again, Dempsey brought his right over to Firpo's jaw, and the Argentine went down for a full count of "Nine." Once more he arose, and this time went down from a left to the body, but he only listened to a count of "Two" before he staggered up, to go down from another left for a count of "Six." And then, marvelous to relate, "the Wild Bull of the Pampas" rushed Dempsey, who had just knocked him down six times, to the ropes, landed a right which was half a shove, and sent the champion flying out of the ring.

This incident has caused more talk than almost anything that ever happened in the American ring. Some sportsmen claim that Dempsey was out of the ring, half-insensible, for twenty or even thirty seconds. The referee, it is said, was rattled and did not start a count. Under the rules, he could not count until the man was back in the ring or had shown signs of not being able to get back. As it was, Dempsey fell in the laps of the newspaper men. Naturally enough, these shoved him off. This was simply self-protection. One reporter who sat next to the man in whose lap Mr. Dempsey landed, has testified that Dempsey got up in perfect possession of all his senses, seized the side of the ring, and scrambled back, saying as he did so, "Allez-up!"[8], the battle cry of acrobats when they make ready for a jump. When he once again got his feet in the ring, Dempsey rushed across at Firpo and landed a terrific right-hander as the bell rang, ending the most sensational round in American ring history.

---

7. Tex Rickard (1870–1929) put boxing matches together and promoted them to the public.
8. allez-up: pronounced "A-lay up"; also "allez hop" or "allez oop"; means "Go, jump!"

When the second round began, Dempsey was like an unleashed tiger. He met Firpo more than halfway across the ring and at once bored through, lashing his right to the body before they clinched. Breaking out of the clinch, Dempsey shot two rights to Firpo's jaw and dropped him for a count of "Four." When the Argentine arose he tried to close in and clinch, but Dempsey met him with a blasting left to the chin, followed by a crashing right directly on the button.[9] The huge Firpo dropped inert, as if he had been one of his own pampas bulls hit by the axe of a butcher. He was out until long after the fatal "Ten" had been counted. So ended one of the most exciting battles in ring history, and Jack Dempsey still remained heavyweight champion.

9. "on the button": on the nose

Baseball: Take Me Out to the Ball Game

—adapted from *Baseball* by Richard George Knowles and Richard Morton and *Babe Ruth as I Knew Him* by Waite Hoyt

George Herman Ruth Jr.—a.k.a. Babe Ruth—is one of the most popular figures in the history of sports. Many consider him the greatest baseball player to ever play the game. Ruth set many records, including career home runs (714), runs batted in (RBIs) (2,213), bases on balls (2,062), slugging percentage (.690), and on-base plus slugging (OPS) (1.164). The last two records still stand today.

Ruth spent most of his career with the New York Yankees. Between 1921 and 1933, the Yankees appeared in the World Series seven times, winning four times. Many sports enthusiasts consider the 1927 Yankees to be not simply the best baseball team, but the greatest *sports* team ever. They won a record 110 games and won the World Series. They were led by two legends of the game, Ruth and Lou Gehrig. That year, Babe Ruth broke his own single-season home run record by hitting sixty home runs, a record which would stand until 1961.

The following selection tells about the game of baseball generally and then more about Babe Ruth as seen through the eyes of Yankees pitcher Waite Hoyt.

Baseball may have evolved from several old English games, but it is the most famous American sport. In the mid-1800s, baseball as we know it began to be played in the United States.

Eighteen players, nine on each side, are required to play the game of baseball, which is traditionally an outdoor sport. One team takes the field, which is shaped like a large diamond. The first man on the other team steps up to the plate[10] with a bat in hand. The batter's teammates take their seats in the dugout,[11] ready to bat in proper order. Their aims are very simple, for each team is engaged in turn in sending as many of their men as they possibly can around the diamond. When the batter hits the ball, he must drop the bat and run to first base. If he can get there before the ball is in the hands of the fielder who stands there, he is safe. If he has hit the ball sufficiently hard or planted it in a corner of the field where it cannot be readily returned, he may be able to reach second base, or even third. If he hits it so far that it goes beyond the outfield fence, he achieves what is called a home run and can advance all runners to home plate. The complete circuit of the bases[12] by a man scores a run for his side.

10. plate: refers to "home base," the plate on the ground where the batter stands to hit the ball
11. dugout: a bench area where team members wait to bat
12. circuit of the bases: refers to the way a player runs around and touches each base

When three men are out,[13] the positions are reversed, the batting side taking the field and the fielders coming in to bat. The retiring[14] of three men brings their inning to a close, and when each team has played nine innings, the team which has scored the greater number of runs wins the game. There is no such thing as a tie game in baseball. If the nine innings of each side result in a tie, another inning is played, and the team scoring the most runs in such innings is the winner. A baseball game usually takes about three hours, but some have lasted as long as eight.

Baseball is a game that enchants those who play it. In the field, no man is idle, and each must catch and throw the ball from his place in the field. That place is like a little kingdom. Whether in left field or second base, it's his to command. The men in the field are all required to be alert and continually on the move.

The very handling of the ball is amazing to watch, especially by the pitcher. The pitcher is trying everything he knows to mislead the batter by throwing fastballs, curve balls, screwballs, sliders, and all sorts of other sneaky pitches. The batter, on his side, is bent upon defeating those wiles and hitting the ball so as to advance the base runners who have been at bat before him. If there is a runner on second base, the idea of the batter is to bat the ball into right field, thus giving a fast runner on second base the opportunity of reaching home and completing a run. On the other hand, the pitcher will be straining every nerve to deliver balls that cannot be batted in the direction desired by the batter. It is a match between the brains of two athletes, each trying to defeat the aim of the other.

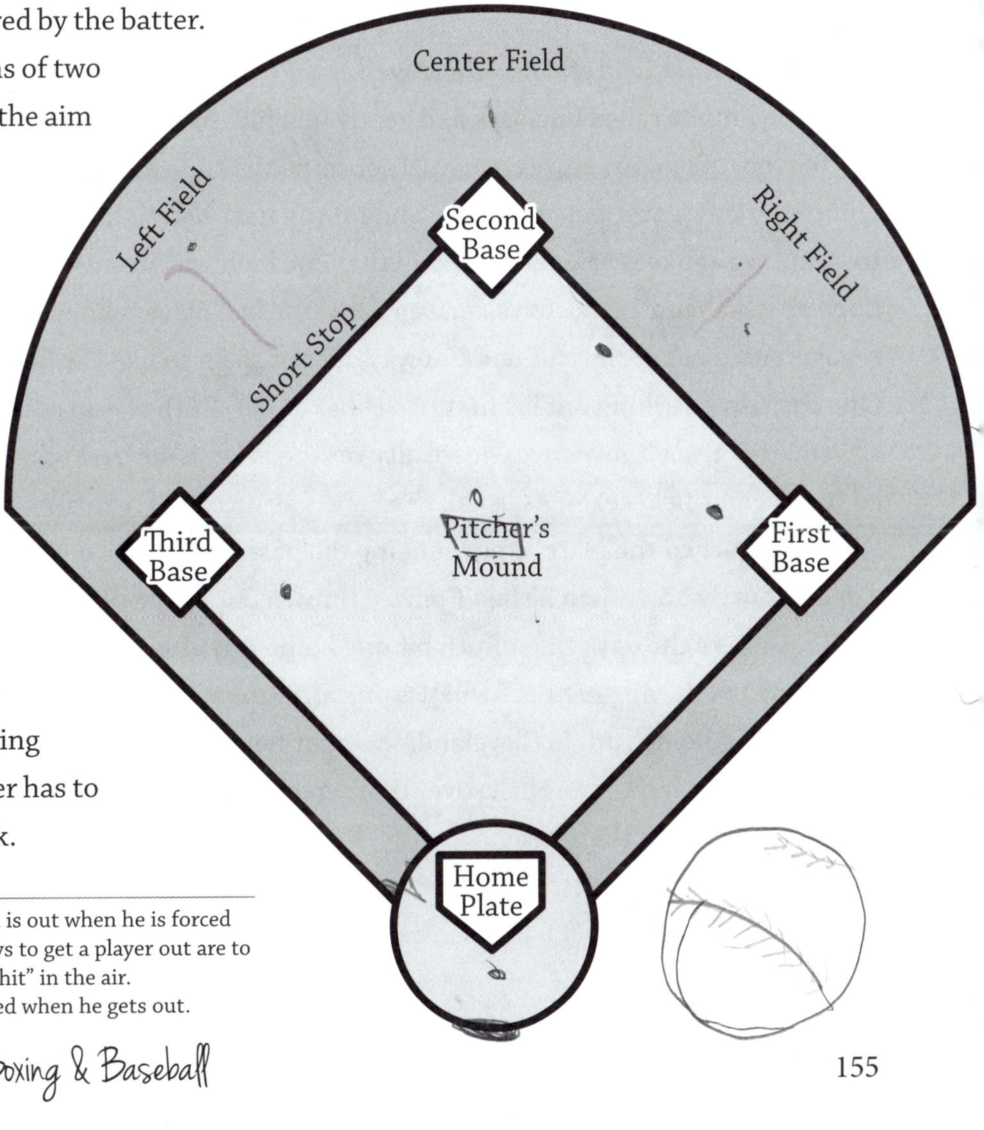

Base-running is also fascinating. Some players will risk getting out (being tagged with the ball) by sprinting for the next base, which is called stealing base. Base runners work together to distract the fielders by running off their bases and back on again until the right moment comes for the steal. In addition to trying to outwit the batter, the pitcher has to watch base runners like a hawk.

13. out: A player on the offensive team is out when he is forced to "retire" from the field. Some ways to get a player out are to tag him with a ball or to catch his "hit" in the air.
14. retiring: A player is said to be retired when he gets out.

Because one team is constantly trying to outwit the other, baseball has been labelled a "thinking man's sport." Strategy and brains are just as important as strength and agility. The pace of the game is slower than that of sports that require constant running, such as soccer or basketball, but the minds of the players are always moving quickly.

Baseball was never more popular than it was in the 1920s when Babe Ruth was playing the game. Known by many nicknames—the Bambino, the Sultan of Swat, the Colossus of Clout, the Big Bam—Ruth also had a reputation for his wild lifestyle. He partied hard, ignored team rules, and spent time schmoozing with gangsters and Hollywood movie stars. He made up for this in the public eye by visiting many orphanages and sick kids in hospitals. Once, Ruth visited a critically injured eleven-year-old boy at the hospital. He promised the boy that he would hit a home run for him that afternoon. Sure enough, he popped one over the fence that day.

Everything the Babe did was fabulous. One day, in Boston, with a strong wind blowing toward the plate, he hit a high towering fly.[15] The left fielder came running in to get it and kept coming. He never got near it—the ball landed in the infield, nearly beaning the shortstop. The ball had been hit so high that Ruth was able to gallop all the way around the bases for a home run. It was probably the first and last infield home run in history.

In the same Fenway Park he pulled another stunt, but this one will never show on the records. He was up at bat with two strikes against him. Just as the pitcher started his windup, a pigeon swooped down from center field and flew directly over the plate. Babe swung and missed, and started to walk away. The umpire called him back and gently told him he'd struck out swinging at a bird.

The most fabulous story circulated concerns the time in the 1932 World Series when Ruth pointed to the center field bleachers and hit the next ball right to that spot. The feat made history, but we Yankees saw the Babe pull that one before. There used to be a horrible drunk named Conway who haunted Boston's Fenway Park. The ball players knew him fairly well, since he was a regular and most vociferous fan. Conway did not seem to like the Babe. He said so loudly and often. One day, after striking out his first two times at bat, Ruth was ushered to the batter's box with a stream of Conway's invectives heard all over the Park. Babe backed away from the plate and pointed to the right field seats. As usual, the Babe was up to the occasion. A deep home run followed. When he reached the plate after rounding the bases, he stopped, turned toward Conway, and made a deep, courtly bow. Then he had Conway thrown out of the place.

Those were the days when Ruth hit one home run after another. When Huggins told Ruth to "push one to left" against the Athletics one afternoon, he pushed it to the left field bleachers for a blockbusting home run. In Cleveland, the right field wall of League Park was heightened by a tall wire screen. Ruth hit many balls over that screen. One fine day he hit one through it. The Cleveland players sadly shook their heads.

In Detroit, Babe had some of his biggest days. One homer he hit in Navin Field carried over the right center field bleachers. It rolled down a street which ran at right angles to the avenue behind

15. fly: a ball hit high into the air that the fielders try to catch

the right field fence. A boy chased it for blocks on a bicycle. The sports writers could see that from the press box. "It nearly went downtown," they wrote.

One time in St. Louis, the King of Swat was in a terrible batting slump. He took up a "fungo stick," a long, thin, underweight bat used to knock flies in practice. He clouted a homer on the roof of the right field stand and snapped his slump.

In Chicago, they renovated Comiskey Park. They added a second tier to the right field stands. The architects said, "No one will ever hit a ball on that roof. Not even Ruth." The first time at bat, Ruth hit a home run over the newly constructed grandstand.

One of his greatest feats was performed in Chicago. Herb Pennock was pitching against Mike Cvengros. The game was nip and tuck.[16] A pitcher's battle all the way. The game was being played on "getaway" day—the last day of the series. The Yankees were to leave on the 6:45 train out of Chicago. An hour's leeway for packing and taxi rides was required to make the train. At 5:30 the game was still in progress and Mark Roth, the Yankees' secretary, was tearing his hair. In desperation Roth paid a visit to the Yankee bench. Roth said to Miller Huggins,[17] "Miller, if this game isn't over soon we'll miss that train. What'll I do?" Ruth was in earshot. In fact, he was the first man up in that inning. He was just picking up his bat. He turned to Roth and said, "Don't worry, Mark. We'll make that train. I'll fix that." Ruth fixed it. He hit a home run which won the game. The Yankees just caught the train.

The Yankees were riding high in 1927, sweeping through the American League like a flight of jet bombers. Ruth, of course, was the bell cow.[18] He was hitting home runs like a man possessed, reaching for his own record of fifty-nine (hit in 1921). When the last game of the season rolled around, the Bam had just reached fifty-nine. We were playing Washington, with wise old Tom Zachary scheduled to pitch against us. Zach wasn't too fast, but he had the type of weird stuff which bothered the sluggers.[19] In the clubhouse before the game, Ruth was holding forth on the possibilities of making a homer. "I'll bet anyone ten bucks I hit one," he said. There were no takers. When Ruth gave voice to one of his inspired hunches, we knew what to expect. The Babe hit no homers the first three times at bat. He had one more chance—just one—to break his record. The crowd was silent, waiting; the boys on the bench watched tensely. Ruth got no instructions from the manager when he strode to the plate. He needed none. And he got his home run, breaking the record with his last at-bat of the season.

It was Miller Huggins who used to describe Babe Ruth's value in the lineup as "the most destructive force ever known in baseball." He didn't mean the force of Ruth's homers alone. The mere presence of the Babe created a disastrous psychological problem for the other team. Even when he wasn't hitting, the opposition was fearful that he might start.

---

16. nip and tuck: neck and neck; very close
17. Miller Huggins: 1878–1929, a professional baseball player and manager
18. bell cow: the lead cow in a herd, wears a bell
19. "he had the type of weird stuff which bothered the sluggers": In other words, Zachary pitched balls that curved or sank or did "tricks" in the air that were hard for batters to hit.

Tell It Back—Narration

1. **MARK UP THE TEXT—Annotation:** Read through the reading selections again. As you read, write in the margin of the text symbols that will help you understand it better and find important details later. The following are some symbols you might use:

   - Underline the main idea of the story or any important point.
   - Put a question mark in the margin to mark any part of the story you don't understand.
   - Write any questions or thoughts you have in the margin.
   - Put an exclamation point in the margin to mark any part of the story you find surprising or particularly interesting.
   - Circle any important or unfamiliar vocabulary words or proper nouns when they are first introduced. Remember, a proper noun is the name for any specific person, place, thing, or idea. How do you know which words to circle? Circle words that appear repeatedly, or words you can't understand from the context of the sentence alone. Look up any unfamiliar words in the glossary, or, if they aren't there, in a dictionary.

2. **ORAL NARRATION:** Look over the annotations you made for *Boxing: Rock 'Em, Sock 'Em*. Then, without looking at the text, retell the story as best you remember it using your own words. Try not to leave out any important details.

   Here are the first two sentences to help you get started:

   Man is a fighting animal. From the teeth and the claws of the caveman to the poison gas of modern warfare, fighting has been one of his principal preoccupations.

3. **OUTLINE:** Create an outline for *Baseball: Take Me Out to the Ball Game* using Roman numerals (*I, II, III*) for the most important events and capital letters (*A, B, C*) for less important events. Use standard numbers (*1, 2, 3*) for minor points.

   ____

   ____

   ____

   ____

   ____

   ____

Talk About It—

1. Look at the painting by George Bellows that depicts the famous fight on September 14, 1923, between Jack Dempsey and Luis Firpo, a fight that has been called the most savage two rounds in boxing history. This painting shows the moment when Firpo knocked Dempsey out of the ring. It does a marvelous job of making the viewer feel as though he is there in the scene, due in part to its low point of view. You can almost see the sweat, hear the noise of thousands cheering and shouting, and smell whiffs of cigar smoke from the men at ringside. What adjectives would you use to describe this scene? Who appears to be the dominant athlete in this moment?

▲ Dempsey and Firpo, by George Bellows June 1924.

2. One important difference between boxing and baseball is that baseball is a team sport, while boxing is an individual sport. What are the major differences between individual and team sports?

▲ Babe Ruth and Lou Gehrig were teammates and star players on the 1927 New York Yankees.

3. Which of the two sports—boxing or baseball—seems more complicated to you? Which seems more dangerous?

4. Do you agree with the first line of *Boxing: Rock 'Em, Sock 'Em*, which says that "man is a fighting animal"? Why or why not?

Memoria—

> You are never really playing an opponent. You are playing yourself, your own highest standards, and when you reach your limits, that is real joy. —Arthur Ashe

1. After reading this quotation by Arthur Ashe, world champion tennis player, define any words you may not know. Then discuss the meaning of the quotation.

2. How does this quote relate to the readings about boxing and baseball?
3. Memorize the quotation and be prepared to recite it during your next class.
4. Write the quotation in your commonplace book, along with any thoughts you have about it.

Writing Time—

1. **SENTENCE PLAY**—"This is a book. It is about comparison. It is part of a series of books on writing and rhetoric."

   Doesn't that sound rather clunky? When you notice that your sentences are short and choppy, that's usually a sign that there is a problem. When there is no variety in sentence length, writing can either feel awkward and choppy (when sentences are too short) or make the reader feel out of breath (when sentences are all way too long). One way to vary the length of your sentences is to combine some shorter sentences into a longer one. For example: "This book, a book about comparison, is part of a series on writing and rhetoric."

   Often you can combine shorter sentences by making one of them an appositive phrase. An appositive is a noun or noun phrase that explains another noun or pronoun. For example:

   My first car, <u>a rusty, old Volkswagen</u>, accompanied me on many road trips.

   "A rusty, old Volkswagen" is an appositive phrase that describes "car" by providing more detail about it. Instead of saying, "My first car was a rusty, old Volkswagen. It accompanied me on many trips," you can combine the two sentences by making the second part of the first sentence into an appositive phrase.

   Take each of the following series of sentences and combine them into one by using an appositive phrase.

   Example: My dog Rosie is a Golden Retriever. She likes to play fetch.
   Change to: My dog Rosie, a Golden Retriever, likes to play fetch.

   A. Lou Gehrig played for the New York Yankees. Gehrig died from a disease called ALS.

   ____

   ____

   ____

B. Lou Gehrig was a talented speaker. He gave a famous inspirational speech.

____

C. Each boxing match has rounds, which are breaks in the match. Baseball has innings.

D. Jack Dempsey was a champion boxer. He held the title for seven years.

E. Babe Ruth is the most famous slugger.[20] He could hit the ball over the fence.

2. **COPIOUSNESS: Active Voice Review—**When writing, you'll mostly want to use active voice. In active voice, the subject of the sentence performs an action. Take this sentence for example: "Dempsey punched Firpo's jaw." In this case, the subject is "Dempsey." The action is "punched." In the sentence "Ruth hit a home run over the newly constructed grandstand," "Ruth" is the subject. The action is "hit."

   In passive voice, on the other hand, the subject of the sentence fails to do the acting and instead is acted upon. Look at the same two sentences in passive voice: "Firpo's jaw was punched by Dempsey." "A home run was hit over the newly constructed grandstand by Ruth." Notice how "Firpo's jaw" and "home run," the subjects of the sentences, are being acted upon by "Dempsey" and "Ruth."

20. A slugger is a baseball player who is a successful hitter, especially of home runs.

As you can see, the passive voice sentences aren't quite as zippy as the two sentences written in active voice. Active voice uses strong verbs and is livelier and less wordy than passive voice. Passive voice uses weak verbs (such as "is," "am," "are," "was," "were," "be," "being," "been").

In the following sentences, change the passive voice into active voice. Write the new sentences in the space provided.

Examples:

> Passive voice: A high-towering fly ball was hit by the Babe.
> Change to: The Babe hit a high-towering fly ball.
> Passive voice: Dempsey was angered by the crowd.
> Change to: The crowd angered Dempsey.

A. The dog was surprised by the hobo's kindness.

____

____

B. The town was leveled by the tornado.

____

____

C. One homer was hit by the Babe over the right center field bleachers.

____

____

D. During his reign of nearly seven years, a number of battles were fought by Jack Dempsey.

____

____

E. All of us have been surrounded by our enemies.

____

____

F. Cavities in the teeth are caused by soda pop and candy.

____

____

G. The crime would have been prevented by a police officer.

____

____

3. **COMPARISON**—The purpose of this lesson's essay is to compare boxing with baseball. Before you start writing, use the following prompts for each paragraph to help you sketch out your ideas. You can use lists, phrases, or complete sentences for your answers. Then compose your full essay on a separate paper or on a computer. Remember that each paragraph has its own job to do.

The paragraphs you write after going through these steps will be your first draft, or your first version of the essay. Assume that your first draft will need some rewriting to make it the best essay it can be.

Prewriting: Begin by making a list of as many similarities and differences between your subjects as you can think of.

Similarities between the two subjects:

____

____

____

____

Differences between the two subjects:

____

____

____

____

Now select two of the most important similarities from your list.

Similarity #1:

Similarity #2:

Select two of the most important differences from your list.
Difference #1:

Difference #2:

Paragraph 1 (Introduction): Start with an introduction that includes an analogy, a narrative overview of each subject, and a topic sentence.

Begin your introduction with an analogy about sports. Remember, a simile uses "like" or "as" to make a comparison, and a metaphor uses one thing to describe another, but without using the words "like" or "as." Include a second sentence that explains your analogy if needed.

Analogy:

Next write a short narrative overview of the two subjects. Consider the questions who, what, when, and where, and tell about each subject in one or two sentences.

Boxing:

Who:

____

____

What:

____

____

When:

____

____

Where:

____

____

Baseball:

Who:

____

____

What:

____

____

When:

____

____

Where:

____

____

Finally, write your topic sentence, which simply states the main idea of your essay.

Topic sentence:

____

____

____

Paragraph 2 (Similarity #1): Write about one major similarity between the two subjects. Start by identifying the similarity you will be describing. Then tell more about the similarity by adding facts, examples, or details from the readings for both subjects.

Details about similarity #1:

____

____

____

____

____

____

Paragraph 3 (Similarity #2): Write about a second major similarity between the two subjects. Start again by identifying the similarity you will be describing. Then tell more about the similarity by adding facts, examples, or details from the readings for both subjects.

Details about similarity #2:

____

____

____

____

____

____

Look in the readings for a quote that gives a supportive fact, example, or detail and include it in your description.

Quote:

____

____

____

Paragraph 4 (Difference #1): Write about one major difference between the two subjects. Start by identifying the difference you will be describing. Then tell more about the difference by adding facts, examples, or details from the readings for both subjects.

Details about difference #1:

____

____

____

____

____

Paragraph 5 (Difference #2): Write about a second major difference between the two subjects. Start again by identifying the difference you will be describing. Then tell more about the difference by adding facts, examples, or details from the readings for both subjects.

Details about difference #2:

____

____

____

____

____

Look in the readings for a quote that gives a supportive fact, example, or detail and include it in your description.

Quote:

____

____

____

Paragraph 6 (Conclusion): Write an epilogue, or concluding paragraph. First, recap the main point of your essay. Then reflect on something important that can be learned from the comparison. Finally, write an observation or question about your subjects that would be interesting to learn more about in the future.

Something that can be learned from the comparison:

____

____

Something to learn more about:

____

____

Once you have completed your prewriting, go through these instructions again and write your paragraphs based on the prompts.

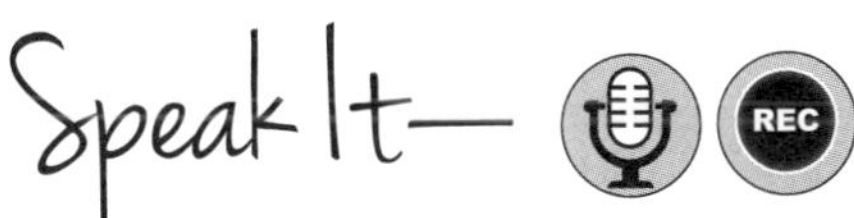

1. Lou Gehrig's Farewell Speech—Although Lou Gehrig stood in the shadow of Babe Ruth, he was one of the most remarkable baseball players of all time. He was a World Series champion six times. As a power hitter himself, he once whacked four home runs in a single game. He was also a top first baseman and base stealer. Sadly, his career ended when he was discovered to have a rare disease called amyotrophic lateral sclerosis, or ALS. Gehrig gave the following famous speech in 1939 to 60,000 adoring fans in Yankee Stadium. Use your skills in elocution to read this speech with humility and touching drama.

Luckiest Man Alive

Fans, for the past two weeks you have been reading about the bad break I got. Yet today I consider myself the luckiest man on the face of this earth. I have been in ballparks for seventeen years and have never received anything but kindness and encouragement from you fans.

Look at these grand men. Which of you wouldn't consider it the highlight of his career just to associate with them for even one day? Sure, I'm lucky. Who wouldn't consider it an honor to have known Jacob Ruppert?[21] Also, the builder of baseball's greatest empire, Ed Barrow?[22] To have spent six years with that wonderful little fellow, Miller Huggins? Then to have spent the next nine years with that outstanding leader, that smart student of psychology, the best manager in baseball today, Joe McCarthy?[23] Sure, I'm lucky.

When the New York Giants,[24] a team you would give your right arm to beat, and vice versa, sends you a gift—that's something. When everybody down to the groundskeepers and those boys in white coats remember you with trophies—that's something. When you have a wonderful mother-in-law who takes sides with you in squabbles with her own daughter—that's something. When you have a father and a mother who work all their lives so you can have an education and build your body—it's a blessing. When you have a wife who has been a tower of strength and shown more courage than you dreamed existed—that's the finest I know.

So I close in saying that I might have been given a bad break, but I've got an awful lot to live for.[25]

2. **FORMAL DISCUSSION:** Your teacher may instruct you to have a formal discussion. This sort of discussion is not a debate. Rather, it is an opportunity for your class to have a conversation around an open question or a controversial topic. Discussion is a great way to hear other people's ideas and to learn to express your own thoughts well. You can take sides as in a debate, but you are also free to agree with one another, enhancing each other's arguments. Usually a teacher will not participate in a formal discussion; instead she stands aside and listens in.

21. Jacob Ruppert: businessman and owner of the New York Yankees from 1915 to 1939
22. Ed Barrow: business manager and team president of the New York Yankees
23. Joe McCarthy: manager of the New York Yankees from 1931 to 1946
24. The New York Giants were a crosstown baseball team and major rival of the New York Yankees. The Giants moved to San Francisco in 1957. There is still a NY Giants football team.
25. Lou Gehrig™ is a trademark of the Rip van Winkle Foundation d/b/a The Lou Gehrig Society. Used with permission. This speech can be found at http://lougehrig.com/about/farewell.html.

Here's how it works: Your teacher will assign you a question or a topic. She might allow you to prepare for the discussion as homework, or she may give you time in class to jot down your thoughts. Either way, you will probably be permitted to keep your notes with you as you discuss. You will then have a conversation about the topic; this conversation usually lasts for fifteen to twenty minutes. Be sure to let everyone have a chance to speak, and if some people are being quiet, feel free to draw them into the conversation by asking them direct questions. If you can support your ideas by quoting a text, so much the better! In the end, your teacher may assign you a score based on the scoring guidelines included with this exercise.

Formal Discussion Scoring Guidelines

Award points based on the following criteria:

- taking a stand by clearly stating an argument (thesis) +2
- providing evidence for the argument +2
- making an analogy +2
- making a relevant comment +1
- asking a clarifying question +1
- inviting another student to participate +1
- interrupting -1
- monopolizing the conversation -2
- making personal attacks -2
- distracting the audience -2

3. **PARTNER FEEDBACK:** With a student partner (or your teacher), take turns reading the rough drafts of your comparison essays. You and your partner should give each other comments about what is more or less effective about your writing. Use the rubric at the back of the book to help you get ideas for your comments. (A rubric is a guide to evaluating and grading writing, and your teacher may use this particular rubric to grade your essay.) Try to say two positive things about your partner's essay, and then come up with at least two suggestions for editing the essay.

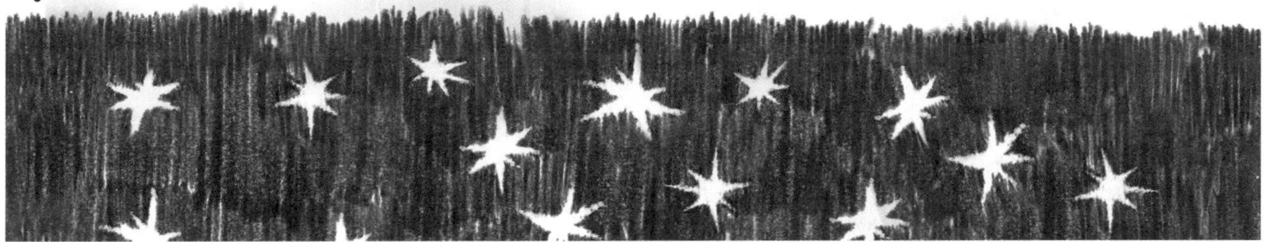

Revise It—

1. In *Encomium & Vituperation* you practiced using transition words and phrases to help your sentences and paragraphs flow together, and you should be continuing to use them with your comparison essays as well. Remember that transition words and phrases can help to smooth over your writing from one sentence to another and one paragraph to another. If you don't use transitions, your writing will be confusing and hard to follow. You might consider transitions to be the "glue" of your essay because they connect the parts of the essay to each other. The following are some examples of good transitions:
   - **Between sentences:** Boxing is an exciting and entertaining sport. <u>However</u>, it can lead to serious injuries.
     The word "however" connects the two sentences. "However" tells us that the author intends to introduce a contrast.
   - **Between paragraphs:**
     Dempsey's endurance was unrivalled for his time. He worked out by jumping rope, by swinging a sledgehammer, and even by chopping wood.
     <u>In addition</u>, Dempsey could land a violent punch with either hand and had a sturdy physique.
     The phrase "in addition" introduces another point. The first paragraph was about Dempsey's endurance. The transition at the beginning of the second paragraph tells us that we will learn about his other remarkable qualities as well.

The following are a list of transition words and phrases you can use:

- To list supportive points:
  - ◊ First,/Second,/Third,
  - ◊ To begin with,/Next,/Finally,
- To draw conclusions:
  - ◊ Hence,
  - ◊ As a result,
  - ◊ Because of this,
  - ◊ Therefore,
  - ◊ Thus,
  - ◊ Finally,
  - ◊ In conclusion,
- To provide a contrast:
  - ◊ By contrast,
  - ◊ In contrast,
  - ◊ On the other hand,
  - ◊ Rather,
  - ◊ Instead,
  - ◊ Just the opposite,
  - ◊ On the contrary,
  - ◊ By comparison,
- To make an additional point:
  - ◊ Additionally,
  - ◊ In addition,
  - ◊ Also,
  - ◊ Furthermore,
  - ◊ At the same time,
  - ◊ Moreover,
- To concede a point:
  - ◊ Nevertheless,
  - ◊ Still,
  - ◊ Yet,
  - ◊ After all,
  - ◊ At any rate,
  - ◊ However,
  - ◊ In any case,
- To provide an example:
  - ◊ For example,
  - ◊ In other words,
  - ◊ For instance,

Be sure to use a comma to offset transition words from the rest of the sentence. For example:

> There have been many star baseball players throughout the game's history. <u>For example</u>, Babe Ruth was the most famous baseball player of the 1920s. <u>Also</u>, Joe DiMaggio won nine World Series titles.

In this passage, the phrases "for example" and "also" help readers ease into the next thought.

Even if you don't use a specific transition word, it is vital for each new paragraph to "take up" the idea of the previous paragraph. Look at your essay and consider where it would benefit from the use of transition words or phrases. Make any changes or additions that will help make smooth connections between the parts of your essay.

A. Use a transition word or phrase from the previous list to connect the following sentences.[26]

Example: Although many sports are played in teams, some sports are played solo. ___For example___, boxers face each other one-on-one.

a. During the game, a player fell down on the field, but later got up and played the game out. ________________________________, he hurt his leg so badly that it never regained its strength.

b. One year, the Giants players weren't as motivated as usual. ________________________________, they lost game after game.

c. During one game, a player named Tinker was struck out three times, but he refused to be discouraged. ________________________________, he kept smiling and tried to change his strategy.

d. Mordecai Brown, the great pitcher of the Chicago Cubs, lost his finger in an accident. ________________________________, he is called "Three-Fingered Brown."

e. A cheering crowd can energize the players, making them play harder and run faster. ________________________________, a silent audience makes for a boring game.

B. Use a transition word or phrase from the previous list to connect the following paragraphs.

Example:

Rocky Marciano was a famous boxer during the 1950s. He was undefeated as a world champion for four years. He was known for his energy and unique fighting style. ___However___, Marciano was not only a boxer. Later in his life, he went on television and even hosted a weekly boxing show.

a. Boxing and wrestling may seem similar at first glance, but there are several important differences between them. In boxing, players stand up and throw punches at one another. They try to knock one another down onto the mat. ________________________________, wrestling is less violent. Wrestlers use their bare hands to grab one another. The goal is to force the other wrestler onto the mat, but the wrestlers are not allowed to hit one another.

26. The sentences in this exercise are adapted from *Pitching in a Pinch, or Baseball from the Inside* by Christy Mathewson.

b. The mouthguard is an important part of boxing. Boxers sometimes take punches to the face, so they wear mouthguards to protect their teeth from getting knocked out.

   ______________________________, boxing gloves reduce impact on the fighter and protect a boxer's lips and cheeks. Even though pain and injury are expected in boxing, no boxer wants his face to be permanently disfigured.

c. The history of boxing has its roots in ancient Greece and Rome. But it wasn't until 1681 in England that the first recorded boxing match took place. On January 6 of that year, a duke arranged the first modern boxing match between his butler and his butcher. Daniel Mendoza, another Englishman, published a book called *The Art of Boxing* in 1789.

   ______________________________, modern boxing is mostly an English sport. The sport that we know today as boxing was completely different before the seventeenth century.

d. Many people like to practice boxing for fun on their own. There are specific kinds of boxing equipment that a person can use to box at home.

   ______________________________, a punching bag is a sturdy bag that hangs from the ceiling. It is filled with materials such as sand, grain, or cloth. A person can put on boxing gloves and practice her punches by repeatedly hitting the bag.

e. Because boxing is a violent sport, there are many rules in place today to protect boxers. For example, boxers can only compete against people of a similar weight. This helps to prevent serious injury. A smaller, lighter boxer would not be able to win against a taller, heavier boxer in the ring.

   ______________________________, despite important innovations, there have been many deaths related to boxing. Since 1884, approximately 500 boxers have died after being severely injured while boxing.

2. Here is what you must do to effectively revise your work:
   a. Get feedback. Use comments from your student partners (or from your teacher) to strengthen and improve your paper.
   b. Wait a day or two before you rewrite your paper. The time away from it will help you to see its problems more clearly.
   c. Read the paper aloud to yourself. This is often the best way to catch mistakes—grammatical errors, as well as words that don't work well—because you will be using two senses—seeing and hearing—instead of one. If something sounds wrong, it probably is.

Once you are ready to rewrite, use the following steps to aid with your revision:

a. *Find your topic sentence and underline it.* There should be one sentence that states the main idea of your essay. Make sure your paper expresses that idea throughout.
b. *Make sure each paragraph gets the job done.* Remember that each paragraph has a special purpose according to the demands of the prompts. Revisit the goal of each paragraph and compare it to what you've written. Does each paragraph successfully accomplish its goal?
c. *Find and fix grammar mistakes.* Make sure all your nouns and verbs agree and that your writing is clear. Fix any fragments or run-ons. In other words, make sure you are writing complete sentences.
d. *Strengthen phrasing.* Are your word choices specific instead of vague? Do you use strong nouns and verbs? Do you vary your sentences and occasionally begin them with a prepositional phrase or a participial phrase? Weed out passive voice and excess adjectives. Use compound sentences, appositives, adverb phrases, and questions to make your writing more interesting. Transition smoothly between ideas and paragraphs using transition words.
e. *Proofread.* Look for any punctuation, spelling, or capitalization errors. Then fix them!
f. *Retype* the draft with the corrections you have made.

Lesson 10

Fifth Comparison: The Love Letters of Napoleon & Keats

Never does a school year go by that I don't find a dog-eared love note lying on my classroom floor. For some **inexplicable** reason, those notes have a way of falling out of folders and hanging around for teachers to find them. Now, you may think words of love all sound pretty much alike, but there's actually quite a bit of variety to them. For example, here's the shy approach:

Guess who likes you? Me! (But you'll never guess who "me" is!)

Or there's the bold approach:

You are cute. I really like you. Do you like me back?

Some notes take a more indirect route:

Jodi says she likes you. Promise! No lies! But don't freak out. She didn't want me to tell you.

As sincere as these love notes may be, they are pretty weak stuff compared to some of the more famous love letters of history. Of course, they may be perfectly fine for middle school, but they would not have satisfied the likes of the French emperor Napoleon Bonaparte or the English poet John Keats. Those gents gushed out words of love like geysers of hot chocolate. Their love letters make for a whole book each.

Now, let me be clear: The purpose of this lesson is *not* for you to learn to write better love letters. For that, you're on your own. There's a time and a place for everything, and *now* is neither the time nor the place. Rather, in this lesson you will compare some love letters written by Napoleon and Keats and figure out how they're similar and how they're different. First, take a look at some of Napoleon's letters, and then move on to Keats.

Millions of Kisses to Joséphine: Napoleon's Letters to His Wife

—from *Napoleon's Letters to Joséphine 1796 to 1812*, compiled by Henry Foljambe Hall

Napoleon Bonaparte was twenty-six years old when he first met thirty-two-year-old Joséphine de Beauharnais in Paris during the summer of 1795. He was a rising star of the French army, and she was a leading socialite. Although he wasn't a handsome man, Napoleon's military victories made him famous and wealthy. Someday he hoped to be a king. Joséphine belonged to the French nobility at a time when France was murdering its nobles. During the Reign of Terror,[1] her husband had been executed and Joséphine thrown in jail. Miraculously she was set free before the revolutionaries could chop off her head. When Napoleon met her, he fell madly in love and swiftly proposed to her. They were married in March of 1796.

Although Napoleon loved Joséphine with wild passion, she seldom returned his affection. While Napoleon was conquering Italy for France, Joséphine was enjoying parties and balls in Milan. He often felt serious pangs of jealousy. Many times she hurt his feelings by ignoring him or not meeting him at appointed times. Although he went on to become emperor of France and crowned Joséphine empress of France, he lost his trust in her. Even so, Napoleon seems to have loved her to the last. With his dying breath he whispered, "Joséphine."

TO JOSÉPHINE, AT MILAN.

Marmirolo, July 17, 1796

I got your letter, my beloved; it has filled my heart with joy. I am grateful to you for the trouble you have taken to send me news; your health[2] should be better to-day—I am sure you are cured. I urge you strongly to ride [your horse], which cannot fail to do you good.

1. Reign of Terror: a time near the end of the French Revolution when priests, nobles, and political prisoners were relentlessly executed
2. More than likely, Joséphine was only pretending to be sick so that she could remain in Milan and enjoy the dinners and dances there.

Ever since I left you, I have been sad. I am only happy when by your side. Ceaselessly I recall your kisses, your tears, your enchanting jealousy; and the charms of the incomparable Joséphine keep constantly alight a bright and burning flame in my heart and senses. When, free from every worry, from all business, shall I spend all my moments by your side, to have nothing to do but to love you, and to prove it to you? Your horse I shall send you, but I am hoping that you will soon be able to rejoin me. I thought I loved you some days ago; but, since I saw you, I feel that I love you even a thousand times more. Ever since I have known you, I worship you more every day; which proves how false is the maxim of La Bruyere that "Love comes all at once." Everything in nature has a regular course, and different degrees of growth. Ah! pray let me see some of your faults; be less beautiful, less gracious, less tender, and, especially, less kind; above all never be jealous, never weep; your tears madden me, fire my blood. Be sure that it is no longer possible for me to have a thought except for you, or an idea of which you shall not be the judge.

Have a good rest. Haste to get well. Come and join me, so that, at least, before dying, we could say—"We were happy for so many days!!"

Millions of kisses, and even to Fortune, in spite of his naughtiness.[3]

BONAPARTE.

TO JOSÉPHINE, AT MILAN.

Verona, November 23, 1796.

I don't love you an atom; on the contrary, I detest you. You are a good for nothing, very ungraceful, very tactless, very tatterdemalion.[4] You never write to me; you don't care for your husband; you know the pleasure your letters give him, and you write him barely half-a-dozen lines, thrown off anyhow.

How, then, do you spend the livelong day, madam? What business of such importance robs you of the time to write to your very kind lover? What inclination stifles and alienates love, the affectionate and unvarying love which you promised me? Who may this paragon be, this new lover who engrosses all your time, is master of your days, and prevents you from concerning yourself about your husband? Joséphine, be vigilant; one fine night the doors will be broken in, and I shall be before you.

Truly, my dear, I am uneasy at getting no news from you. Write me four pages immediately, and some of those charming remarks which fill my heart with the pleasures of imagination.

I hope that before long I shall clasp you in my arms, and cover you with a million kisses as burning as if under the equator.

BONAPARTE.

3. Napoleon seems to be saying that fortune (or fate) is keeping him apart from Joséphine, which is why he calls it naughty.
4. tatterdemalion: ragamuffin; a person who wears tattered, worn-out clothes

I Almost Wish We Were Two Butterflies: John Keats's Letters to Fanny Brawne

—from *The Complete Works of John Keats, Volume 5: Letters 1819 and 1820*, edited by H. Buxton Forman

In the fall of 1818, John Keats first met Fanny Brawne. It was a difficult time for Keats, as his brother Tom was dying of tuberculosis. Fanny's friendship became for Keats a distraction from his grief.

When they first met, Fanny was flirtatious with different men and Keats was more attached to her than she was to him. But, eventually, the two fell deeply in love. Fanny inspired many of Keats's best-known poems, and in October 1819 they became officially engaged.

Sadly, the pair's happiness could not last. Keats began to experience symptoms of the same deadly disease that had killed his brother. Once he realized he was dying, Keats wrote to Fanny, telling her she was free to break off their engagement. Fanny refused, continuing to visit and nurse him. One of Keats's friends decided that he must go to Rome to receive top medical care, and in the last month before Keats left, he and Fanny were inseparable. She never left his bedside.

Once he arrived in Italy, Keats stopped writing to Fanny. He knew that he would never see her again, and it would be too painful to correspond. But a piece of marble that was her parting gift to him never left his hands. On February 23, 1821, Keats died in Rome after two years of suffering. He was buried with a lock of Fanny's hair.

TO FANNY BRAWNE

Postmark: Newport, July 3, 1819
Shanklin, Isle of Wight, Thursday

My dearest Lady — . . . The morning is the only proper time for me to write to a beautiful Girl whom I love so much: for at night, when the lonely day has closed, and the lonely, silent, unmusical Chamber is waiting to receive me as into a Sepulcher, then believe me my passion gets entirely the sway, then I would not have you see those Rhapsodies which I once thought it impossible I should ever give way to, and which I have often laughed at in another, for fear you should [think me] either too unhappy or perhaps a little mad.

I am now at a very pleasant Cottage window, looking onto a beautiful hilly country, with a glimpse of the sea; the morning is very fine. I do not know how elastic my spirit might be, what pleasure I might have in living here and breathing and wandering as free as a stag about this beautiful Coast if the remembrance of you did not weigh so upon me. I have never known any unalloy'd

Happiness for many days together: the death or sickness of someone has always spoilt my hours—and now when none such troubles oppress me, it is you must confess very hard that another sort of pain should haunt me.

Ask yourself my love whether you are not very cruel to have so entrammeled me, so destroyed my freedom. Will you confess this in the Letter you must write immediately, and do all you can to console me in it—make it rich as a draught of poppies to intoxicate me—write the softest words and kiss them that I may at least touch my lips where yours have been. For myself I know not how to express my devotion to so fair a form: I want a brighter word than bright, a fairer word than fair. I almost wish we were butterflies and liv'd but three summer days—three such days with you I could fill with more delight than fifty common years could ever contain. But however selfish I may feel, I am sure I could never act selfishly. . . . Though I could center my Happiness in you, I cannot expect to engross your heart so entirely—indeed if I thought you felt as much for me as I do for you at this moment I do not think I could restrain myself from seeing you again tomorrow for the delight of one embrace.

But no—I must live upon hope and Chance. In case of the worst that can happen, I shall still love you . . . !

Some lines I read the other day are continually ringing a peal[5] in my ears:

To see those eyes I prize above mine own
Dart favors on another—
And those sweet lips (yielding immortal nectar)
Be gently press'd by any but myself—
Think, think Francesca, what a cursed thing
It were beyond expression!

John

TO FANNY BRAWNE

Kentish Town, July 1820

My dearest Fanny,

My head is puzzled this morning, and I scarce know what I shall say though I am full of a hundred things. 'Tis certain I would rather be writing to you this morning, notwithstanding the alloy of grief in such an occupation, than enjoy any other pleasure, with health to boot,[6] unconnected with you.

Upon my soul I have loved you to the extreme. I wish you could know the Tenderness with which I continually brood over your different aspects of countenance, action and dress. I see you

5. ringing a peal: sounding like a bell
6. to boot: in addition

come down in the morning: I see you meet me at the Window—I see everything over again eternally that I ever have seen. If I get on the pleasant clue[7] I live in a sort of happy misery, if on the unpleasant 'tis miserable misery. You complain of my ill-treating you in word, thought and deed—I am sorry,—at times I feel bitterly sorry that I ever made you unhappy—my excuse is that those words have been wrung from me by the sharpness of my feelings. At all events and in any case I have been wrong; could I believe that I did it without any cause, I should be the most sincere of Penitents. I could give way to my repentant feelings now, I could recant all my suspicions, I could mingle with you heart and Soul though absent, were it not for some parts of your Letters. Do you suppose it possible I could ever leave you? You know what I think of myself and what of you. You know that I should feel how much it was my loss and how little yours.

. . . Do nothing but love me—if I knew that for certain life and health will in such event be a heaven, and death itself will be less painful. I long to believe in immortality. I shall never be able to bid you an entire farewell. If I am destined to be happy with you here—how short is the longest Life. I wish to believe in immortality—I wish to live with you forever.

. . . I am strong enough to walk over—but I dare not. I shall feel so much pain in parting with you again. My dearest love, I am afraid to see you; I am strong, but not strong enough to see you. Will my arm be ever round you again, and if so shall I be obliged to leave you again? My sweet Love! I am happy whilst I believe your first Letter. Let me be but certain that you are mine heart and soul, and I could die more happily than I could otherwise live. If you think me cruel—if you think I have slighted you—do muse it over again and see into my heart. My love to you is "true as truth's simplicity and simpler than the infancy of truth" as I think I once said before. How could I slight you? How threaten to leave you? not in the spirit of a Threat to you—no—but in the spirit of Wretchedness in myself. My fairest, my delicious, my angel Fanny I do not believe me such a vulgar fellow. I will be as patient in illness and as believing in Love as I am able.

Yours forever my dearest
John

7. "If I get on the pleasant clue": A clue (or clew) is a helpful track or guide. It was originally a ball of thread such as the one that helped Theseus escape the labyrinth. It appears that Keats is essentially saying, "If I can follow a pleasant way of thinking, I live in a sort of happy misery. If I follow an unpleasant way of thinking, it's misery upon misery."

Tell It Back—Narration

1. **MARK UP THE TEXT—Annotation:** Read through the reading selections again. As you read, write in the margin of the text symbols that will help you understand it better and find important details later. The following are some symbols you might use:
   - Underline the main idea of the story or any important point.
   - Put a question mark in the margin to mark any part of the story you don't understand.
   - Write any questions or thoughts you have in the margin.
   - Put an exclamation point in the margin to mark any part of the story you find surprising or particularly interesting.
   - Circle any important or unfamiliar vocabulary words or proper nouns when they are first introduced. Remember, a proper noun is the name for any specific person, place, thing, or idea. How do you know which words to circle? Circle words that appear repeatedly, or words you can't understand from the context of the sentence alone. Look up any unfamiliar words in the glossary, or, if they aren't there, in a dictionary.

2. **ORAL NARRATION:** Without looking at the text, retell the biographical introductions to the love letters of Napoleon and Joséphine and Keats and Fanny as best you remember them using your own words. You do not need to narrate the letters themselves.

   Here is the first sentence of each brief bio to help you get started:

   Napoleon Bonaparte was twenty-six years old when he first met thirty-two-year-old Joséphine de Beauharnais in Paris during the summer of 1795.

   In the fall of 1818, John Keats first met Fanny Brawne.

Talk About It—

1. Napoleon says to Joséphine, "Ever since I left you, I have been sad. I am only happy when by your side." John Keats says to Fanny, "Though I could center my Happiness in you, I cannot expect to engross your heart so entirely." Is there anything unhealthy about being happy only when by the side of a loved one? Is there anything unhealthy about centering one's happiness in one person? Why or why not?

2. Look at the official royal portrait of Napoleon and the painting of John Keats. Describe the two pictures. What can you tell about the men's personalities from their portraits?

▲ Napoleon on his Imperial throne by Jean-Auguste-Dominique Ingres, 1806

▲ John Keats by Joseph Severn, 1819.

3. Before ways of communicating such as e-mail and text messaging became popular, writing love letters was a common way for people to express their affection. Do you think love letters can still be a good way for lovers to express their feelings today? Are they better than e-mails and texts? Why or why not?

Memoria—

More than kisses, letters mingle souls. —John Donne

1. After reading this quotation by John Donne, a famous English poet, define any words you may not know. Then discuss the meaning of the quotation.
2. Do you agree that words can powerfully express love just as much as a physical embrace? Why or why not?
3. Memorize the quotation and be prepared to recite it during your next class.
4. Write the quotation in your commonplace book, along with any thoughts you have about it.

Writing Time—

1. **SENTENCE PLAY**—John Keats's letters are beautifully written. They make generous use of rhetorical devices such as metaphor and parallelism. In this exercise you will imitate some of the more poetic sentences by this famous poet.

   A. Parallelism isn't just created by repeating words, phrases, clauses, verb forms, and sounds within a single sentence. Parallelism can also be created by making a pattern with more than one sentence. Keats does it here:

      I see you come down in the morning. I see you meet me at the window. I see everything over again eternally that I ever have seen.

      Do you see the repeating pattern of the subject pronoun "I" and the verb "see"? By repeating "I see," Keats is telling Fanny that there is something relentless, something unwavering in his love for her. It is a very powerful, attention-grabbing technique. Give this pattern a try yourself by creating parallelisms with similar sentence beginnings.

      a. In the space provided, create a series of parallel sentences using "I hear" at the beginning of each sentence. The subject does not have to be about love.

      ____

      ____

      ____

      b. In the space provided, create a series of parallel sentences using "we must" at the beginning of each sentence.

      ____

      ____

      ____

      c. In the space provided, create a series of parallel sentences using "you can't" at the beginning of each sentence.

      ____

      ____

      ____

B. Another type of parallelism that Keats uses involves placing an explanation between two sentences with similar beginnings. For example, look at the following paragraph, in which Keats repeats the phrase "I am strong":

> I am strong enough to walk over, but I dare not. I shall feel so much pain in parting with you again. I am strong, but not strong enough to see you.

In the first sentence Keats makes a statement. In the second sentence he explains his statement. In the third sentence he repeats the idea of the first sentence with a slightly different spin. This repetition reinforces the idea that Keats really wants to see Fanny, but doesn't feel that he can take the pain of parting from her again.

a. In the space provided, follow Keats's pattern by creating two parallel sentences starting with "I am thankful, but" and placing an explanation between the parallel sentences.
Example: I am thankful for my dad, but I think he's a little crazy. He sings at the top of his lungs in the shower. I am thankful, but his voice hurts my ears.

____

____

____

b. In the space provided, follow Keats's pattern by creating two parallel sentences starting with "you are hungry, but" and placing an explanation between the parallel sentences.

____

____

____

2. **COPIOUSNESS**—A normal sentence structure goes as follows: subject, verb, object. Take this sentence for example:

SUBJECT — I shall send you your horse — OBJECT

VERB

Anastrophe is a rhetorical device that inverts, or turns around, the normal structure. It makes an ordinary sentence more dramatic. Here is the same sentence with the object first:

Your horse I shall send you.

And here is anastrophe with the verb first:

Send you your horse I shall.

As with every rhetorical device, you will not want to use anastrophe excessively. If you do, you will start sounding like Yoda from *Star Wars*: "Powerful you have become. The dark side I sense in you." A little anastrophe, however, can give your writing some extra zing.

Make the following ordinary sentences more interesting by using anastrophe. Either place the object or the verb first in the sentence.

Example:

You should play your guitar.
Change to: Your guitar you should play. (object inversion)
Or change to: Play your guitar you should. (verb inversion)

A. We must visit Mexico soon.

____

____

____

B. We will eat homemade *dulche de leche*.

____

____

____

C. We should climb a Mayan pyramid.

____

____

____

D. When we get to Cancun, we will hit the beach.

E. I absolutely love wearing coral jewelry.

3. **COMPARISON**—The purpose of this lesson's essay is to compare Napoleon's love letters with Keats's love letters. Before you start writing, use the following prompts for each paragraph to help you sketch out your ideas. You can use lists, phrases, or complete sentences for your answers. Then compose your full essay on a separate paper or on a computer. Remember that each paragraph has its own job to do.

   The paragraphs you write after going through these steps will be your first draft, or your first version of the essay. Assume that your first draft will need some rewriting to make it the best essay it can be.

   Prewriting: Begin by making a list of as many similarities and differences between your subjects as you can think of.

   Similarities between the love letters of Napoleon and Keats:

Differences between the love letters of Napoleon and Keats:

Now select two of the most important similarities from your list.

Similarity #1:

Similarity #2:

Select two of the most important differences from your list.

Difference #1:

Difference #2:

____

____

____

Paragraph 1 (Introduction): Start with an introduction that includes an analogy, a narrative overview of each subject, and a topic sentence.

Begin your introduction with an analogy about romantic love. Remember, a simile uses "like" or "as" to make a comparison, and a metaphor uses one thing to describe another, but without using the words "like" or "as." Include a second sentence that explains your analogy if needed.

Analogy:

____

____

____

Next write a short narrative overview of the two subjects. Consider the questions who, what, when, and where, and tell about each subject in one or two sentences.

Napoleon's letters:

Who: ______________________________

____

What: ______________________________

____

When: ______________________________

____

Where: ______________________________

____

Keats's letters:

Who: ______________________________

____

What: ______________________________

____

When: ______________________________

____

Where: ______________________________

____

Finally, write your topic sentence, which simply states the main idea of your essay.

Topic sentence:

____

____

____

Paragraph 2 (Similarity #1): Write about one major similarity between the two subjects. Start by identifying the similarity you will be describing. Then tell more about the similarity by adding facts, examples, or details from the readings for both subjects.

Details about similarity #1:

____

____

____

____

____

____

Paragraph 3 (Similarity #2): Write about a second major similarity between the two subjects. Start again by identifying the similarity you will be describing. Then tell more about the similarity by adding facts, examples, or details from the readings for both subjects.

Details about similarity #2:

Look in the readings for a quote that gives a supportive fact, example, or detail and include it in your description.

Quote:

Paragraph 4 (Difference #1): Write about one major difference between the two subjects. Start by identifying the difference you will be describing. Then tell more about the difference by adding facts, examples, or details from the readings for both subjects.

Details about difference #1:

Paragraph 5 (Difference #2): Write about a second major difference between the two subjects. Start again by identifying the difference you will be describing. Then tell more about the difference by adding facts, examples, or details from the readings for both subjects.

Details about difference #2:

____

____

____

____

____

Look in the readings for a quote that gives a supportive fact, example, or detail and include it in your description.

Quote:

____

____

____

Paragraph 6 (Conclusion): Write an epilogue, or concluding paragraph. First, recap the main point of your essay. Then reflect on something important that can be learned from the comparison. Finally, write an observation or question about your subjects that would be interesting to learn more about in the future.

Something that can be learned from the comparison:

____

____

____

Something to learn more about:

____

____

____

Once you have completed your prewriting, go through these instructions again and write your paragraphs based on the prompts.

Speak It—

1. Practice your elocution, and especially your inflection, by reading the following scene aloud. The scene is adapted from *Cyrano de Bergerac* by Edmond Rostand, and it has three speaking parts: Narrator, Cyrano, and Roxane.

NARRATOR. Cyrano de Bergerac is a delightful play that is both comedy and tragedy. Cyrano is a famous French soldier and duelist, the most gifted swordsman of his day. He is deeply in love with his distant cousin, the beautiful Roxane. Despite his many talents, Cyrano is insecure about his very large nose, which he calls "a rock, a peak, a cape" and "a dwarf pumpkin" and "a prize turnip." Because he doesn't see himself as handsome, he doesn't believe that Roxane could ever love him.

Roxane falls in love with a handsome, empty-headed soldier by the name of Christian. He is such a dunce that he never has anything romantic to say to her. Whenever Christian wants to write a love letter to Roxane, he asks Cyrano to do the work. Cyrano gladly writes beautiful poetry to his beloved Roxane, but—sadly for him—Christian gets all the credit. Roxane tells Christian that at first she fell in love with his face, but now she doesn't care whether he's handsome or ugly. She loves "his soul." In other words, she's really in love with Cyrano, the poet, but doesn't know that he's the one writing her the beautiful letters.

After a while, Christian dies in battle, and Roxane grieves for him. Cyrano realizes that he can't add to her grief by telling her that Christian never wrote her a single letter. He remains her friend, but never dares to tell Roxane that he loves her. Then one evening, a heavy log strikes Cyrano on the head. Realizing he is dying, he goes to see Roxane one last time. He asks to hear "Christian's dying letter" one last time. As he reads the letter aloud in the dark, Roxane realizes that Cyrano was her poet and the man whose soul she loved all along. Here's that final scene:

ROXANE. Each of us has his wound; ay, I have mine,—
Never healed up—not healed yet, my old wound!
'Tis here, beneath this letter brown with age,
All stained with tear-drops, and still stained with blood.

NARRATOR. Twilight begins to fall.

CYRANO. His letter! Ah! you promised me one day
That I should read it.

Roxane. What would you?—His letter?

Cyrano. Yes, I would **fain**,—to-day . . .

Roxane (*giving the bag hung at her neck*). See! here it is!

Cyrano (*taking it*). Have I your leave to open?

Roxane. Open—read!

Cyrano (*reading*). "Roxane, **adieu**! I soon must die!
This very night, beloved; and I
Feel my soul heavy with love untold.
I die! No more, as in days of old,
My loving, longing eyes will feast
On your least gesture—ay, the least!
I mind me the way you touch your cheek
With your finger, softly, as you speak!
Ah me! I know that gesture well!
My heart cries out!—I cry 'Farewell'!"

Roxane. But how you read that letter! One would think . . .

Cyrano (*continuing to read*). "My life, my love, my jewel, my sweet,
My heart has been yours in every beat!"

Narrator. The shades of evening fall **imperceptibly**.

Roxane. You read in such a voice—so strange—and yet—
It is not the first time I hear that voice!

Narrator. She comes nearer very softly, without his perceiving it, passes behind his chair, and, noiselessly leaning over him, looks at the letter. The darkness deepens.

Cyrano. "Here, dying, and there, in the land on high,
I am he who loved, who loves you, —I . . ."

Roxane (*putting her hand on his shoulder*). How can you read? It is too dark to see!

Narrator. He **starts**, turns, sees her close to him. Suddenly alarmed, he holds his head down. Then in the dusk, which has now completely enfolded them, she says, very slowly, with clasped hands:

Roxane. And, fourteen years long, he has played this part
Of the kind old friend who comes to laugh and chat.

Cyrano. Roxane!

Roxane. 'Twas you!

Cyrano. No, never; Roxane, no!

Roxane. I should have guessed, each time he said my name!

Cyrano. No, it was not I!

Roxane. It was you!

Cyrano. I swear!

ROXANE. I see through all the generous **counterfeit**—
The letters—you!
CYRANO. No.
ROXANE. The sweet, mad love-words!
You!
CYRANO. No!
ROXANE. The voice that thrilled the night—you, you!
CYRANO. I swear you err.
ROXANE. The soul—it was your soul!
CYRANO. I loved you not.
ROXANE. You loved me not?
CYRANO. 'Twas he!
ROXANE. You loved me!
CYRANO. No!
ROXANE. See! how you falter now!
CYRANO. No, my sweet love, I never loved you!
ROXANE. Ah! Things dead, long dead, see! how they rise again!
—Why, why keep silence all these fourteen years,
When, on this letter, which he never wrote,
The tears were your tears?
CYRANO (*holding out the letter to her*). The bloodstains were his.
ROXANE. Why, then, that noble silence, —kept so long—
Broken to-day for the first time—why?
CYRANO. Why?
ROXANE. Live, for I love you!
CYRANO. No, In fairy tales
When to the **ill-starred** Prince the lady says
"I love you!" all his ugliness fades fast—
But I remain the same, up to the last!
ROXANE. I have **marred** your life—I, I!
CYRANO. You blessed my life!
Never on me had rested woman's love.
My mother even could not find me fair:
I had no sister; and, when grown a man,
I feared the mistress who would mock at me.
But I have had your friendship—grace to you
A woman's charm has passed across my path.
And now I must die. . . .
ROXANE. No! I loved but once, yet twice I lose my love! No! No!

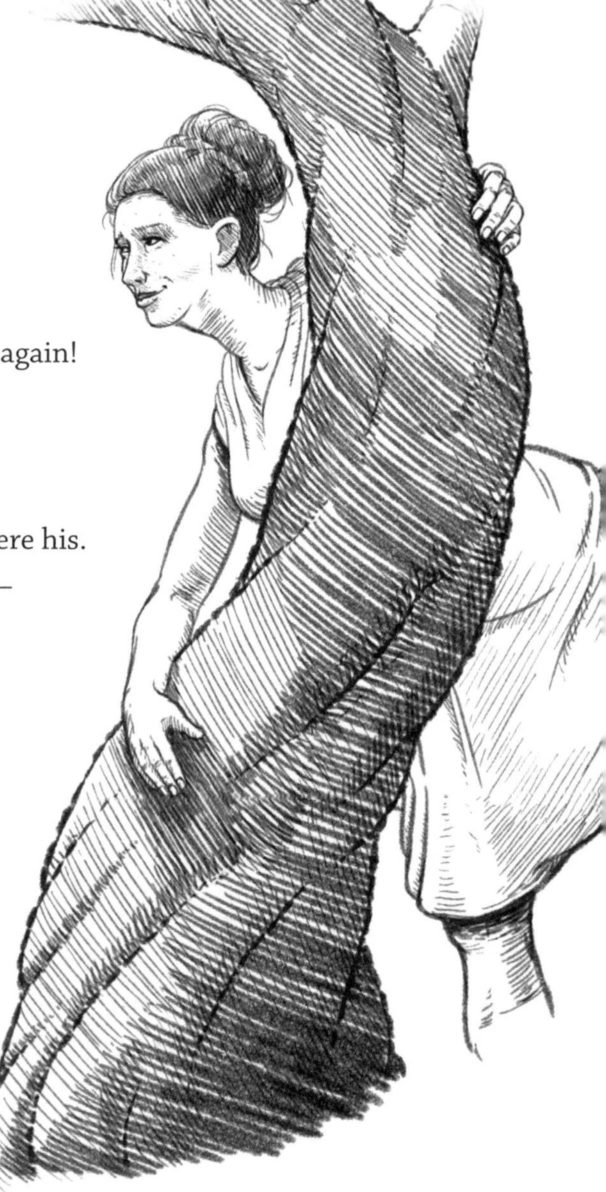

2. **FORMAL DISCUSSION:** Your teacher may instruct you to have a formal discussion. This sort of discussion is not a debate. Rather, it is an opportunity for your class to have a conversation around an open question or a controversial topic. Discussion is a great way to hear other people's ideas and to learn to express your own thoughts well. You can take sides as in a debate, but you are also free to agree with one another, enhancing each other's arguments. Usually a teacher will not participate in a formal discussion; instead she stands aside and listens in.

   Here's how it works: Your teacher will assign you a question or a topic. She might allow you to prepare for the discussion as homework, or she may give you time in class to jot down your thoughts. Either way, you will probably be permitted to keep your notes with you as you discuss. You will then have a conversation about the topic; this conversation usually lasts for fifteen to twenty minutes. Be sure to let everyone have a chance to speak, and if some people are being quiet, feel free to draw them into the conversation by asking them direct questions. If you can support your ideas by quoting a text, so much the better! In the end, your teacher may assign you a score based on the scoring guidelines included with this exercise.

Formal Discussion Scoring Guidelines

Award points based on the following criteria:

- taking a stand by clearly stating an argument (thesis) +2
- providing evidence for the argument +2
- making an analogy +2
- making a relevant comment +1
- asking a clarifying question +1
- inviting another student to participate +1
- interrupting -1
- monopolizing the conversation -2
- making personal attacks -2
- distracting the audience -2

3. **PARTNER FEEDBACK:** With a student partner (or your teacher), take turns reading the rough drafts of your comparison essays. You and your partner should give each other comments about what is more or less effective about your writing. Use the rubric at the back of the book to help you get ideas for your comments. (A rubric is a guide to evaluating and grading writing, and your teacher may use this particular rubric to grade your essay.) Try to say two positive things about your partner's essay, and then come up with at least two suggestions for editing the essay.

Revise It—

1. In lesson 9 you had some practice with transition words and phrases—but once is not enough! Transition words and phrases take a fair bit of practice before they come naturally. Sentences occasionally need transition words if the connection between them needs to be clarified. Transition words can also smooth out the flow between paragraphs. The following are two examples of good transitions:

   - **Between sentences:** John Keats's short life was marred by tragedy. When he was eight years old, his father fell from his horse and died. Additionally, his mother died of tuberculosis.

     The word "additionally" connects the second and third sentences. It tells us that the author wants to make a second and similar point supporting the idea that John Keats had a tragic life.
   - **Between paragraphs:**

     John Keats died when he was only twenty-five. He didn't live long enough to write thick volumes of poetry like Wordsworth or Byron. He was frequently too sick and weak to concentrate on his writing, and he would sometimes have to put his pen down to cough blood up from his lungs. All in all, he published only fifty-four poems.

     Yet, it is remarkable that John Keats is considered one of the greatest poets in the history of English poetry.

     The word "yet" concedes a point. The first paragraph was about the short, sickly life of John Keats and his meager output as a poet. The transition word tells us that in the next paragraph we will see that, despite the few poems he published, Keats still ranks as a great poet.

   The following are a list of transition words and phrases you can use:

   - To list supportive points:
     - ◊ First,/Second,/Third,
     - ◊ To begin with,/Next,/Finally,
   - To draw conclusions:
     - ◊ Hence,
     - ◊ As a result,
     - ◊ Because of this,
     - ◊ Therefore,
     - ◊ Thus,
     - ◊ Finally,
     - ◊ In conclusion,
   - To provide a contrast:
     - ◊ By contrast,
     - ◊ In contrast,
     - ◊ On the other hand,
     - ◊ Rather,
     - ◊ Instead,
     - ◊ Just the opposite,
     - ◊ On the contrary,
     - ◊ By comparison,

- To make an additional point:
  - ◊ Additionally,
  - ◊ In addition,
  - ◊ Also,
  - ◊ Furthermore,
  - ◊ At the same time,
  - ◊ Moreover,
- To concede a point:
  - ◊ Nevertheless,
  - ◊ Still,
  - ◊ Yet,
  - ◊ After all,
  - ◊ At any rate,
  - ◊ However,
  - ◊ In any case,
- To provide an example:
  - ◊ For example,
  - ◊ In other words,
  - ◊ For instance,

Be sure to use a comma to offset transition words from the rest of the sentence. For example:

> George Gordon, Lord Byron, was a vigorous poet, a man of action who could never control his wild and stormy moods. Just the opposite, Keats was a quiet, loyal man given to times of sorrow and deep reflection. However, Keats's poetry was every bit as strong and passionate as Byron's.

In this passage, "just the opposite" and "however" help readers ease into the next thought.

Even if you don't use a specific transition word, it is vital for each new paragraph to "take up" the idea of the previous paragraph. Look at your essay and consider where it would benefit from the use of transition words or phrases. Make any changes or additions that will help make smooth connections between the parts of your essay.

A. The following sentences are based on the life of Napoleon Bonaparte. Use transition words or phrases from the previous list to better connect the sentences.

   Example: Napoleon Bonaparte was one of the most famous military men in history, and he held many positions throughout his life. __To begin with__, he was a student, the first from his island to graduate from the military school in Paris. __Next__, he was promoted to the rank of general at the young age of twenty-four. __Additionally__, he became the first French emperor on May 14, 1804.

   a. Napoleon was an arrogant man. ______________________________,

      he did not let anyone stand in his way. ______________________________, rumors that he was a man of short stature were not true. He was five feet and seven inches tall.

b. Napoleon was born on the small island of Corsica and grew up speaking Corsican, so French was his second language. ______________________________, he always had trouble spelling words in French.

c. Napoleon won many amazing military victories for France. ______________________________, he defeated the Austrian army in Italy at the Battle of Borghetto in 1796.

d. Napoleon loved his second wife, Marie-Louise. ______________________________, Josephine remained the great love of his life.

e. Napoleon lost the Battle of Waterloo in 1815. ______________________________, he was exiled to the island of Saint Helena, where he later died.

B. In the following exercises, join the two sentences with a transition word or phrase. Take your best guess whether the author intended to list supportive points, draw a conclusion, provide a contrast, concede a point, or provide an example, and write your guess in the space provided. Discuss with your teacher and your classmates why you chose the transitions you did.

Example: John Keats and Fanny Brawne were apart for much of their courtship. ___Therefore___, they had to write letters to one another.
___drawing a conclusion___

a. Keats was sickly for many years. ______________________________, he was able to write poetry that celebrated the beauty of life.

____

b. Several of Keats's poems rank among the most famous English poems of all time.

______________________________, "Ode on a Grecian Urn" is still beloved and taught in schools today.

____

c. When he was a youth, Keats's personality changed dramatically.

______________________________, he was lazy and hotheaded.

______________________________, he became more studious and quiet.

____

d. When Keats and Fanny first met, Keats fell deeply in love with her charms.

______________________________, Fanny took longer to realize her feelings for Keats.

____

e. There was no effective treatment for tuberculosis until after Keats's death.

______________________________, Keats, his mother, his two brothers, and his sister-in-law were not able to recover from the disease.

____

2. Here is what you must do to effectively revise your work:
   a. Get feedback. Use comments from your student partners (or from your teacher) to strengthen and improve your paper.
   b. Wait a day or two before you rewrite your paper. The time away from it will help you to see its problems more clearly.
   c. Read the paper aloud to yourself. This is often the best way to catch mistakes—grammar errors, as well as words that don't work well—because you will be using two senses—seeing and hearing—instead of one. If something sounds wrong, it probably is.

   Once you are ready to rewrite, use the following steps to aid with your revision:
   a. *Find your topic sentence and underline it.* There should be one sentence that states the main idea of your essay. Make sure your paper expresses that idea throughout.
   b. *Make sure each paragraph gets the job done.* Remember that each paragraph has a special purpose according to the demands of the prompts. Revisit the goal of each paragraph and compare it to what you've written. Does each paragraph successfully accomplish its goal?
   c. *Find and fix grammar mistakes.* Make sure all your nouns and verbs agree and that your writing is clear. Fix any fragments or run-ons. In other words, make sure you are writing complete sentences.
   d. *Strengthen phrasing.* Are your word choices specific instead of vague? Do you use strong nouns and verbs? Do you vary your sentences and occasionally begin them with a prepositional phrase or a participial phrase? Weed out passive voice and excess adjectives. Use compound sentences, appositives, adverb phrases, and questions to make your writing more interesting. Transition smoothly between ideas and paragraphs using transition words.
   e. *Proofread.* Look for any punctuation, spelling, or capitalization errors. Then fix them!
   f. *Retype* the draft with the corrections you have made.

Comparison Essay Rubric

Name: ______________________ Date of Assignment: ______________________

Content ________ /80

Introduction (15 points)

Does the paragraph begin with an analogy? (5 points) ________

Does the writer include short narrative overviews of each subject? (5 points) ________

Is there a topic sentence that states the main idea of the essay? (5 points) ________

Body Paragraphs (50 points)

Do the four body paragraphs, and the information they present, clearly and strongly expand on the topic sentence found in the introduction? (10 points) ________

Does the first body paragraph identify a major similarity between the two subjects? Does it provide additional facts, examples, or details? (10 points) ________

Does the second body paragraph identify a second major similarity between the two subjects? Does it provide additional facts, examples, or details? Does it use a quote from the readings? (10 points) ________

Does the third body paragraph identify a major difference between the two subjects? Does it provide additional facts, examples, or details? (10 points) ________

Does the fourth body paragraph identify a second major difference between the two subjects? Does it provide additional facts, examples, or details? Does it use a quote from the readings? (10 points) ________

Epilogue (15 points)

Does the conclusion—the epilogue—clearly restate the topic using different words? (5 points) ________

Does it state something important that can be learned from the comparison? (5 points) ________

Does it state something that would be interesting to learn more about? (5 points) ________

Style & Form ________ /20

Style (12 points)

Are the sentences varied? (4 points) ________

Do the paragraphs follow each other in a way that makes sense? In other words, do they flow together? (4 points) ________

Does the writer use strong and specific words (vocabulary)? (4 points) ________

Form (8 points)

Number of spelling, punctuation, capitalization errors ________

2 or fewer per page: 4 points   5–6 per page: 2 points
3–4 per page: 3 points   More than 6 per page: 0 points

Number of sentence errors (run-ons or fragments) ________

1 or fewer per page: 2 points   2–3 per page: 1 point   More than 3 per page: 0 points

Is the handwriting neat and legible? Or, is the paper typed according to the teacher's requirements?   Yes: 2 points   No: 0 points ________

Total: ________ /100

Get to the Point: Tips for Summarizing

Every morning the president of the United States receives a daily brief on his desk. The brief contains a summary of the most important happenings in the world and the biggest threats to the nation's security. It's the king of all summaries. It's the whole world shrunk down to a few pages.

Many reasons exist for summarizing, and they mostly boil down to a matter of time. While the president needs to be informed about world events, he doesn't have time to read about every detail every morning. In the same way, your audience doesn't have endless hours to devote to your speech or essay. Sometimes you will want your work to include information from another source, but what if that information is too detailed to share in full? By summarizing you can share the main idea of the information without overwhelming your audience.

Do you need to communicate only the most important facts? Summarize! Do you need to tell a long story in just a few words? Summarize! Do you need to hold your audience's attention and not bore them to death? Summarize! As an added bonus, summarizing can help you to understand something better because it forces you to focus on the most essential details.

Here's a list of tips to help you summarize:

1. Ask yourself, "Is a summary necessary?"
   - Is the information too detailed to include without summarizing?
   - Do you need to retell a longer story in shortened form?
   - Do you want to avoid using a quotation by using your own words instead?

   You might want to include a summary of an article or story in your essay if it:
   - engages the emotions of your audience (pathos).
   - strengthens the logic of your thesis (logos).
   - helps you to have better credibility with your audience (ethos).

Pathos, logos, and ethos are three ways to persuade or appeal to your audience. Pathos seeks to engage the heart. It appeals to the positive (happiness, sympathy) or negative (anger, fear) emotions of the audience and often makes use of stories to do so. Logos seeks to engage the head. It appeals to the reason of the audience and often uses facts, logic, numbers, and research. Ethos seeks to engage the trust of the audience. It points to the credibility of the person who is writing and speaking to build the audience's confidence that he or she has authority on the subject.

2. Read the article or story you intend to retell very carefully. Note the main points. If you want to summarize something lengthy, it can be helpful to create an outline first.

3. Eliminate unnecessary description, dialogue, or less important ideas. By doing this, you are making sure that your summary contains only the most significant parts of the story.

4. Put the important parts of the article or story into your own words. This is called paraphrasing. When you summarize, it's your turn to tell the story. How would you retell the story so that it makes the most sense to you? Give yourself a reasonable number of sentences with which to summarize and try to stick to that number.

5. Finally, cite the source of your summary.

The following passage is from *Babbitt* by Sinclair Lewis. In it a woman named Zilla tells her friends about her experience trying to board the trolley to go to the movies. Read the passage and then look at the example of a good summary that follows.

> "I was standing on the platform waiting for the people to let me into the car, and this beast, this conductor, hollered at me, 'Come on, you, move up!' Why, I've never had anybody speak to me that way in all my life! I was so astonished I just turned to him and said—I thought there must be some mistake, and so I said to him, perfectly pleasant, 'Were you speaking to me?' and he went on and bellowed at me, 'Yes, I was! You're keeping the whole car from starting!' he said, and then I saw he was one of these dirty ill-bred hogs that kindness is wasted on, and so I stopped and looked right at him, and I said, 'I—beg—your—pardon, I am not doing anything of the kind,' I said, 'it's the people ahead of me, who won't move up,' I said, 'and furthermore, let me tell you, young man, that you're a low-down, foul-mouthed, impertinent skunk,' I said, 'and you're no gentleman! I certainly intend to report you, and we'll see,' I said, 'whether a lady is to be insulted by any drunken bum that chooses to put on a ragged uniform, and I'd thank you,' I said, 'to keep your filthy abuse to yourself."

Summary:

> In the novel *Babbitt*, a prideful lady tells about her conflict with a trolley conductor. The conductor yelled at her to move out of the way, and she responded by insulting his manners and appearance, calling him a "foul-mouthed, impertinent skunk." (Lewis 145)[1]

1. It is important to cite (or give credit to) the source of your information, and this is an example of a citation. For a review of how to write source citations, see *Writing & Rhetoric, Book 7: Encomium & Vituperation*. For an additional resource on MLA style, we recommend the *MLA Handbook for Writers of Research Papers* by the Modern Language Association. Purdue's Online Writing Lab (OWL) can also be helpful: https://owl.english.purdue.edu/owl/section/2/11/.

Outlines: Your Very Own Story Maps

Have you ever been lost? When I was a kid, I wandered into the toy department of a huge store without telling my parents. Next thing I knew, my parents were gone and I was racing madly through the store trying to find them. Come to think of it, I got lost a lot—in flea markets, in parades, and in the woods. I always wished I had a map or a GPS for finding my parents.

When you're somewhere you don't know very well, a map is an essential tool to help you understand where you are. Similarly, an outline is your very own "map" of what you read. When you create an outline, you are drawing a map that helps you navigate the different parts of a story or essay. Important points in the essay and important events in the story are like landmarks that stand out and can be seen from miles around. Smaller points are the streets and back alleys you explore as you move through a story.

In this book, you will outline some of the stories and articles you read.

Writing an Outline

Outlines are summaries of a story that look like organized lists. To create an outline, use Roman numerals (*I*, *II*, *III*, *IV*, *V*, etc.) to list the biggest, most important points. Then, list the next important points using the letters of the alphabet (*A*, *B*, *C*, *D*, *E*). Next, use numbers for even smaller points that help to establish the larger points by telling more about them (*1*, *2*, *3*, *4*, *5*). Note, however, that some outlines may not need all these levels of detail. Your teacher will set a standard for the level of detail required in your classroom.

The following famous Arabian story was retold by American writer W. Somerset Maugham and is adapted here. Take a look:

> There was a wealthy merchant in Baghdad who sent his servant to the **bazaar** to buy fresh fruits and vegetables. In a little while, the servant came back with his baskets empty. He was trembling with fear, and said, "Master, just now when I was in the bazaar, I was bumped by a woman in the crowd. When I turned around, I saw it was Death who had bumped into me, and she gave me a threatening look! Now, let me borrow your horse, and I will ride away from this city and avoid dying. I will flee to Samarra, and in that city Death won't find me." The merchant let him borrow his horse, and the servant jumped upon it, and he dug his heels in its flanks. He rode away as fast as the horse could gallop. Then the merchant went down to the bazaar and he saw Death standing in the crowd. He marched up to Death and said angrily, "Why did you give my servant a threatening look when you saw him this morning?" "That was not a threatening look," Death said. "It was merely a

start of surprise. I was astonished to see him in Baghdad, for I had an appointment with him tonight in Samarra."[1]

Now here is an outline based on the story:

I. The servant of a merchant was bumped by Death in a Baghdad bazaar.
  A. Death gave him a threatening look.
  B. The servant returned to his master, terribly frightened.
II. The servant fled to Samarra in fear.
  A. He begged for a horse to get away from Baghdad.
  B. He told the merchant his destination was Samarra.
  C. The merchant lent him a horse.
    1. The servant dug his heels into the horse's flanks.
    2. The horse galloped fast.
III. The merchant confronted Death.
  A. He found her in the bazaar.
  B. He demanded to know why Death gave a threatening look to his servant.
  C. Death assured the merchant that she had not given a threatening look, but had merely been startled to see the servant there.
IV. Death told the merchant she was surprised because she had expected to meet the servant that night in Samarra.

1. adapted from *Sheppey*, a play by W. Somerset Maugham (copyright 1933 by W. Somerset Maugham), published in 1933 by William Heinemann Ltd., London

Memoria: Building Memory Muscle

Our word "memory" comes from the Latin word *memoria*, which means "mindful" and "remembering." The Greek poet Aeschylus said that memory is the "workmaid and mother of the Muses." By this he meant that memory works for us and inspires us just as the nine Muses, Greek goddesses, were thought to inspire artists. In Greek times, and for many centuries afterward, people understood that to memorize beautiful and instructive words is helpful to life and work.

In this book you will memorize significant quotes, which will help you in your writing and in your life. You will be surprised how often these insightful and beautiful words will surface in your mind and on your tongue at just the right moment because you have spent time thinking about them and committing them to memory.

There are many things you can do to help you with memorization:

- Go to a place where you will not be distracted. We retain information better when we have learned it in a quiet space.
- Repeat the piece multiple times out loud. Practice it in front of family or friends.
- Create hand motions that help you to remember words and phrases, and repeat the words as you perform the motions. For example, consider the famous quote attributed to Edmund Burke: "All that is necessary for the triumph of evil is that good men do nothing." To help you remember this quote, you could cup the fingers of one hand into a claw (representing evil) and hold the fingers of your other hand upright (representing good men); then have those claw fingers snatch the upright fingers, showing their "triumph." Or, you could make a fist with one hand to represent evil and use it to pound down the upright fingers on the other hand to show evil's triumph. Be creative and have fun! Motion can be a wonderful jog to your memory.
- Discuss the piece with someone else, explaining what the piece means and describing your feelings about it. Thinking through a piece will help it to stick in your mind.
- Think about places (rooms in your house, for instance) and connect them in your mind with different parts of the text. For instance, for the previous Edmund Burke quote, you could think of the kitchen, and specifically, the garbage disposal in your kitchen sink. The disposal represents evil that triumphs over (grinds up) good men (the good food that goes down the drain).
- Write a journal entry on the quote, poem, or speech you want to memorize. Not so long ago, it was popular for people to keep "commonplace books." These books were essentially scrapbooks of quotes, poems, ideas, prayers, and notes of music. A person who kept a commonplace book expected that these bits of knowledge would be useful in conversation, in thought, and for writing. By jotting down the ordinary or "commonplace" stuff of life, people hoped to remember their thoughts for future reference. We have included the prac-

tice of keeping a commonplace journal in this book in order to strengthen your memory for writing and speaking.

Elocution Electrifies

Elocution is the skill of clear and powerful public speaking. Elocution is the way you thrill your audience with your words and make them sit up and pay attention. You might call it the current of electricity in a speech that gives everyone listening a lovely jolt.

Elocution has always been a vital part of rhetoric. In fact, it is really a combination of two of the five laws of rhetoric: *memoria* (memory) and *actio* (delivery). When you deliver a speech or a dramatic reading, you rely heavily on your memory and on the way you speak (delivery) to make a good impression on your audience.

Almost all public speaking is rehearsed ahead of time, so whether or not you actually learn a speech by heart, memory is still very important. You have to try to remember when to use gestures or when to change the emotion in your voice. When you read from a script, you want to remember the script well enough to look up and make eye contact with your audience.

Delivery involves a number of different skills: breathing, articulation, posture, eye contact, expression, and gesture. Take a quick look at each one of these.

- **Breathing:** To make your voice sound loud or soft, and to give it emotion, you will need to have a good volume of breath in your lungs. Empty your lungs of air and then try to speak with force and expression—it can't be done! Now fill your lungs with air and listen to all the wonderful things you can do with your voice. Make sure you draw full breaths as you are speaking.
- **Articulation:** In delivering your speech, you want to speak each word clearly and crisply so that your audience understands you. You must avoid mumbling or slurring your words together. Audiences have a hard time understanding mumbling, even with a microphone to amplify the voice. Enunciate each and every word, and you will surely sound like you know what you're talking about.
- **Posture:** You can't hope to avoid mumbling if you are hunched over while you recite. When you stand erect, straight and tall, you can fill your lungs more easily. You can speak with greater power and articulation. When you square your shoulders and keep your chin up, you will feel confident that you have something important to share. Your audience will also feel confident that something extraordinary is about to happen.
- **Eye contact:** Making eye contact is like having good posture for your eyes. You don't want your eyes to "stoop" any more than your shoulders. Unless you are saying something very sad or shy, keep your eyes off the floor and on the faces of the people in your audience. People like to feel as if you are speaking to them. It helps them to feel as if you recognize them and like them. If looking people in the eye is difficult at first, go ahead and look at their foreheads or at their ears. People won't know that you aren't peering directly into their eyes.

- **Expression:** In previous Writing & Rhetoric books, you've learned that you need to use your voice to convey emotion to the audience. Tone is the most important part of giving your voice an emotional quality or expression. Whether you speak loudly, softly, or somewhere in between (volume), whether you speak rapidly or slowly or at a moderate speed (pace), or whether you speak in a high voice or a low voice (pitch), you are giving your audience cues about how they should feel about what you are saying. (You are also helping to keep them awake.) Often it is important to pause at important moments in your speech to allow your words to sink in. Volume, pace, and pitch all make up the tone of a speech.

  Another important part of expression is inflection. When you use inflection, you are changing the pitch (the highs and the lows) of your voice to grab the audience's attention. Inflection helps the audience know when it needs to be excited or laugh or get serious. We know that when a person asks us a question, his voice will get a little higher at the end of his sentence. A person also sounds more uncertain or more excitable when the voice goes up. We know we're about to hear a strong statement or bad news when a person's voice goes lower. Inflection is one way to make a speech more powerful.
- **Gestures:** Beyond good posture, speakers can add extra emphasis to their words by using gestures. A raised hand or raised eyes, a fist pounding in one's hand or on a podium, arms wide open or rigidly shut—these are ways to convey new levels of meaning. It's important not to overdo gestures during a speech, because that can get a little distracting, but a well-timed gesture can really highlight an important point in a speech or recitation.

People use breathing, articulation, posture, eye contact, expression, and gestures every day when talking to one another. This is how all human beings communicate. When we deliberately use all of these tools together, when we seek to speak skillfully to an audience, we are practicing elocution.

Glossary

Literary and Rhetorical Concepts

Active voice—wording in which the subject of a sentence does the action of the action verb (e.g., The spider ate the fly.)

Adjective—describes a noun and helps us to "see" it more clearly: e.g., happy, silly, strange

Adverb—usually describes a verb and answers the questions how, when, and where; can also describe adjectives or other adverbs: e.g., shakily, lazily, sometimes

Analogy—a broad term for a comparison between two ideas, events, or objects that is used to describe or explain one of those things

Anastrophe—a rhetorical device that inverts the typical sentence structure

Annotations—notes added to a text to help understand or explain it

Appositive—also an appositive phrase; a noun or a noun phrase that explains another noun

Argument—a clear line of thinking aimed at proving a point

Autobiography—a description of someone's life that is written by the person himself, usually in the first person

Biography—a description of someone's life that is written by someone else, usually in the third person

Body paragraphs—all the paragraphs of an essay between the introduction and the conclusion

Character—a person who has a role to play in a story; can also refer to a person's moral strengths or weaknesses, as in "good character" and "bad character"

Chiasmus—a pattern in which the words in the first half of a sentence are reversed in the second half of the sentence (e.g., "Fair is foul, and foul is fair.")

Citation—used in writing to identify a source of information

Comparative adjective—an adjective used to compare, or show the differences between one person and another person, or one thing and another thing: e.g., larger, smaller, faster, higher ("That piece of cake is *larger than the other one.*")

Comparison—a way of looking at two or more people, objects, ideas, or events to identify how they are alike and different

Compound sentence—two independent simple sentences combined by a linking word called a conjunction

Conflict—a clash between people or ideas

Conjunctions—connecting words such as "and," "or," and "but"

Copiousness—stretching exercises for students of rhetoric whereby students reach for new words to express variations of the same idea*

Dialogue—a conversation between two or more people

Elocution—the art of public speaking

Eloquence—skillful and persuasive speech and writing

Encomium—warm, glowing praise about a specific person or thing, usually in the form of a speech or an essay

Enunciation—clear and articulate speech

Epilogue—a tidy ending to a written work

Ethos—a type of appeal that attempts to persuade the audience that the writer or speaker is a trusted authority on her subject

Evaluate—to weigh the good and bad of two or more persons, objects, or events

Evidence—facts and ideas that support the truth or validity of an argument

Fable—a short story that teaches a simple moral lesson, usually with talking animals

Fact—a truth, something known to exist or to have happened

Fairy tale—a fanciful story for children, usually with magical people or creatures

Fiction—any imaginative story

Figurative language—wording that suggests an imaginative meaning that goes beyond what the actual words say

Fragment—a sentence that is incomplete

Hyperbole—deliberate exaggeration for the sake of emphasizing an idea or of appealing to the emotions of an audience (e.g., "Her sneeze could be heard for miles around.")

Hypophora—a rhetorical device in which the speaker asks a question and then immediately supplies the answer (e.g., "Are we afraid? No, we're terrified!")

Improbable—not likely

Improper—inappropriate or immoral

Inflection—the change in pitch or tone of the voice that is used to make spoken words more meaningful

Logos—an appeal to reason that is often made using facts, numbers, logic, and research and helps strengthen the logic of a thesis; the content of a speech

Main idea—the most important thought in a story, speech, or essay; what the story, speech, or essay is all about

Memoria—Latin for "memory," one of the five canons or laws of rhetoric

Memorize—to learn something by heart

*A broad definition of copiousness is "any large quantity or number." Food, birds, or bubbles can be copious. In rhetoric, copiousness is aimed at developing a richness and flexibility of language so that many words and many ways of phrasing those words are available to the writer and speaker.

Metaphor—a comparison in which one thing is used to describe another thing that appears to be different but that actually has some similarities (e.g., "That test was a breeze," "Love is a rose, a red and thorny flower"). Metaphors do not use the comparison words "like" or "as."

Narrative—noun: all forms of story, from fairy tale, to history, to myths, to parables, to fables; adjective: story-telling

Noun—a person, place, thing, or idea: e.g., astronaut, island, sled, love

Nuance—a small similarity or difference between two things

Opinion—a personal claim, not necessarily based on fact

Outline—the skeleton of a story that tells what comes in the beginning, the middle, and the end

Paragraph—a group of sentences that form an idea together

Parallelism—a rhetorical strategy in which words, phrases, or clauses form a recognizable pattern; includes a number of different rhetorical devices, including anaphora

Paraphrasing—using one's own words and writing style to express ideas that are similar to the ideas in a source text

Participial phrase—a phrase that begins with a present participle

Passive voice—wording in which the subject of a sentence fails to do the acting and instead is acted upon (e.g., "The fly was eaten by the spider.")

Pathos—an appeal to the emotions of an audience

Preposition—a word that shows location (on, in, under), direction (to, into, onto, from), or time (before, after, during). Some prepositions can also connect a verb to a direct object (e.g., "I'm tired <u>of</u> this opera.") or introduce an amount of something or a length of time (e.g., "She ate three teaspoons <u>of</u> sugar.").

Prepositional phrase—a phrase that begins with a preposition: e.g., over the moon, toward the castle, after midnight

Present participle—a verb form that ends in *-ing*

Proofreading—looking for mistakes in written material

Proper noun—names a specific person, place, thing, or idea: e.g., Henrietta, Spain, Kleenex

Proverb—a wise saying

Refutation—a short essay that attacks certain parts of a narrative as unbelievable, improbable, unclear, or improper

Repetition—repeating a word, phrase, or idea to make a stronger point (e.g., "Slavery is a blot on human history. It is evil. It involves capturing and trafficking human beings. It is evil. It destroys dreams and tears families apart. It is evil.")

Rhetoric—the art and practice of persuasive writing and speaking

Rhetorical device—also known as a rhetorical figure; uses words in clever ways to be more persuasive; simile and hyperbole are two examples of rhetorical devices

Run-on sentence—a sentence that lacks proper punctuation and should really be divided into separate sentences, either with punctuation or a conjunction

Simile—a comparison using the words "like" or "as" (e.g., "I'm as silly as a clown with a fire hose.")

Stanza—a section of poetry similar to a paragraph in prose

Subject—what the sentence is about; either a noun, a pronoun, or a noun phrase

Summary—a shortened or concise version of a longer story

Superlative adjective—an adjective used to describe a person or thing as having more of a quality than all of the other people or things in a group: e.g., tallest, smallest, fastest, highest ("China has the largest population in the world.")

Synonym—a word that has nearly the same meaning as another word

Testimony—the expert opinion or evidence of a credible witness

Thesis statement—the main idea or argument of an essay or oration

Topic sentence—a sentence that tells the main idea of an essay

Transition sentence—a sentence that bridges the ideas in one paragraph and the ideas in the following paragraph

Unbelievable—hard to believe, seeming to be impossible

Unclear—hard to understand

Verb—the action word of a sentence: e.g., pass, kick, dash

Vituperation—condemnation of a specific person or thing, usually in the form of a speech or an essay

Vocabulary—a collection of words

Vocabulary Builder

Abroad—in foreign countries

Adieu—good-bye, from the French *a Dieu* or "to God"

Adroit—skillful

Aerodrome—a landing field for planes

Agitation—the state of being bothered or distressed ("Snarling dogs cause me a lot of agitation"); or, a concern and call for action about a particular issue ("The suffragettes led the agitation for votes for women.")

Aggravated—made worse

Aghast—filled with horror or shock

Agility—the ability to move quickly and easily

All-engrossing—completely absorbing, obsessive

Alloy—mixture

Amendment—a change to the Constitution or to a law

Anguish—mental pain and suffering

Animated—expressive, lively

Annals—historical records

Apparatus—machinery

Apprehensions—worries or fears

Arrest—to slow down or stop

Aspirations—desires or goals

Audacious—extremely bold or daring

Backwater—a motionless part of a river

Bazaar—an open-air market with many stalls of sellers

Beckoned—lured, summoned

Bleach—to lighten or whiten

Blockbusting—spectacular

Boiling point—the temperature at which water boils

Botany—the science of plants

Braille—a written language made up of raised dots, used by blind people

Breadth—a span or range, often a long distance

Brigadier—a commander in charge of a brigade of soldiers or police

Brood—to think deeply

Buoyed—lifted

Chasm—a deep gorge, a wide gap between two things

Cinders—small pieces of partly burned coal or wood

Clamored—made a loud uproar or cry

Clouted—smacked hard

Combustible—capable of catching fire and burning

Commercial—relating to finance and business

Commonwealth—a group of sovereign states associated by their own choice and linked with common interests

Composite—a combination of two or more things into one

Confinement—the state of being confined or imprisoned

Conflagration—an extensive and destructive fire

Conjure—to effect or produce, sometimes by magic

Constitute—to make

Contour—the outline of a shape

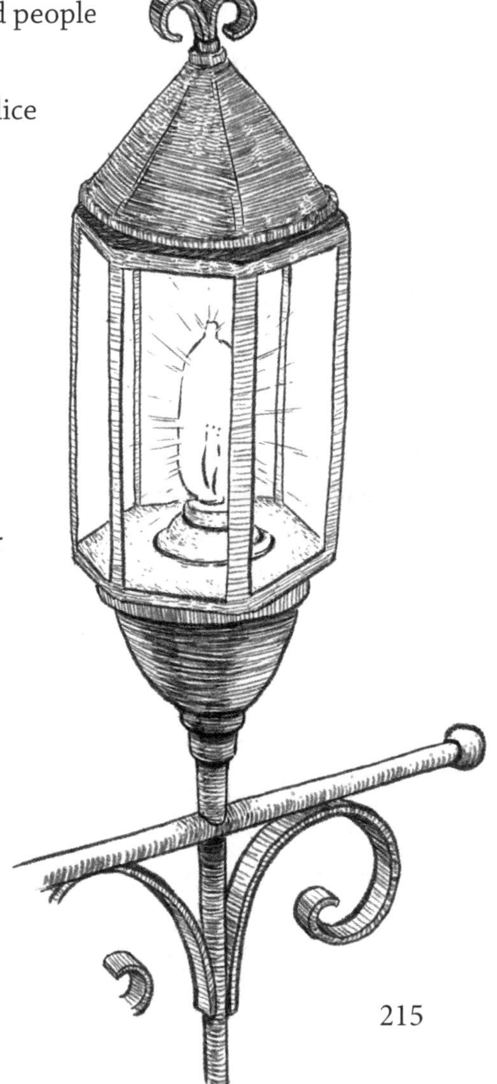

Contradictions—statements that are opposed to one another; or, a combination of qualities that don't usually go together

Countenance—facial expression

Counterfeit—fakery, deceit

Coursing—flowing

Crevasse—a deep cleft in the earth or in ice

Culminating—reaching the highest point or climax

Cunning—skillful, adept, crafty, sly

Decry—to condemn or criticize in a public way

Delirium—a state of mental disorder that might involve fever, disturbances, hallucinations, or even violence

Democracy—self-rule; government of the people, by the people, for the people

Desolation—devastation or ruin

Destiny—future fortune or purpose

Diaphragm—a thin sheet of material much like the skin stretched over a drum

Dictum—a saying; a proverb

Direst—most hopeless

Discontented—unhappy or dissatisfied

Discourse—speech

Dismembered—chopped into pieces

Distilleries—places where liquor is brewed

Dogged—persistent, stubborn

Draught—a gulp; a deep drink

Drought—a long, severe lack of rainfall

Dumb—mute

Electromagnet—a device made of an iron or steel core that is magnetized by electric current in a coil that surrounds it

Eloquent—expressive, clearly revealing feelings or ideas

Embark—to start a journey

Embossed—refers to letters raised on paper by pressure so that they can be felt with the fingers

Encase—to enclose in

Endeavoring—trying hard

Endowed—given as a gift

Engross—to captivate

Enraptured—completely excited, delighted

Entrammeled—trapped, tangled

Exclusion—leaving or shutting out

Exhibition—a display or show

Exodus—a flight from a place; often used to refer to the flight of the Israelites from slavery in Egypt or the flight of other people groups from dire situations

Expedition—a journey or voyage, often of exploration

Expel—to eject, cast out

Extremity—the most extreme point or degree

Faculty—mental or physical power; tendency

Fain—gladly

Feat—an achievement

Feline—catlike

Fiend—a diabolically cruel or wicked person

Fiendish—diabolically cruel or wicked

Foe—an enemy

Forked—split, divided

Formidable—intimidating, fearsome, difficult to conquer

Franc—a French unit of money, almost equal to one dollar

Frock—a gown or dress

Gait—body posture

Gale—a very strong wind

Gallant—brave, noble, chivalrous

Gesticulate—to make gestures

Grotesque—curved and distorted

Gusto—enthusiasm

Hammock—a web of ropes stretched between posts for the purpose of rest or sleep

Hangar—a shelter for housing aircraft

Haze—light fog

Homer—a home run

Humanitarian—a person who helps other people in need

Hypocrite—someone who is fake or who puts up a false front

Idealist—a person with high hopes for the world

Idle—inactive

Ill-starred—unlucky

Illusion—a false hope

Immediacy—urgency

Immitigable—relentless, impossible to lessen the intensity (in this case, the intense desire for revenge)

Imperative—absolutely necessary, essential

Imperceptibly—unnoticeably, without being detected

Impromptu—unrehearsed or not planned carefully

Impunity—freedom from punishment
Incorporated—combined into one body
Indifference—an attitude of uncaring
Indignity—an injury to one's dignity
Industrial—relating to labor or factory work
Inexplicable—unexplainable
Infatuated—passionately obsessed
Insufferable—unbearable and unpleasant
Interfusing—blending or fusing with another thing
Intimate—close, personal
Intimidate—to make timid or afraid
Intoxicate—to fascinate, enchant
Intrepid—fearless, dauntless
Invectives—insults
Inventor—someone who creates new devices
Ire—intense anger, wrath
Languished—faded, fell behind, lost vitality
Larynx—also known as "the voice box"; a hollow organ in the throat that contains the vocal folds
Latent—hidden, potential
Leaden—heavy, like lead
Leeway—space or room; particularly, the space of free time
Levite—a priest from the Israeli tribe of Levi
Luminosity—something lit up or bright
Lunatic—can be used negatively to refer to a mentally ill person; more often used to describe someone foolish
Magnitude—greatness of size or importance
Maiden—first
Marred—spoiled, blemished
Mastiff—a breed of large dog
Mates—short for "shipmates," the sailors on board a sailing ship
Membrane—a thin layer of material
Menacing—threatening
Militant—aggressive and violent
Mint—a place where money is legally produced
Mitigation—the act of excusing or lessening something
Mongrel—of mixed breed, nature, or origin
Monomania—an obsessive passion for one thing or idea
Monotonous—lacking variety, tedious

Nationalities—particular nations in the world

Obliged—required or forced

Obscure—to block, as in "to block from view"

Optimist—someone who takes a favorable view of life and circumstances

Origin—the beginning of something

Pangs—sharp pains

Paragon—a perfect person

Parceled out—divided

Patent—the exclusive right granted by a government to an inventor to manufacture and sell an invention

Pathological—caused by disease

Penitents—people who are sorry for their misdeeds or sins

Phenomenon—an event, sometimes an unusual happening

Philanthropists—people who donate money or property for the welfare of others or for civic good

Physique—physical body or appearance

Picketing—protesting or demonstrating against a government, business, etc.

Plateaus—raised land with a flat, level surface

Populous—having a large population, crowded

Precursors—ones who go before another

Preoccupations—obsessions

Primal—original, first

Projected—took on

Projectiles—generally refers to weapons thrown or shot through the air, but can also be debris that rains down with great force

Prolific— productive

Prostrate—completely flat

Psychopathic—mentally disturbed, dangerously insane

Pyrotechnic—spectacular by way of resembling firework

Quarry—a pit where rocks are mined

Quota—a specified number

Recant—to deny or turn away from (as in to deny one's beliefs)

Recuperative—having the power to recover health or strength

Reimburse—to pay back

Relentlessly—unceasingly

Relish—great enjoyment

Reluctant—hesitant

Reminiscences—recalled memories

Renegades—traitors, rebels
Resolute—resolved, determined
Resolve—determination, a definite decision
Rhapsodies—joyful emotions
Righteous—virtuous or moral
Samaritan—a person from Samaria, near Israel; Samaritans were enemies of the Jews
Schmoozing—hanging out and chatting cozily
Segregation—separation; specifically a separation of races; the system in which black and white people live, work, eat, and go to school separately
Separatism—the separation of people according to race, gender, or ethnicity
Sepulcher—a tomb built of stone
Shorthand—a quick way to write using abbreviations and symbols
Silhouette—the shadowy outline of something
Skepticism—doubt
Sledge—a sled or sleigh pulled by dogs
Socialite—a fashionable person, known for being the center of many parties and social gatherings
Stag—an adult male deer
Start—to jerk suddenly from being startled
Stenographer—a person who takes dictation in shorthand
Stoker—a laborer who stokes a ship's furnace with coal, producing steam that drives the ship
Straitjacket—a device used to wrap the arms of a violent person and bind them tightly against his body
Strivings—efforts, struggles
Stupefaction—a state of being baffled or amazed
Sublime—awe-inspiring
Submerged—completely hidden from view as if immersed under water
Supernatural—"beyond the natural"; usually refers to spiritual things: God, angels, ghosts, etc.
Swells—large bulges of water on the ocean's surface
Tactful—thoughtful and sensitive
Tactile—relating to the sense of touch
Tantalizingly—temptingly
Telegraphy—the passing of information over long distances without physical messages
Throes—violent emotions; struggles, great pains
Tier—a row or level
Tolerant—open-minded, considerate of those with whom one disagrees
Traitor—a person who betrays another
Tranquil—calm
Transfigured—changed in form or shape

Transmission—the spread or carrying of something

Traverse—to go across

Trifling—very small, trivial

Trumped-up—invented to falsely accuse

Tuberculosis—a bacterial infection that inflames the lungs and causes them to bleed

Unabated—undiminished

Unalloy'd (unalloyed)—unmixed, pure

Uniformity—the condition of being the same

Unreconciled—opposed, divided

Uppercut—a swinging blow directed upward to an opponent's chin

Urchins—mischievous youngsters

Ushered—led by an escort

Utility—the state of being useful

Valiant—brave, courageous

Vainly—without success

Vigilant—alert, watchful

Vigils—watches kept during ordinary sleeping times

Vital—energetic and lively

Vocal chords—known today as vocal folds; vibrating muscles and tissue in the throat that give us speech

Vociferous—loud and enthusiastic

Vulgar—rude and crude

Wheedling—persuading or pleading

Wiles—crafty plans

Wrenched—seized, pulled away violently

Yawned—opened wide

So Long

I'm going out for dinner tonight, and I have a decision to make. What'll it be? Mexican or Italian? On the one hand, I really like the fiery flavors of Mexican food and heaps of fresh salsa on everything. On the other hand, what could be better than the mellow pastas and rich tomato sauces of Italian food? When it comes to picking out a restaurant, I have to think hard about what I'm most in the mood for.

As I mentioned in the introduction, life is full of decisions, and the way to arrive at answers is through comparison. You may not have the opportunity to decide between driving a Ferrari or a Lamborghini, and you may not get to choose between a vacation in Nepal or Tahiti, but most of the important decisions are yours to make. Will you live with bitterness or with joy? Will you be stingy with your time or generous? Will you seek to be selfishly comfortable or seek to be useful to others? Will you envy your neighbors or rejoice with them? Those decisions will shape who you are and who you become. They are much more significant decisions than what tie or necklace to wear to a dance. I sincerely hope that these comparison exercises help you to be better at making decisions, both the life-changing kind as well as the more mundane where-will-I-dine-tonight ones.

Speaking of dining, most people like food with lots of flavor, and in the same way, writing that has flavor is more interesting to readers than a bland essay. In this book, you learned how to carefully compare two things by explaining their similarities and differences. Along the way, you discovered that you can spice up an introduction with an attention-getting analogy. Whether you chose a simile with the words "like" or "as," or a metaphor without them, your comparison started off with some commendable zing. You also learned that a narrative overview of your subject gives your readers the basic facts, while the topic sentence explains what information will be presented in your paper.

When you moved on to your body paragraphs, you balanced the flavor of your essay by writing two paragraphs about similarities and two about differences. You also sprinkled in a few quotations along the way. These quotes gave your writing credibility as you borrowed from the authority of an expert source. At the end of your essay, you threw in a pinch of reflection and a dash of curiosity as you thought about what you learned from the readings and what you might want to explore in the future.

Is that all? Ha! Not by a long shot! You reviewed some of the rhetorical devices from the last book, such as parallelism and hypophora, and you learned a few new ones, such as anastrophe, chiasmus, and answering a question with another question. You played with all sorts of sentences by making them longer and more elegant or shorter and more succinct. You used appositive phrases to help your writing flow well, and you strengthened your sentences by switching from passive voice to active voice.

As you compared your way through time and space, you met some colorful characters from history, from a daring pilot to a steadfast suffragette to a lovesick poet. If your imagination was hard at work, you heard the ring of the world's first telephone, shivered on the deck of a sinking ship, and cheered in the stands of a baseball stadium. You experienced the thrill of new ideas, new records broken, and new kinds of entertainment as you entered the twentieth century.

Now you're ready to take on the new creative challenge of description and impersonation in the next book. These are two of my favorite exercises in this whole series of books. Till we meet again to learn more about those exercises, *adios* and *arrivederci*! Mexican or Italian? I can't decide!

Ahab's Madness

This passage from the novel *Moby-Dick* by Herman Melville is the same passage that is found in lesson 3 (see page 32), but it has been "translated" into more current English.

For long days and weeks, Ahab lay tormented in his hammock. His torn body and soul blended together and drove him crazy. On the voyage home, after the encounter with the whale, an obsession with killing the whale seized him. Sometimes during the passage, he was a raving lunatic; and, even though he only had one leg, he was still quite strong, and he became stronger in his fits of insanity, so that his mates were forced to tie him fast there. As he sailed, he babbled in his hammock. In a jacket of ropes, he swung back and forth as the ship hit the waves. Now and then the ship floated across a peaceful sea, and the old man's insanity apparently disappeared when they came to Cape Horn. Ahab came forth from his dark room into the blessed light and air, looking firm and collected, though pale, and gave his calm orders once again; and his mates thanked God that his madness was now gone. But even then, Ahab babbled on inside his head. Human madness is often a crafty, cat-like thing. When you think it's gone, it may just be changing into something less obvious.

Certainly, Ahab had sailed upon this voyage with the sole and obsessive goal of hunting the White Whale. If any of his old acquaintances on shore could guess what was going on in his head, their shocked and sensitive souls would have protected the ship from such an evil man! They sailed to earn money, but he was intent on a daring and deadly revenge.

Often Ahab was forced to get out of his hammock by exhausting and realistic dreams during the night. When he woke, his thoughts would whirl round and round in his blazing brain, till the throbbing of his head became torture. Sometimes he felt as if he were being dragged up from his hammock, and a great pit seemed to open up in him, from which spiky flames and lightning shot up, and terrifying demons summoned him to leap down among them. When this happened, a wild cry would be heard through the ship; and with glaring eyes Ahab would burst from his room, as if he were escaping from a bed that was on fire.

Here, then, was this grey-headed, ungodly old man, chasing with curses a whale around the world, at the head of a crew, too, chiefly made up of wanderers and castaways and cannibals. Such a crew seemed specially picked to help him have his obsessive revenge. Sometimes they seemed to share his hate, and the White Whale seemed to be as much their foe as his. How all this came to be—what the White Whale was to them, or how the Whale seemed to be the gliding great demon of the seas of life—to explain all this would be to dive deeper than I can go.

Dr. Jekyll and Mr. Hyde

—adapted from *The Strange Case of Dr. Jekyll and Mr. Hyde* by Robert Louis Stevenson

This passage from the novel *The Strange Case of Dr. Jekyll and Mr. Hyde* by Robert Louis Stevenson is the same passage that is found in lesson 1 (see page 4), but it has been "translated" into more current English.

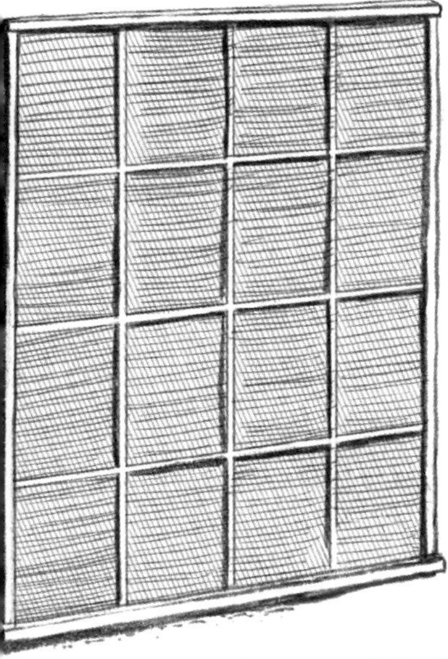

It seemed to me that I was steadily losing Dr. Jekyll, the good side of me, and slowly turning into Mr. Hyde, the evil side of me. Between these two men, I felt I needed to choose. Whether I was Jekyll or Hyde I still had the same memories, but otherwise the two men didn't think alike at all. When I was Jekyll, I remembered my adventures as Hyde, sometimes with excitement and sometimes with dismay. When I was Hyde, I didn't worry at all about Jekyll. I merely remembered Jekyll the way a robber remembers a cave—the respectable doctor was a good place for me to hide my evil side out of sight. Jekyll indulged Hyde the way a father might indulge his son; Hyde didn't care at all about his "father."

I didn't know which side to choose. If I embraced being Jekyll, I would need to put to death all those cravings and lusts that I cherished secretly inside of me. If, instead, I embraced being Hyde, I had to let go of my career and my reputation and all of my friendships. I wanted to choose the better part of me, but I lacked the strength to remain good and keep my resolution.

Of course I liked the doctor better than Hyde, even though Jekyll was a dissatisfied old man. He was surrounded by friends and had honest hopes for the future. But whenever I said good-bye to the freedom of being young, thoughtless, and shameless, I longed to become Hyde all over again. It tortured me to let go of my wickedness, and so—in moments of weakness—I drank down the brew that turned me into Hyde.

When a drunk does stop to think about his problem, not one time in five hundred does he pay any attention to the harm drinking does to him. That was me. Whenever I thought about Edward Hyde, I didn't give enough credit to the damage he was doing to my morals and my good self. Yet this is how I kept hurting myself. I had locked up my evil side for a long time, and now he came out of his cage roaring.

Notes

Notes

Notes

Notes

Notes

Notes

Logic

We use logic every day, especially to distinguish *logical* arguments from those that are unreasonable. As a fundamental part of the trivium, logic is a paradigm subject by which we evaluate, assess, and learn other subjects, growing ever closer to their mastery.

Informal Logic
(Grades 7–12)

Formal Logic
(Grades 8–12)

Logic/Pre-Rhetoric
(Grades 8–12)

Speech & Debate
(Grades 8–12)

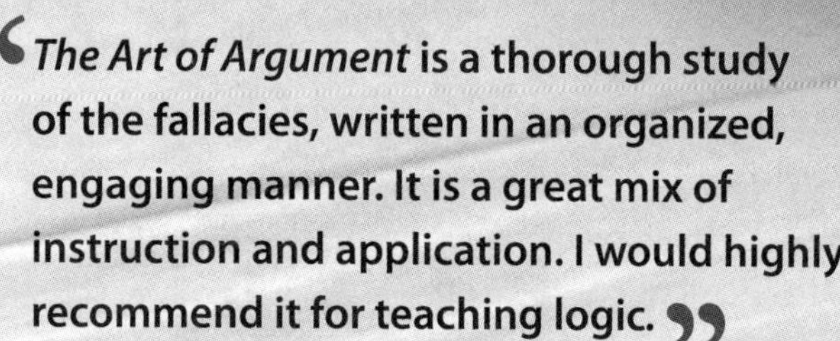